T0277988

Temple
of the
STARS

Temple
of the
STARS

The Astrological Decans

MARTIN GOLDSMITH

REDFeather™
MIND | BODY | SPIRIT

4880 Lower Valley Road, Atglen, PA 19310

Other REDFeather Titles by the Author:
Moon Phases: A Symbolic Key, ISBN 978-0-914918-83-7

Cover design by Danielle Farmer
Type set in Hypatia Sans Pro/Bell MT

ISBN:
978-0-7643-6842-4
978-1-5073-0404-4 (Epub)
Printed in India

Published by REDFeather Mind, Body, Spirit
An imprint of Schiffer Publishing, Ltd.
4880 Lower Valley Road
Atglen, PA 19310
Phone: (610) 593-1777; Fax: (610) 593-2002
Email: Info@redfeathermbs.com
Web: www.redfeathermbs.com

For our complete selection of fine books on this and related subjects, please visit our website at www.redfeathermbs.com. You may also write for a free catalog.

REDFeather Mind, Body, Spirit's titles are available at special discounts for bulk purchases for sales promotions or premiums. Special editions, including personalized covers, corporate imprints, and excerpts, can be created in large quantities for special needs. For more information, contact the publisher.

We are always looking for people to write books on new and related subjects. If you have an idea for a book, please contact us at proposals@schifferbooks.com.

ACKNOWLEDGMENTS

*I would like to extend warm thanks to my brother
Ken for his tireless efforts in collecting data, and
for his help on some of the more difficult decans.
I would also like to thank Craig Boswell for editing.*

CONTENTS

The Round Zodiac of Denderah

Introduction: Decans in Babylon and Egypt

Astrologers divide each of the twelve signs of the zodiac into three parts called decans. Each decan represents 10 degrees of the 360-degree circle of the zodiac. The sun's passage through a decan therefore lasts approximately ten days. Though modern astrologers make little use of the thirty-six decans, they were of great importance until the late Renaissance. At that time, they were attacked by Catholics and Protestants alike, for as the most overtly magical element of astrology, they were considered a form of "Egyptian necromancy." As a result of these attacks, the tradition was essentially dead by the end of the seventeenth century.

The decans emerge from two different traditions, one originating in Babylonia and the other in Egypt. The Babylonian tradition has many variants, but all of them involve planetary rulers for each of the decans. The most popular of these was the "Chaldaean" system, which held sway throughout the Renaissance but is now completely out of use. To the small degree that modern astrologers use the decans, they use an Indian system, originally of Greco-Babylonian origin. This system was known to medieval Europe through the work of Al-Biruni and is to this day an important part of Vedic, or Indian, astrology. It was popularized in the West in the early twentieth century by Alan Leo and his followers.

In the Indian system of decans, the first decan of a sign is ruled by the ruler of the sign as a whole, the second is governed by the ruler of the next sign of the same element, and the third is governed by the ruler of the third and last sign ruled by that element. For example, the first decan of Taurus, which is an earth sign, would be ruled by Venus, which is the traditional ruler of Taurus. The second decan of Taurus would be ruled by Mercury, which is the traditional ruler of the next earth sign— Virgo. The third decan of Taurus would be ruled by Saturn, which is the traditional ruler of the third earth sign, Capricorn. This is an enticingly simple system but has never been all that influential. The rulerships of

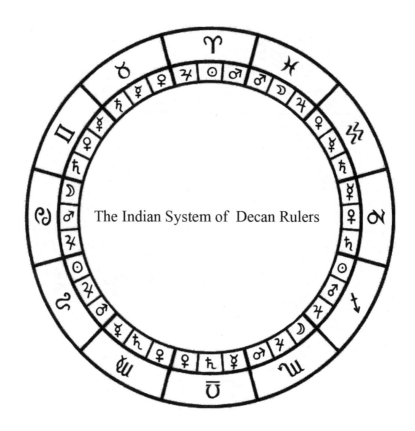

The Indian System of Decan Rulers

the Indian system are definitely more accurate than those of the Chaldean system but are still not particularly illuminating in astrological readings.[1]

The second tradition of decans comes from ancient Egypt and is much more interesting. Egyptian astrology developed independently of Greco-Babylonian astrology. It was not used to predict the will of the gods, nor was it used as a way of determining a person's innate character. Egyptian astrological diagrams appear almost exclusively on the ceilings of tombs and on the inside of coffin lids. They are impersonal sky maps meant to guide the soul of the dead person through the netherworld or "Duat." These sky maps depict approximately thirty-six gods, who rule over thirty-six small constellations through which the sun passes in its journey across the sky. After a person died and was encoffined, their soul would be looking up at this "sky map" on the tomb ceiling or coffin lid, and getting its orientation in the starry realms through which it was about to travel.[2] The soul would then leave the body and travel through each of the decans, following the path of the sun. If the soul survived the many perils of the Duat, through the protective powers of the decan gods, it would eventually catch up with the sky boat of the sun god, Re. By merging with Re, the soul would become immortal; it would join the undying light force to be resurrected with the sun at dawn.[3] Because these esoteric mysteries were at the core of the Egyptian religion, astrology was an important element of that religion, albeit a secret discipline in the special care of the funerary priests.[4]

These religious doctrines took pictorial form in Egyptian coffins and tombs. Typically, we see the elongated figure of Nut, the sky goddess, bent around the figures of the thirty-six decan gods. In a text found in almost every coffin, Nut proclaims: "I shall bear thee anew, rejuvenated. . . . I have spread myself over thee, I have born thee again as a god."[5] As a personification of the night sky, Nut "eats" the decans, one after another, as they set in the western sky. Then, at dawn, she gives birth to them again. Similarly, the soul of the deceased, traveling alongside the planets and decanal constellations, would be reborn in the light of the morning sky. It would become an immortal star god—known in ancient Egypt as an *akh*.

Even as late as the fourth century CE, long after Egypt had been taken over by the Greeks and Romans, we find a magical text that outlines this journey of the soul. After a period of prayer and purification, the soul of the living initiate is lifted into the heavens, where it beholds the starry constellations of the decan gods. The initiate proclaims that he too is a star, wandering among other stars. He then encounters and merges with the sun god.[6] It is interesting to note that this late text has a living person leaving his body and "astral traveling" through the heavens.

This indicates that the journey through the decanal constellations was not limited to the dead but could also be undertaken by the living through magical rites.[7] Jeremy Naydler, in his excellent book *Shamanic Wisdom in the Pyramid Texts*, argues convincingly that the sarcophagi in the pyramids were essentially isolation chambers, used by the living pharaoh as an aid to leaving the body and gaining a revitalizing spiritual contact with the gods of the Duat. According to Naydler: "The king must first of all go into the Osirian realm, following the decanal constellations in the southwestern sky as they are enveloped by the Dwat, and there meet the forces of death but not succumb to them. He becomes a 'living Osiris' . . . not in virtue of having died, but rather in virtue of having ventured into

Nut surrounds nine decan gods, in the tomb of Ramses VI.

the spirit world alive and having become solarized there as an *akh*. The fruit of this experience is his spiritual rebirth . . . and precisely as such he is qualified to wear the crown of Egypt."[8] These metaphysical ideas are a bit difficult for the modern mind to fathom, particularly the Egyptian association of the night sky with the Duat or netherworld. We are used to the dead inhabiting an underworld that is basically in another dimension. The ancient Egyptians, by contrast, saw very little divide between the physical and astral realms.

To summarize: the decan images in ancient Egyptian tombs had two main religious functions. First, they served as a map of the heavens through which the sun god Re passed, along with the souls of the righteous dead. Second, the decan images secured the protection of the gods ruling each of the thirty-six decanal regions of the heavens. As the soul passed through each decan of the sky, it would be protected by the god of that decan, magically invoked by its image within the tomb.

Because the decan images were essentially magical talismans, the order in which they were placed was of far less importance than their mere presence. For this reason, we find all kinds of discrepancies between different decanal systems. There is very little agreement between one system and another. About the only constants are Isis and Osiris, who were regularly identified with the star Sirius and the constellation Orion. Outside of these constants we find different families of decan systems, with plenty of variations even within a single family. Often, there are missing decans or extra decans. In fact, some depictions include whole throngs of extra decan gods. Egyptian astrology was not precise; it was a form of theurgy or religious magic and had little in common with the astronomically accurate astrology of the Greco-Babylonian tradition. In fact, the *mathematical* division of the heavens, which is so basic to Greco-Babylonian astrology, was foreign to Egyptian astrology.

Regrettably, for many centuries there has been a tendency to project the mathematical consciousness of Greek astrology back into Egyptian astrology. This misunderstanding can still be found in the works of Schwaller de Lubicz and certain New Age interpreters of Egyptian astrology. This overly mathematical conception of Egyptian astrology was already present during the Italian Renaissance. Renaissance astrologers were very interested in the Egyptian decans but didn't realize that the images they had inherited from Arabic sources were actually Greco-Egyptian hybrids that had been created during the Ptolemaic period, after the Greeks had taken over Egypt. In the Ptolemaic period, Greek astrologers brought the funerary decans of Egypt into their own mathematically sophisticated astrology and applied them to the concerns of the living. None of this was known to the Renaissance intelligentsia, who did not have enough understanding either of Egyptian religion or Egyptian astrology to recognize that the "Egyptian decans," which they had inherited from Arabic sources, were far removed from the funerary decans of authentic Egyptian astrology.

The Purpose of This Book

I have spent thirty years researching the decan traditions of Egypt, and their medieval and Renaissance descendants. I began this study with the intent of modernizing the ancient Egyptian system and reintroducing it into Western astrology. At the time, however, I did not understand the funerary nature of Egyptian astrology, and I made the mistake of assuming that it was much like Greco-Babylonian astrology. Furthermore, as my research progressed, I became aware that even the best of the many Egyptian decanal systems were not all that accurate. At times, the Egyptian gods fit well with the decans with which they were associated, but often they did not. Though it was clear that a study of ancient Egyptian decans could reveal a lot about the religious mythology of the Egyptians, it did not seem particularly relevant to modern natal astrology. In the end, I saw no point in resurrecting a system just because it was ancient. Old ideas are not necessarily true. If everything old were true, our medicine would still be based on bleeding people at certain phases of the moon!

The revival of Egyptian astrology would also bring with it another danger—that of passing on outdated cultural prejudices. The Egyptians often portrayed the first decan of what we call Aquarius as a group of bound prisoners about to be beheaded. My research shows that this is a Uranian decan associated with rebels and progressive pioneers. For the highly conservative Egyptians, rebels of this sort were considered subversive enemies of the state. This is hardly the sort of astrological interpretation one would want to inflict on a modern client. The Egyptians were at home with water signs such as Scorpio and Cancer but had a poor understanding of the sign Aquarius.

Once I had abandoned the project of resurrecting Egyptian astrology, I decided to take a modern empirical approach to the subject. This involved collecting long lists of people with planets in particular decans. For each of the thirty-six decans, I collected lists of people who had the sun, Mercury, Venus, Mars, Jupiter, Saturn, Uranus, and the North Node in these decans. For some decans, I also looked at Chiron and the moon. There were over two hundred people in each of these lists. The current book is based on an analysis of these lists. I may still discuss the Egyptian gods associated with a decan, if they are either relevant or interesting, but I ultimately defer to the results of my empirical research. This has always been my method. I always accept the results of my research, even when these results contradict traditional astrological beliefs—whether Greek or Egyptian. You will consequently find many unorthodox ideas in this book, including the idea that each sign and each decan has multiple planetary influences and can not be identified with a single ruler.

My decan research did, however, confirm the validity of the traditional zodiacal signs. It also showed unequivocally that each sign is composed of three distinct zones of spiritual influence. These decans are very different from one another. Moreover, they often reveal features of the signs that are unknown to traditional astrologers.

Unlike the Egyptians, I have not associated each decan with a god. After a lot of thought, I decided that the decans do not exhibit enough independent will to be characterized as gods but have more in common with the complex symbols found in Tarot cards. I have therefore given each decan a Tarot-like symbol, which attempts to sum up the spiritual nature of that decan. These symbols deliver far more information and insight than either the gods of ancient Egypt or the planetary rulers of Greco-Babylonian astrology.

The Decans as They Passed out of Egypt

Modern astrology is essentially Greco-Babylonian and has taken very little from Egypt. This is obvious on many levels. It is mathematical rather than talismanic; it is predictive; it stresses the importance of the planets; it is oriented toward the living rather than the dead. Still, for a long period of history, corrupted forms of the Egyptian decans were integrated into the Greco-Babylonian astrological tradition. These decan images became very important in the Renaissance. However, they were embedded within a tradition of magic rather than within the astrological tradition. In fact, the most important astrological authority of the ancient world, Claudius Ptolemy, doesn't even mention them.[9]

The absorption of the Egyptian decans into Greco-Babylonian astrology is an interesting if murky tale. The one thing we know for sure is that this amalgamation occurred only after Alexander the Great conquered Egypt in 332 BCE. At that time, a far-reaching synthesis began to take place between the Greek and Egyptian religions. The Greeks brought with them their philosophy, their mathematics, their astronomy, and their astrology. Yet, for all their intellectual prowess, the Greek conquerors were in awe of the Egyptian religion, which they considered more powerful than their own, and which they also considered the ancient *source* of their own religion.[10] In fact, once they had conquered Egypt, they began to associate and combine their own gods with Egyptian gods. Dionysius was combined with Osiris, Helios with Re, and Hermes with Thoth. This last identification engendered a new mystery religion based on the composite god Hermes/Thoth, who came to be known as Hermes Trismegistus—or "Hermes, Thrice Great." This new religious tradition was centered on magic and, in this sense, had more to do with Thoth than it did with Hermes, since Thoth, as scribe of the Egyptian gods, presided over all the temple rituals as well as the magical formulas accompanying these rituals. In Hermopolis Magna, Thoth was worshiped as the creator god. He was pictured as an all-powerful magician, who called things into being by the mere sound of his voice.[11]

Hermeticism—the religion of Hermes Trismegistus—had a strong metaphysical component but was centered largely on magic. The Egyptians were renowned throughout the world for their magic. Thus, not long after the Greek conquerors arrived, they began to translate Egyptian magical spells into Greek. Since it was already the Egyptian habit to attribute all spells and sacred literature to Thoth, the Greeks, by way of imitation, began to produce a magical literature that was written under the name "Hermes Trismegistus." Many of these Greek books of spells have come down to us. This Hermetic literature represents Hermes Trismegistus in the same broad strokes as the Egyptian Thoth: he is the creator of heaven and earth and presides over fate, justice, death, and the afterlife. He is also the guardian of magical knowledge, and the divinatory and ritual practices through which this information could be gained.[12]

Since the Egyptian priesthood already used decan images in their magic, it is not surprising that the decan gods entered quickly into the Greek Hermetic literature. The Egyptians had long been using decan figures as protective amulets. By 850 BCE, at the time of Pharaoh Osorkon II, we see decan images appearing on statues, amulets, and bracelets. The most popular were decanal statuettes of Sekmet-Bastet. These amulets featured a cat-headed or lion-headed goddess seated on a throne decorated with decanal images.[13] The Greeks, in their studies of Egyptian magic, would have run into these decan images as a matter of course. They would also have encountered decan images in Egyptian tombs, where their astrological nature would have been obvious. The appropriation of the thirty-six decans of Egypt into the twelve-signed Greek zodiac was therefore a natural step. After all, they fit perfectly into the Greek zodiac, three to a sign. In this way, the funerary decans of ancient Egypt were absorbed into an astrological tradition that focused on the living rather than the dead.

In the end, the two astrological traditions never fully merged. Egyptian funerary astrology continued long after the Greek conquest, often with the simple addition of Greek zodiacal figures over the Egyptian decan gods. In the Denderah round zodiac, pictured on page 8, we see Egyptian decan gods along the rim of the circle, and the Greek zodiacal images closer to the center. However, there are *not* exactly thirty-six decan gods, nor do these gods occupy equal sections of the circle. The word *decan*, which is derived from the Greek word for "ten," was not an Egyptian concept. The Egyptians never saw the so-called decans in a mathematical light. Even in the Ptolemaic period, Egyptian temple priests did not consign the decan gods to 10-degree arcs within a circle but continued to practice the funerary astrology of their forebears. Thus, in the Denderah round zodiac, some decan gods occupy four and five times more space than others.

Greek astrologers, for the most part, never fully embraced the decans and their corresponding Egyptian gods. Claudius Ptolemy doesn't mention them, and they are almost never mentioned in the collection of surviving Greek horoscopes from the Ptolemaic period.[14] Though the most influential Greco-Roman astrologers may have ignored the decans, the decan images received quite a prominent place in the magical literature of Greek Hermeticism. A regular feature of these books was the association of specific stones and medicinal herbs with each of the astrological decans. These books also explained how to create magical talismans by engraving occult images on the proper stones. Through sympathetic magic, it was thought that these talismans would draw down the powers of the decans. One such spell book was the *Sacred Book of Hermes*, or *Liber Sacer*. This book gives instructions on how to engrave a decan image on the appropriate precious stone and then fit this stone into a magic ring. Spell books like the *Liber Sacer* were the main source of decan images throughout the Hellenistic, medieval, and Renaissance periods. Thus, while the decans are astrological in nature, they were never fully integrated into traditional Greco-Babylonian astrology but remained embedded within a tradition of Hermetic magic.

In addition to the texts of practical magic associated with Hermeticism, there were also a number of philosophical treatises, known collectively as the *Corpus Hermeticum*. These texts, which were written between 100 and 300 CE,[15] generally took the form of a dialogue between Hermes Trismegistus and a disciple to whom he was teaching the mysteries of the cosmos. While some scholars point to native Egyptian elements within this literature,[16] most Egyptologists see these writings as creations of the Greek invaders. The Hermetic dialogues were written in Greek and relied heavily on the Greek philosophy of Neoplatonism.[17] The texts basically carried forward and developed metaphysical ideas found in Plato's *Timaeus*. However, as Hermetic literature, they gave great importance to the decans, which they generally placed on a higher level than the planets. Thus, in one text, Hermes Trismegistus describes the decans in this way:

> The force which works in all events that befall men collectively comes from the Decans; for instance, overthrows of kingdoms, revolts of cities, famines, pestilences, overflowings of the sea, earthquakes—none of these things, my son, take place without the working of the Decans. . . . For if the Decans rule over the seven planets, and we are subject to the planets, do you not see that the force set in action by the Decans reaches us also, whether it is worked by the Decans themselves or by means of the planets?[18]

Though the decans were never fully integrated into Greco-Babylonian astrology, Hermetic versions of the Egyptian decans became tremendously popular throughout the ancient world. Versions of the Hermetic decans traveled into many European countries, as well as Assyria, Persia, India, and even China. In these travels, the decans were translated and retranslated into different languages and different traditions. Not surprisingly, this led to a dramatic and ongoing corruption of the source material. For instance, in one Indian version of the decans, the first decan of Cancer is symbolized by "a terrible woman with a noose." In Egypt, this decan was almost always portrayed as Isis holding an ankh. Clearly, the Indians had received this lore in the form of pictures and did not understand what the picture portrayed. They mistook the looped cross of the ankh for a hangman's noose, thus changing a symbol of life into a symbol of death. The corruption of the decan images, as they passed from hand to hand, might be compared to the children's game of "telephone." Every time the decans passed through new hands, they were further distorted.

The names given to the decans in the Hermetic literature also underwent corruption. In genuine Egyptian sources, the names of the decans were written in hieroglyphics and were often just descriptive phrases such as "the divider of the sheep," "the beginning of the jar stand," or "Osiris's right arm." In the Hermetic literature these names degenerated into barbarous names of power. They were transformed into nonsensical but supposedly magical words, the modern equivalent of which is "abracadabra." The Greeks were in awe of the Egyptian religion but didn't understand it all that well, since very few of them could actually read hieroglyphics.

The decans arrived in medieval Europe through Islamic scholars who had absorbed and developed Greco-Egyptian astrology and Greco-Egyptian magic. When Islamic Spain was reconquered by Christian rulers in the eleventh and twelfth centuries, Islamic books on magic, medicine, and astrology were translated from Arabic into Latin. These books, in fact, were among the first of the Arabic books to be translated. Christian monks of the High Middle Ages were apparently gluttons for magic, and while the Egyptian decans were seen as pagan, and even evil, they were also considered very powerful.

During the Christian Middle Ages, astrology became central to the worldview of western Europe. However, the Egyptian decans were still considered too demonic to be included in this worldview. After all, the decans had been received in large part through textbooks on magic, most especially the notorious *Picatrix*, where one finds spells to "liquidate one's enemy" and to "destroy a city." Since Europe's literate population, in the High Middle Ages, was largely clerical, they could hardly embrace this form of astrology. Moreover, Saint Augustine himself had associated the Egyptian decan gods with demons.[19] Of course, at the time, Christians represented every pagan god as a demon, and the Egyptian decans, with their exceptionally powerful pagan gods, were considered particularly dangerous.[20]

The Decans in the Renaissance

Saint Augustine was the most influential of the Church Fathers during the early Middle Ages. He attacked the whole of astrology and astronomy as sinful, since it led the mind into the "sin of curiosity."[21] In fact, despite his high reputation as a medieval intellectual, Augustine may have been the most important source of Christian anti-intellectualism in the medieval period. Because of Augustine's attacks on astrology and astronomy, religious intellectuals of the High Middle Ages had to find moral and theological justifications for the study of physical science. These intellectual gymnastics resulted in the production of a great deal of convoluted theology, which blended Aristotelian and Neoplatonic philosophy with Christian angelology and Greco-Babylonian astrology. This philosophical amalgamation contained a great deal of ancient science and philosophy, but was essentially a *theological* system, and as such was dogmatic and authoritarian. Moreover, even after physical science had been clothed in Christian trappings, it suffered continual attack from the Catholic establishment, especially the lower clergy.

With the advent of the Renaissance, the Augustinian prejudice against astrology, magic, and science began to break down. Frances Yates, in *Giordano Bruno and the Hermetic Tradition*, asserts that the recovery of the *Corpus Hermeticum* in Florentine intellectual circles was very important to the Renaissance reevaluation of human potential. Augustine's doctrine of original sin pictured man as sinful and fallen, even at birth. By contrast, some of the Hermetic texts pictured people as potential magi, who could become masters of their fate and rise above the level of the planets and the decans to participate directly in the creative powers of God.[22] These ideas were embraced by the Florentine intelligentsia and were spelled out in Pico della Mirandola's influential *Oration on the Dignity of Man*. Pico's *Oration* was the clarion call of the era, announcing that humanity's potentials are unlimited, and that people should aspire to new heights. This new stance toward the world was reflected in the Renaissance reexamination of traditional teachings in religion, medicine, science, and art. Compared to the Middle Ages, the Renaissance was an era of great progress and optimism, and it is Frances Yates's contention that this was due, in part, to the rejection of the hopeless portrait of mankind embedded in Augustinian Christianity and its replacement by positive Gnostic ideas found in the Greco-Egyptian *Corpus Hermeticum*.[23]

Renaissance intellectuals such as Marsilio Ficino and Pico della Mirandola were enthusiastic about the ideas in the *Corpus Hermeticum*. However, they mistakenly identified these philosophical works as genuine products of ancient Egypt. Actually, they were written centuries after the birth of Christ, by Greco-Egyptian intellectuals steeped in the philosophy of Neoplatonism. Because Marsilio Ficino and Pico della Mirandola recognized both Platonic and Christian ideas in these texts, they believed that the ancient Egyptian religion contained precursors of the more evolved teachings of Christianity and could therefore be studied without spiritual danger. The Renaissance was an era of great syncretism—where Hebrew, Egyptian, Christian, and Greek ideas were absorbed into a single worldview. This stance—which had the sanction of many ancient church authorities—led to a passion for Egyptian wisdom. In fact, Egyptian art and religion became something of a fad.[24]

Obelisks, transported from Egypt, decorated city squares. One was even placed next to the Vatican. Famous artists put Egyptian hieroglyphics in their paintings. One painting in the Vatican depicts the pagan sage Hermes Trismegistus. Another painting shows the conquest of Italy by the Egyptian god Osiris. Much of this Egyptian lore was hopelessly inaccurate. For instance, artists and intellectuals were using a book called *Hieroglyphica* to translate Egyptian writing. Unfortunately, the author of the *Hieroglyphica* had absolutely no understanding of the Egyptian language. Hieroglyphics would not, in fact, be successfully translated for several centuries.[25]

One of the most impressive monuments to emerge from Renaissance Egyptomania is the *Sala dei Mesi*, in Ferrara's Palazzo Schifanoia. This gigantic astrological painting covers all four walls of a 72-foot-long room. It was completed in 1470 and prominently features the thirty-six Egyptian decan gods. The walls are divided into three tiers. The topmost tier depicts the life of the Greco-Roman gods. The middle tier shows the zodiac divided into the thirty-six Egyptian decans.[26] The bottommost tier pictures the court life of Ferrara's rulers—the Estes. The general idea was that magical force would pass from the pagan gods on the top tier, through the decan images in the middle tier, and on to the rulers of Ferrara, on the bottom tier. Since the room was a council chamber used for political decision-making, the rulers of Ferrara were making use of "Egyptian magic" in their exercise of government. (These remarkable paintings can be viewed by looking up the Palazzo Schifanoia on the web.)

Egyptomania, and the syncretic religion of which it was a part, was brought to an end by the Protestant Reformation. During the period leading up to the Reformation, the popes, though often quite corrupt, were sympathetic to the intellectual and scientific interests of the intellectual class. Compared to the heresy-hunting popes of the late Middle Ages, they were quite tolerant and did not interfere with the intelligentsia's exploration of Greek, Egyptian, and Hebrew religions. However, when the firebrand Protestant reformer Martin Luther appeared on the scene, this picture began to change. At the beginning of the rebellion, Pope Paul III sent a broad-minded humanist cardinal to negotiate with Martin Luther. When this man failed to bring Luther back into the fold, the church began to adopt a hard-line policy. The Dominican Order, which was associated with the Inquisition, came to the fore, and with them the rigidly Aristotelian worldview of their medieval intellectual authority, Saint Thomas

Aquinas. As Aristotelians, the Dominicans opposed any form of Neoplatonism—which was the Greek philosophy that had always undergirded astrology and magic. As the Dominicans gained more power, they began to systematically repress books and teachings informed by Neoplatonism. In fact, astrology was banned by the Catholic Church, outside of its use for medical or meteorological purposes—this, despite the fact the popes of the era, like the kings, always had personal astrologers.

In the era of the Counter-Reformation, the Church became overtly anti-intellectual. Giordano Bruno was burned at the stake, and Galileo was threatened with torture. In fact, if one takes a close look at the record, one finds that almost *every* innovative Italian philosopher and scientist during the late sixteenth and early seventeenth centuries was attacked by the Inquisition.[27] Due to this repression of free thought, Italy became something of an intellectual backwater over the course of the seventeenth century, and progressive thinking moved to the less repressive Protestant countries in the North, notably England and the Netherlands.

During the sixteenth century, the most-important proponents of the "Egyptian" decans were arch-magician Cornelius Agrippa and Neapolitan philosopher Giordano Bruno. Bruno is known to modern historians as an early champion of Copernicus's sun-centered universe. He was also the first to declare that the universe was infinite in extent, and not a closed system bounded by "crystal spheres." These seemingly modern ideas, however, must be put in context. Bruno was a thoroughgoing Egyptianist, and as such, saw Copernicus's system as part of a general reformation of knowledge that would include the resurrection of the sun-centered religion of ancient Egypt.[28] In fact, while Marsilio Ficino and Pico della Mirandola were very careful to address Augustine's injunctions against decanal magic, Bruno openly championed the Egyptian magic of the *Hermetica*. Frances Yates tells us that Bruno was trying to reform Christianity by marrying it with the magical religion of the Egyptians. He may have even wanted to *replace* Christianity with Egyptian solar worship. He was especially committed to the idea that the divine spirit was immanent in animals and plants—an idea that had a central place in the ancient Egyptian religion.[29]

Bruno included the "Egyptian" decans in several of his books, using a version of the decan symbols taken from Cornelius Agrippa. The decans were especially prominent in Bruno's *De umbris idearum* (*On the Shadows of Ideas*), which was published in 1582. This book begins as a dialogue between several people, one of them being Hermes Trismegistus. In the book, the decan images are represented as Platonic Ideas or heavenly archetypes. Bruno believed that the imprinting of these images on one's mind would draw down, in talismanic fashion, the powers of the decans and the planets. In other words, by focusing one's mind on the true heavenly archetypes—the Egyptian decans—one would become identified with Thoth and begin to absorb his knowledge and magical powers.

Bruno's *De umbris idearum* fit the decans into the classical tradition of "memory palaces." Memory palaces were invented by Greek and Roman orators as a way to memorize speeches. In works by Quintilian and pseudo-Cicero, the orator was taught to practice his speech while passing through a large building. When he came to a window or a door, he would make up a symbol that alluded to whatever was going on in the speech. Later, when he actually gave the speech, he would be going through the building in his mind. The sequence of symbols would jog his memory about what he should be talking about. Though this technique sounds too complicated to actually work, variants of the technique are used even now by contestants in memory competitions.[30]

The memory tradition of ancient Rome was resurrected in the Middle Ages by Albertus Magnus and Thomas Aquinas. In the same general period, Dante wrote his *Divine Comedy*, which is essentially a huge memory palace organizing various virtues and vices. With the resurrection of Hermeticism and Neoplatonism in the High Renaissance, the memory tradition took a new turn. It became allied with talismanic magic. Classical and medieval memory palaces employed symbols that were purposely grotesque, so they could be easily recalled. In the Renaissance, however, these artificially devised symbols were replaced by occult symbols, including the Egyptian decans. This new type of memory palace did not function as an aid to memorization but was constructed to channel heavenly information and power. By meditating on these symbols, people sought to harmonize their minds with the mind of God. This new type of memory palace takes a physical form in the astrological paintings of the Palazzo Schifanoia but is also evident in Bruno's *De umbris idearum*.

Ficino and Pico had been careful to put their ideas in a Christian framework. Moreover, they enjoyed the protection of the powerful Medici family. Giordano Bruno, by comparison, was very rash. He championed the Egyptian religion *over* Christianity at a time when even Christian Neoplatonism was being attacked by the Church. Not surprisingly,

Bruno was accused of heresy by the Inquisition. He was condemned for dealings in magic, holding opinions contrary to the Catholic faith, and claiming the existence of the plurality of worlds. Refusing to recant, he was burned at the stake in the Campo dei Fiori in Rome, on February 17, 1600. When Italy became a republic in the nineteenth century and was freed from the domination of the pope, Italian nationalists erected a statue to Giordano Bruno in the place of his execution, where it stands to this day. For nationalists and Freemasons, Bruno symbolized the victory of free thought over the intellectual repression of the church.

The burning of Giordano Bruno signaled an end to the Egyptian decan tradition, at least within astrology. Decanal astrology was simply too dangerous to practice. However, other aspects of Hermetic culture continued to thrive, at least for a while. Alchemy, which was another important element in the Hermetic culture of the Renaissance, grew in importance in the seventeenth century and was embraced by ground-breaking scientists such as Boyle and Newton. Alchemy had always had an element of practical chemistry but in this period became allied to an occult form of Christianity called Rosicrucianism. In Rosicrucian texts, alchemical processes symbolized internal spiritual transformations, the final stage of which was the "red tincture," or Christ consciousness. In the 1620s, however, Rosicrucianism was attacked by the Catholic Church as a form of Satanism, and it too began to wither.[31] Alchemy was increasingly divested of its spiritual orientation and began its transformation into modern materialistic chemistry. Newton, who was an avid student of spiritual alchemy, was too cautious to speak of these things openly. Simson Najovits says of Newton: "Publicly, he hypocritically professed an orthodox, and even aggressive, Protestant religion." Privately, he denied the Trinity and had many other unorthodox religious views. In fact, in his unpublished *Chronology of Ancient Kingdoms Amended*, Newton claims that the Egyptian religion had been the true religion before it was corrupted by star worship and the belief in Osiris, Isis, Horus, and Amun.[32]

The Enlightenment began as a reaction to the terrible religious wars and witch hunts of the seventeenth century. These excesses of belief led to a general skepticism about any invisible reality. Witches, magic, and even the Christian religion were increasingly seen as products of the human imagination. With the Enlightenment's turn toward physical science, astrology also suffered a dramatic loss of prestige. It lost its credibility with the intelligentsia and within academia, and began to devolve into fortune-telling. Divorcing itself from metaphysical and religious issues, it increasingly concerned itself with predictions about health, romance, and money. The magical element disappeared, and with it, the Egyptian decans.

During this period, Hermeticism started to go underground. It found its most undiluted expression in the Freemasons, a secret society that spread rapidly through the aristocracies of Europe and America. The Freemasons were unabashed Hermeticists and, as such, were still rooted in the syncretic religion of the Renaissance, which combined Christian, Jewish, and Egyptian elements. Since the Freemasons were practitioners of ritual magic, and devotees of "Egyptian" wisdom, it is not surprising that they embraced the decans. Even as late as 1871, the decans are discussed in *Morals and Dogmas of the Ancient and Accepted Scottish Rite of Freemasonry*. Here they are related to a Masonic grade called the "Knight of the Brazen Serpent."

The Freemasons, as heirs of the magical tradition of the Renaissance, viewed the decans as tools of magic and ignored their astrological uses. Through Freemasonry, the "Egyptian" decans were transmitted to a few writers in the Golden Dawn. However, as much as the Golden Dawn effectively promoted the Kabbalah and the Tarot, they had little influence on modern astrology and did nothing to promote the use of the decans.

Methodology

I came up with my interpretations for the thirty-six decans by studying lists of examples. Using AstroDatabank and tens of thousands of solar charts, I collected lists of famous people with planets in the decans. For instance, for the first decan of Aries, I collected separate lists for people with the sun, Mercury, Venus, Mars, Jupiter, Saturn, Uranus, and the North Node in this decan. Each of these lists included over two hundred famous people, as well as data about people I know personally. For the more difficult decans, I also made lists for Chiron and the moon. I analyzed each of these lists separately and then began to identify characteristics and themes common to each of these planetary placements. What I found right away—and this was very curious—was that it made little difference which planet was in a decan; every planet seemed to express the decanal energy in much the same way.

Before analyzing the lists, I tried to void my mind of all preconceptions. This would allow me to see what was actually there, rather
than seizing on a few examples to confirm what I already believed, or
what I *wanted* to believe. Voiding the mind was not an easy thing to do.
For before I began this undertaking, I had made a thorough study of the
Egyptian decan gods, as well as the more famous decan systems of the
Middle Ages and the Renaissance. In other words, I had lots of ideas
about each decan before I began my formal analysis. This proved to be
a major problem. I found that I had to go over the examples in each list
several times, with months in between each assessment, so I could look
at the material freshly. Not surprisingly, I found it particularly difficult
to rid myself of preconceptions about decans that are prominent in my
own chart. When I got stuck or was torn between rival interpretations, I
turned to my brother Ken for aid, sending him example lists of problem
decans and conferring with him at length about the nature of these decans.

The analytical phase of my research produced about twenty pages
of notes, single spaced, for each decan. After reading these over, I began
to identify the basic themes of each of the decans. I created subheadings
and grouped my insights under the appropriate subheading. The creation
of the decan symbols was probably the most difficult part of the work—
and also the most important. Sometimes the images came to me out of the
blue; in other cases, I came up with a number of different symbols and
lived with them awhile until it became clear which symbol made the best
fit with the examples. In deciding upon a symbol, I would sometimes ask
questions of the examples. I might ask: "Is the chief figure in this decan
an artist or is it a teacher?" I would then look at the examples and count
how many of them did some kind of artwork and how many did some kind
of teaching. The advantage of this approach is that it helped me discredit
symbols that, though incorrect, had a kind of hypnotic fascination. Certain images had so much power that it was easy to think that they had
to be right. This kind of error was a common occurrence when I was
entertaining the idea that I was channeling the "one cosmically correct
symbol." In the end, I found it more useful to come up with a number of
different decan images. After coming up with several, I would simply
ask myself which of the images best described the examples.

Sources

There really aren't a lot of modern astrology books on the decans. There is a book by Gary Goldschneider called the *Secret Language of Destiny*, which stands entirely outside the decan tradition but provides insightful descriptions of the decanal areas of the zodiac.[33] Goldschneider's work is especially useful because it is derived from empirical research. Austin Coppock's *36 Faces*, which is intuitively rather than empirically based, is informed by the decan tradition. However, unlike my own book, which emphasizes ancient Egyptian decan systems, Coppock's work emerges from the magic tradition of the Middle Ages and Renaissance. Like medieval spell books, *36 Faces* gives instructions for engraving appropriate stones with decanal images. Unfortunately, both the text and illustrations of Coppock's book are decidedly morbid, with frequent references to Aleister Crowley and decans named "A Cup of Blood" and "An Executioner's Sword." Though the book is well written and fairly insightful, it is hard to imagine that a book so spiritually dark could have a positive influence.

While there is very little *astrological* literature on the decans, there is a great deal of academic literature on ancient Egyptian astrology. For practical reasons, I will mention only a few of the most important academic treatments of Egyptian astrology. The most important book for any serious research into the Egyptian decans is Otto Neugebauer's *Egyptian Astronomical Texts*. Neugebauer lists the decan gods depicted in each of eighty-one extant archaeological sources. For instance, he gives the names and arrangements of the gods of the round zodiac of Denderah, the rectangular zodiac of Denderah, etc. He also lists the gods on the interiors of coffin lids, some of them as late as the Roman period. Since photographs of all these monuments are found in his books, it is possible to check his attributions, which are generally quite accurate. Neugebauer's lists are basic, since they show which Egyptian gods are associated with each decan.

Perhaps the chief breakthrough in the understanding of the decans is found in Sophie-Anne von Bomhard's *The Naos of Decades*.[34] This is a detailed description of a decanal monument that was recently brought up from the bottom of the harbor of Alexandria. The book's publisher is the Oxford Centre for Maritime Archaeology. While von Bomhard does not lay out her thesis very clearly, she has a deep understanding of the place of the decan images within the funerary religion of ancient Egypt.

To get more of a handle on the mythology of the decan gods, I have employed the books of Wilhelm Gundel and Franz Boll, two German academics who wrote before World War II.[35] These works focus on post-Ptolemaic decan lists that had already been assimilated into the Greco-Babylonian astrological tradition. Still, there is a great deal of erudition here. There are many more academic studies of the Egyptian decans, some of them very modern. However, the majority of them show no understanding of the talismanic nature of the decans and tend to view these systems as extremely inaccurate forms of mathematical astrology. See the bibliography at the end of this book for some of the more interesting articles and books on this subject.

The Nature of Decan Symbols

For each of the decans I have created a symbol, reminiscent of an image from the Tarot. To me, this seems the most useful and accurate way to describe the energy of the decans. This approach to the decans is not exactly new. In the Renaissance, the decans were also given pictorial symbols. The Egyptians, of course, saw each of the decans as a god—most of them minor gods, but gods nonetheless. For a while, I considered assigning gods to the various decans, but in the end I did not feel that there was enough *active will* in the decans to justify this approach. The decans simply aren't godlike. On the other hand, the Greek approach, which assigns planetary rulers to the decans, is even less compelling. There have been many systems of decan rulers. The only one now in use is the Indian system described at the very beginning of this book. I researched this system thoroughly but found it highly inaccurate. I then tried to come up with my own system of decan rulers. Ultimately, I failed to discover any simple system of rulers that fits the data. The one regular rule I did find was that the first decan of a sign is often dominated by the traditional ruler of the sign as a whole. Even when there are multiple planetary influences in the first decan, this traditional ruler is almost always strongest. In the signs Scorpio, Aquarius, and Pisces, whose traditional rulers have been replaced by more recently discovered planets, we find Pluto dominant in the first decan of Scorpio, Uranus dominant in the first decan of Aquarius, and both Neptune and Jupiter influencing the first decan of Pisces.

As for the second and third decans, these do not follow any obvious pattern. In discussing these decans, I might mention a ruler—for instance, Venus for Virgo 2 and Saturn for Virgo 3—but I have based these attributions entirely on the examples and am not following any system. I treat planetary rulers at length only when it significantly adds to our understanding of a decan. In some cases, I mention planetary influences only in passing, in some cases not at all. Modern astrologers are rather addicted to systems of rulership and may be frustrated by my failure to provide single decan rulers. However, my research shows that there are multiple planetary influences in most decans. To speak of a single planetary ruler is therefore misleading. It is not just an oversimplification but actually prevents one from understanding the subtler dynamics of the decan. Perhaps it would be best to throw out the term "ruler" entirely and speak instead of "dominant planetary powers." Some readers may also object to the fact that I haven't assigned an Egyptian god to each decan. To begin with, the idea that each decan has a single "correct" decan god is not authentically Egyptian. In the highly variable decan systems, any number of gods may occupy a single decan. Only Isis and Osiris regularly occupy specific decans. I have assigned an Egyptian god to a decan only if this significantly aids in one's understanding of that decan. In fact, in some cases I have assigned Egyptian gods that are almost never actually found there. It is not my purpose to resurrect an authentically Egyptian astrology. I make use of Egyptian ideas to the degree that I think them useful to the aims of modern astrology. In any case, I do not consider the decans godlike and therefore feel no compunction to represent them as Egyptian gods. I find the "Tarot symbol" approach far more useful.

In each decan image, it is the human situation in the symbol that seems to be the most important element of the decan, with the planets functioning as subordinate elements of the story, which often take specific roles within the decan picture. Take, for instance, the first decan of Pisces. The decan symbol has a woman arguing with the captain of a ship and pointing to a world globe. In the symbol, the rebellious woman represents an aspect of Mars, the globe represents Jupiter, and the ocean represents Neptune. Thus, beneath the decan symbol, we can detect the decan's "ruling" planets interacting with each other in fairly specific ways.

The "Tarot card" approach came to me a long time ago when I was researching the phases of the moon. When I studied lists of people born during a certain moon phase, Tarot-like images often came to me. Some of these were so close to the Major Arcana of the Tarot that I wondered whether the moon phases were not the ultimate *source* of the Major Arcana. In *Moon Phases*, which was published in 1988, I argued that the 10-degree moon phases are related to the decans of the zodiac. I said, "As I did more charts I realized that there is, in fact, a strong connection between the decanates and the smaller [moon] phases—even if it doesn't follow any easily grasped system of planetary rulerships. People with the Sun in the last decanate of Scorpio actually do seem to show a lot of the characteristics associated with Phase 21, the third Scorpio moon phase. And people with the Sun in the second decanate of Cancer actually do show a lot of characteristics of Phase 10, the second Cancer phase."[36] At the time I wrote *Moon Phases*, I also wondered whether the symbols I had come up with were specific to the moon phases, or whether they were also valid for the zodiacal decans. Since I had not yet done much research on the decans, I left the question open.

Now that I have done a lot of research on the decans, I realize that the moon phases *are* decanal, and that the symbols I created for them are essentially decan symbols! It would have been nice if the symbols I came up with for the current book were the same as the ones I created for my book on the moon phases. And while there are strong similarities for almost every decan, there are also important discrepancies. The new symbols, however, are definitely superior. I am a better researcher now and have better data to work with. When I researched *Moon Phases*, I was not yet in possession of Lois Rodden's *AstroDatabank*, for instance. In researching the current book, I used *AstroDatabank* and a huge collection of solar charts compiled by my brother, then checked all this data with the Wikipedia and Find a Grave websites.

To return to the symbolic element of the decans, the Tarot-image approach definitely works, but one must still ask what these symbols actually tell us. First of all, each symbol represents an archetypal situation that people of that decan seem to live through again and again. The symbol is representative of that person's consciousness and concerns—and to some degree what they are trying to master in their current incarnation. It is an interior landscape that they inhabit and tend to project onto the outside world. They live into these images because, for them, the decan image is a very real aspect of the world as they perceive it. It is a colored lens or filter that makes some things appear important and other things unimportant.

The decans deal with the way we experience the world, but they also indicate the kind of life lessons we need to learn. Each decan offers the possibility of mastering certain kinds of life situations. In the process, we also learn to use the planetary energies intrinsic to these decans. These lessons are provided by life itself in the rather repetitive challenges that define our lives—challenges that mirror the decan images of our astrological charts.

Curiously, the decans seem to behave in much the same way *no matter what planet is involved*. The planets seem to act as energizers, without adding much of their own personality to the way the decan is expressed. Yet, it gets even more curious. Any planet in a decan seems to activate the planets identified with that decan. Thus, because the second decan of Capricorn is "ruled" by Chiron, any planet that lands there expresses itself *as* Chiron. Venus in the second decan of Capricorn activates the phase image and also the planetary archetype of Chiron. It would seem that the Chiron archetype is locked within the decan itself and operates independently of the position of Chiron in the heavens. Each decan seems to contain planetary archetypes as pools of energy and thought without reference to the *physical* planets. For a deeper exploration of this issue, see the final essay of this book, which discusses the nature of planetary influence.

The decan image provides the most comprehensive characterization of a decan, but the decan's dominant planets help flesh out the story—a story that people tend to live out in real life. Referring once more to the first decan of Pisces, the rebellious woman is Mars, the stubborn captain is Jupiter, and the world globe is also Jupiter. These planetary energies will be easily accessible to people who have *any* planets in this decan; any planet will tune these individuals in to Martian and Jupiterian archetypes. In the course of their lives, they may also encounter a lot of Martian and Jupiterian individuals, who will also serve to bring these energies into their lives.

The presence of planetary archetypes within each decan seems inescapable, but the human situation in the decan image is what defines the particular ways that these planetary archetypes play out. Jupiter could be a teacher in one decan and a crusader in another. The decan image frames and defines the planetary energies and also shows *how* its most influential planets relate to one another. This very specific information about planetary relationships exposes the crudity of the Greek approach with its single planetary decan ruler. To say that Mars rules the first decan of Aries, without mentioning the strong influence of Mercury, is to give a grossly simplified and highly inaccurate portrait of the decan.

The decans can provide many analytical insights in chart readings. However, each person has many decans in his or her chart. There is not just the sun and moon, but all the planets, as well as points such as the Midheaven and Ascendant. In fact, it might be said, without much exaggeration, each person has *all* the decans in his or her chart. Thus, while the decans are very useful in chart interpretation, they have other important uses. The decans can also be studied as abstract archetypes. They can be studied as one might study the *I Ching* or the Tarot—not as a divinatory system, but as a way to rise to a higher level of spiritual understanding.

In *The Wisdom of the Tarot*, by Paul Foster Case, he expounds upon the implicit teachings of each card of the Major Arcana, with the goal of connecting the reader to the energies and consciousness of these archetypes. Case's approach is gnostic and, ultimately, religious. Case was the founder and leader of a spiritual society called the Builders of the Adytum. The adytum is the innermost sanctuary of an ancient temple. At a certain point in my own decan research, I realized that I too am building a temple, an astral temple that can connect the reader to the archetypes of the thirty-six decans.

Through my decan images, descriptive essays, and famous examples, I am providing a way for people to familiarize themselves with the astrological archetypes—to be able to walk in, around, and through them. The decan images are intended to draw down both energy and wisdom from these archetypes through sympathetic magic. They are intended to serve as a conduit or lens to archetypes that are repositories for specific types of consciousness and wisdom. Still, access to these archetypes is not a given. Short of meditating on the symbols, it is unlikely that the reader will connect with the archetypes. I have provided symbols, keywords, and examples to make this process easier, but if the reader does not meditate on these things, it will be difficult for him or her to forge strong connections with the archetypes and to extend and personalize the material found in this book.

Identifying Your Decans

It is easy to use this book if you have a fairly accurate astrological chart. If you don't, you can get one at astro.com. The most-important decans for an individual will be the decans of the Ascendant, Sun, Moon, and other important planets. There are 30 degrees in a sign. The first 10 degrees (00°00'–9°59') compose the first decan, the second 10 degrees (10°00'–19°59') compose the second decan, and the third 10 degrees (20°00'–29°59') comprise the third decan. Retrograde planets very close to the cusp between decans may require a bit of thought before one can decide to which decan a planet belongs.

Aries, 1st Decan

IMAGE: *A boy puts together a pirate costume out of various scraps laid out on a table. He then joins his friends, raises his wooden sword aloft, and commands them to attack a rival group of youngsters.*

People with an emphasis here are in a lifelong battle against falsehood, for whenever they encounter dishonesty, they get angry and go on the attack. The sword of the decan symbol is the "sword of truth," which cleanly separates truth from lies. It skewers false representations of reality as well as underhanded dealings. The sword also represents the ability to sever ties to people, ideas, or emotions that are holding one back. People of this decan are initiating a new cycle; it is therefore important that they "cut the umbilical cord" by turning their backs on their parents' expectations. Parents always have a lot of ideas about who their children are, and what they should do with their lives. The courage to rebel is therefore necessary for true individuation. One cannot expect to be given the freedom to be oneself by one's parents or by society. One has to claim this freedom for oneself, even when that requires a fight.

The first decan of Aries marks the beginning of spring, when new shoots are rising through the ground and pushing aside obstacles in their path. People of this decan have a great deal of natural vitality, for they are connected to the primal generative forces of the universe. As embodiments of the "divine child," they feel entitled to do and say whatever they want. They see no need to second-guess their impulses and reactions, and demand of themselves only that they meet each situation honestly, however much courage that requires. Aries 1 individuals want to live a life that is adventurous and free. As rambunctious individuals, they have a good idea what they can get away with, for they are constantly testing the boundaries of what is allowed. Generally, they're able to run circles around their opponents, deftly sidestepping every effort to contain their rebellious energies.

Mars and Mercury are the two most influential planets in this decan. Mars gives these people clarity of perception—an ability to reduce the situation to its most important operant elements. By simplifying the situation, Mars provides enough clarity for people to decide upon the best course of action. It also gives them enough courage to act on that decision. Aries 1 individuals know how to think on their feet and are therefore able to maneuver through fast-moving or dangerous situations. This is apparent in the decan symbol, where a would-be warrior maneuvers through a crowd of combatants. As quick-witted individuals, Aries 1 individuals are at an advantage in any fast-moving situation and may speed things up or mix things up in order to gain an edge on their opponents.

As youngsters, people of this decan resist socialization, which they experience as bullying and repression. Parents and teachers seem to think they have a right to dictate what children say or do, but people of this decan don't buy it. They cannot be dissuaded from their own reading of their situation and play it as they see it. They know that theirs is a superior interpretation and refuse to be won over by those who would rob them of their freedom. As far as they are concerned, to acquiesce to the established "realities" of the adult world is to be defeated before one has begun. It is tantamount to surrendering one's "magic wand"—one's ability to conjure up a new reality and act out a part within that vision.

As the first decan of the first fire sign, this is an extremely creative decan. And the most important thing these people create is their own *identity*. Aries 1 individuals find joy in creative self-expression and love to experiment with different identities. Often they refuse to commit to any one persona for quite some time. Instead, they play around with different social stances, clothing choices, and personal myths. Eventually, they decide which of these roles feels most real and most enjoyable, and go with it. In the decan image, we see a boy choosing different clothes and props from a square table. He is choosing which elements he wants to include in his ego image and which elements he rejects. Whoever he decides to be, he has to muster up enough confidence to *be* that person. This will be the focus of his personality—what he insists upon and will fight to defend. Self-assurance, however, is not something Aries 1 individuals are born with. It's something they must develop. They do this by proving to themselves, through small heroic acts, that their chosen role is not just a pose, but a reality.

In the horoscope, the Ascendant of the chart is associated with the first degree of Aries. Like the first decan of Aries, the Ascendant is concerned with a person's sense of identity. Most astrologers view this identity as something of a fixed quantity; they see it in terms of innate or inborn character traits. Missing from this picture is the creativity of early Aries. Aries is a fire sign and is therefore intensely inventive and creative. Admittedly, there are inborn factors at the Ascendant, but there is also an element of artistry and choice. At the Ascendant, individuals take an inventory of the traits they admire and the traits they scorn and then choose which traits they want to take as their own.[37] Through their efforts to express these traits, they slowly *become* the people they have decided to be. The traditional view of the Ascendant, with its emphasis on fixed or inborn character, is a relic of the highly fatalistic perspective of ancient Greek astrology. The Greeks believed that one's character was fixed at birth. People had no hand in who they became. They did not create themselves but could only be who they already were.

In my book on the moon phases, I identified the second moon phase with the first decan of Aries and the Magician card of the Tarot. My image for the first decan of Aries is also suggestive of the Magician card, since both picture a youth standing before a table on which there are a number of objects from which to choose. Like the children playing pirates, these people have great imaginative power. It is easy for them to *conjure up* a vision of the person they want to become and the life they want to live. Initially, this is a vaguely imagined ideal, but with maturity, it takes a more definite form. As opposed to Libras, who tend to worship admirable qualities in others, Aries 1 individuals are focused on new potentials within themselves, for it is basic to their nature to bring new things into the world.

Concentrated will and intention are what gives this decan its force. When one focuses on a single goal, all of one's energy can be brought to bear on that goal. Energy and will are brought to a single point—much like the point of a thrusting sword. My own symbol for the first *degree* of Aries shows a military leader with a sword striding down a gangplank onto enemy territory. Concentrating one's force and limiting one's focus to a single well-thought-out goal make for great potency of action. Thus, military leaders limit their focus to the battle at hand, in order to give it their full energy and attention. Violence is never entirely "off the table" for people of this decan, for their impulse is to cut through obstacles as quickly and decisively as possible. However, as youthful, innocent souls, they are not given so much to *physical* attacks as to intellectual attacks upon lies and falsehoods.

Aries 1 individuals realize that reality is up for grabs. They are constantly promoting their own slapdash vision of life and simultaneously skewering society's shabby myths with the sword of truth. These people are always making a point. They are involved in a war against falsehood. In this battle, one of their chief weapons is satire. A short overview of Western history shows that it was the satirists who most effectively punctured the Establishment worldview—not the scientists, theologians, or philosophers. What would the world be like if it had not been for Boccaccio, Rabelais, Voltaire, Swift, Diderot, Twain, or the cartoonists at *Mad Magazine* and *South Park*? These satirists ridiculed the views of the Establishment so effectively that it became difficult for their audience to return to their old way of seeing things. Through their brutal caricatures, they were subtly commanding others to see the situation as they did. They were daring them to say that it was otherwise. The following satirists have planets in this decan: John Cleese, Terry Southern, Eugene Ionesco, George Bernard Shaw, Carl Reiner, Paul Krassner, Peter Bergman (Firesign Theatre), Jules Feiffer, Tom Lehrer, John Waters, Lily Tomlin, Jay Leno, Neil Simon, and Günter Grass.

In medieval and Renaissance versions of this decan, the most common symbol was a Black man with fiery-red eyes, holding a curved sword above his head. This figure may have originated with the Egyptian war god, Montu, who was often pictured carrying a curved sword called a *khepesh*. In decan lists from the Ptolemaic period, this decan is sometimes represented by Herakles, as a child, strangling two snakes. This is a Greek version of an authentic Egyptian source, which shows the young Khonsu standing atop two crocodiles.[38] Khonsu was originally a moon god, known as "the Traveler," and was usually depicted wielding a sickle-shaped sword.

EXAMPLES

Hunter S. Thompson (Saturn. "Gonzo" journalist—*Fear and Loathing in Las Vegas*.)
Erica Jong (Sun. Novelist—*Fear of Flying*.)
Warren Beatty (Sun. Actor—*Shampoo*, *Reds*.)
Kate Hudson (Mercury, Mars. Actress—*Almost Famous*.)

Tom Wolfe (Moon, Uranus. Journalistic writer—*The Electric Kool-Aid Acid Test*.)

William Shatner (Sun, Mercury. Actor, writer—*Star Trek*.)

Dean Stockwell (Mars. Actor—*Quantum Leap*.)

Douglas Adams (Mercury. Sci-fi writer—*Hitchhiker's Guide to the Galaxy*.)

Michael Pollard (Jupiter. Actor—*Bonnie and Clyde*.)

Bob Crane (Uranus. Actor—*Hogan's Heroes*; sex addict.)

Lily Tomlin (Moon, Jupiter. Comedian, actress—*All of Me*, *9 to 5*.)

Vince Vaughn (Sun, Chiron. Actor—*DodgeBall*, *Swingers*.)

Steve McQueen (Sun. Actor—*The Great Escape*; violent, with an explosive temper.)

Paul Krassner (Mars. Editor of *The Realist*.)

Agnès Varda (Uranus. Feminist film director; influenced New Wave films.)

Lina Wertmüller (Uranus. Filmmaker—*Seven Beauties*, *Swept Away*.)

John Waters (Mercury. Guerrilla filmmaker—*Pink Flamingos*, *Hair Spray*.)

Robert Carradine (Sun. Actor—*Revenge of the Nerds*.)

Winfield Scott Hancock (Pluto. Commander of the Union army at the Battle of Gettysburg.)

Jennifer Aniston (Venus, Chiron. Actress—*We're the Millers*, *Friends*.)

John Cleese and Eric Idle (Jupiter and Sun for Cleese and Mercury for Idle. *Monty Python* comedians.)

Chico Marx (Sun, Mercury, Mars. Manic comic—the Marx Brothers.)

Philip K. Dick (Ascendant, Uranus. Metaphysical sci-fi author.)

Günter Grass (Uranus. Novelist—*The Tin Drum*.)

Tom Stoppard (Saturn. Playwright—*The Real Thing*, which examines honesty and the difference between reality and appearance.)

Ishmael Reed (Saturn. Poet, novelist—*Mumbo Jumbo*, *Going Too Far: Essays about America's Nervous Breakdown*.)

Ilona Staller (Jupiter. Italian porn star and later a member of Parliament.)

Maureen Dowd (Jupiter. Progressive political columnist for the *New York Times*.)

Rachel Maddow (Venus. Leftist political columnist.)

Max Scherr (Jupiter. Founded the *Berkeley Barb*.)

Eugene McCarthy (Sun. US senator, antiwar candidate for president.)

Al Lewis (Venus. Actor—*Car 54 Where Are You?*, *The Munsters*; Green Party candidate; has made up a fictitious past for himself.)

Janet Guthrie (Saturn. Race car driver.)

Corliss Lamont (Sun, Mars. President of the Humanist Association, socialist philosopher, civil rights activist.)

Bette Davis (Saturn. Actress—*Marked Woman*.)

Bob Ezrin (Sun, Mars. Producer, creative catalyst for Alice Cooper, Lou Reed, KISS, Nine Inch Nails.)

Aries, 2nd Decan

IMAGE: *A go-kart race under sunny skies. After crossing the finish line, the winner—an immigrant of mixed race—receives a gold trophy from the judge. He holds it aloft amid the cheers of the crowd.*

The ruler of this decan is the sun, though Mars is also strong. The Tarot card associated with the decan is the Sun, with its smiling sun and joyous children at play. As solar types, Aries 2 individuals are bright, confident, openhearted, and psychologically integrated. They have a great deal of *integrity*, for there is little disconnect between who they are, what they believe, and how they act.

People of this decan know what they want from life and actively pursue it. As self-confident individuals, they don't mind pushing through a crowd of other competitors to "win the prize." Scrappy, willful, and eager to make their mark, they are nonetheless popular with the public, due to their sincerity and openheartedness. Admittedly, they want their moment in the sun, but they also want to make a significant contribution—to succeed in a way that benefits the public. In the decan image, the trophy held up by the boy is a testimony to his victory, but it is also a gift to a public that admires him for having won the race, and for having done so in an honorable and sporting way.

People of this decan are highly individualistic, yet they have a universal quality that everyone can appreciate. The boy in the decan image is of mixed race. He is different from the people in the crowd but is nonetheless easy to relate to. Among the examples, one finds many people who championed racial, national, or sexual minorities, including Kal Penn, Rosa Parks, Pete Seeger, Amy Tan, and Randy Shilts. These people were not just representing their own people; they were championing the human race as a whole.

Because Aries 2 individuals apply themselves to their ventures with energy and enthusiasm, they tend to rise in life. Natural charisma also figures in their success. Even when these people aren't particularly good looking, they are unusually appealing, for they seem to radiate their innermost identity in their faces. The Sun, as the most expressive of the astrological "planets," rules the face, which is the most expressive part of the human body. Aries 2 individuals have striking and memorable faces. Thus, among the examples one finds people who were so widely admired that they became role models. Examples include Steve McQueen, Bette Davis, Queen Latifah, Jerry Garcia, Johnny Depp, Charlton Heston, Doris Day, Shirley MacLaine, Jackie Kennedy, Elizabeth Taylor, Marlon Brando, Winona Ryder, Molly Ringwald, Sigourney Weaver, and Willie Nelson (the list could go on).

As motivated, self-confident people, Aries 2 individuals may enter into politics, acting, or other highly competitive fields. However, they are competing chiefly with themselves, for they hold themselves to very high standards. Aspiring to a kind of moral heroism, they are trying to become their best selves—their noblest and most admirable selves. People of this decan are self-aware, proud, and even a bit vain. But they are also honest, for they readily admit when they have failed and are always trying to better themselves.

Through self-observation, Aries 2 individuals become aware of their inborn talents. This knowledge allows them to actively pursue their destiny—to follow a course that will culminate in the full embodiment of their highest self. In ancient Greece, this process was called *eudaimonism*. The Greeks believed that each person had a good genius or "daimon" that could direct them toward the realization of their destiny. In one Greek tale, the good genius was represented as a human statue made of gold that had to be chipped out of a coating of old pottery. On a symbolic level, this refers to the discovery of one's best or "golden" self by progressively freeing it from personal shortcomings and petty entanglements. People of this decan have a strong sense of personal nobility. Austin Coppock, in *36 Faces*, calls this decan "The Crown" and says of it: "Here the individual struggles with their potential—what is truly royal inside them."[39] The crown is a symbol of mastery: mastery over oneself and mastery in the outer world. The trophy in the decan image, in fact, could easily be replaced by a crown being presented to a king. The crown, like the trophy, is also a solar symbol, whose golden points suggest the rays of the sun.

Because Aries 2 individuals think that the truth is simple and straightforward, they assume that their path in life should also be straightforward. This "road to success" is symbolized, in the decan symbol, by the straight racecourse. People of this decan have clear goals and an intelligent, straightforward strategy to reach these goals. They understand that there will be obstacles to their success, yet they are also confident in their ability to get past these snags. Aries 2 individuals are often talented problem-solvers, for being mechanically-minded, they instinctively break down problems into their component parts. This gives them an ability to fix things as trifling as household appliances, or as important as problematic relationships or matters of public policy. Like the junior mechanic of the decan image, Aries 2 individuals shine a bright light on difficulties that are stalling progress. First, they identify the broadest outlines of the problem, then they focus on particulars, identifying which elements of the situation are critical and which can be effectively ignored. Having figured out what is not working properly, they sum up the problem in a few well-chosen words. Looking up from a murky problem "under the hood," their face clears, and they explain what needs to be done.

Aries 2 individuals recognize when things are not well integrated—when there is a loss of information or energy within a system. Because the Sun represents the integrative center of personal consciousness, it has the best natural perspective for understanding any complex system. It is this solar perspective that allows Aries 2 individuals to reintegrate malfunctioning parts so they support the central purpose of a system. They see the system as a whole but also see how each component must operate if the system is to function smoothly.

Aries 2 individuals have an intuitive understanding of the *proper order* of things and are optimistic enough to believe that this order is attainable. Like the sun, which circles the sky every day, these people try to achieve a broad, global perspective. They are interested in the world situation and keep informed about local and international news. Since they have a good sense of the general trajectory of "the ship of state," they are particularly interested in matters of policy: where current policies are heading, and what alternatives might work better. They recognize when the rationale of the nation's leaders is faulty, either because it is founded upon incorrect readings of the situation or because it is based on immoral motives. Thus, one often finds these people shining a bright light on questionable political policies and practices. They have a confident grasp of the overall situation and express their opinions in forceful, well-articulated language.

The appreciation that Aries 2 individuals have for ideal order is especially obvious in their love of music. Many excellent musicians and songwriters have planets here, including Bach and Haydn. The famous astronomer Johannes Kepler associated music with the sun, which he pictured as Apollo with his lyre. Kepler thought that solar consciousness was the basis of the mathematical harmonies that bind together the solar system, as well as the "music of the spheres" created by these harmonies.[40] He was not wrong in attributing this integrative force to the sun, for it is the sun's gravitational force that establishes and stabilizes the paths of the planets within the solar system.

Aries 2 individuals have a very idealistic approach to their relationships. They are honest, often confessional, and speak directly from the heart. Since they themselves are great talkers, it is important that they marry someone who is open and communicative. These people are good

listeners with a real desire to help. At times, they can be a bit meddlesome, but this is because they care about right relationship and tend to jump in whenever they see transgressions. Many of the Sabian symbols in this decan deal with relationships—and even family life. These people are not rule bound in their approach to relationships but are willing to try anything that brings about mutual happiness and enjoyment.

In Egypt, this decan was often pictured as the youthful sun god Horus, seated on a lotus flower. In the illustration, the forelock indicates that he is still a child. He points to his mouth to show he is still suckling; he is still absorbing the bright rays of the supernal sun.

EXAMPLES

Willie Nelson (Mercury. Country and folk singer/songwriter; activist for Farm Aid and the legalization of marijuana.)

Rosie O'Donnell (Venus. Comedian, talk-show host, open lesbian, philanthropist.)

Elvira (Jupiter. Campy horror host, AIDS activist.)

Kal Penn (Venus. Indian American actor—*Harold and Kumar Go to White Castle*; activist for Syrian refugees, appointee in the Obama administration.)

Queen Latifah (Venus. Black rap star, songwriter, actress—*Beauty Shop*; autobiography titled *Ladies First: Revelations of a Strong Woman*.)

Annette Funicello (Moon. Disney child star, beach movies; advocate for victims of multiple sclerosis.)

David Frost (Sun. Sketch-show host—*That Was the Week That Was*.)

W. O. Bentley (Jupiter. Car manufacturer.)

Neil Armstrong (Uranus. First astronaut to walk on the moon.)

Bette Davis (Sun. Actress—*Dark Victory*, *Marked Woman*; cofounded the Hollywood Canteen for servicemen.)

Jerry Garcia (Moon. Songwriter and leader of the Grateful Dead; drug problems.)

George Clooney (Venus. Actor—*Three Kings*; philanthropist.)

Betty Ford (Sun. First lady, ERA supporter, and founder of a rehab center.)

Robert Scheer (Sun. Radical political writer—*Ramparts*, *The Nation*.)

Camille Paglia (Sun. Trenchant social critic who takes on feminist extremism and poststructuralism.)

Hugh Hefner (Sun. Head of the *Playboy* empire; the magazine dealt with many controversial issues in a straightforward way and promoted tolerance for gays and Blacks.)

Al Gore (Sun. Liberal US senator; climate change activist.)

Ernest Callenbach (Sun. Wrote *Ecotopia*; promoted simple living.)

Daniel Perkins (Sun. Surrealistic political cartoonist—*Tom Tomorrow*.)

Michael Moore (Mercury. Muckraking leftist filmmaker—*Bowling for Columbine*, *Sicko*.)

George Bernard Shaw (North Node. Socialist playwright—*Man and Superman*.)

Ellen Goodman (Venus. *Boston Globe* political columnist.)

Baba Ram Dass (Sun, Uranus. Harvard professor who became a psychedelicist and then a spiritual guru.)

Jerry Brown (Sun. Democratic mayor of Oakland and later governor of California.)

Debbie Reynolds (Sun, Uranus. Popular actress and singer—*The Unsinkable Molly Brown*, *How the West Was Won*.)

Will Rogers (Saturn. Cowboy humorist, social commentator; part Cherokee.)

Arianna Huffington (Moon. Conservative political columnist who became a liberal and cofounded the *Huffington Post*.)

Johnny Cash (Venus, Uranus. Country-western singer—"Folsom Prison Blues.")

Jesse Jackson (Mars. Reverend and civil rights leader—the Rainbow Coalition.)

Loretta Lynn (Mars. Country-western singer/songwriter—*Coal Miner's Daughter*.)

Odetta (Uranus. Black folk singer.)

Johann Sebastian Bach (Sun. Classical composer, known for his fugues.)

Franz Josef Haydn (Sun. Classical composer.)

Gregory Peck (Sun, Jupiter. Actor—*To Kill a Mockingbird*.)

Jackie Gleason (Venus. Television comic—*The Honeymooners*; high liver.)

Tony Blair (Venus. Labour Party prime minister; instituted a minimum-wage act and a human rights act; established quasi-independence for Scotland, Wales, and Northern Ireland.)

James Garner (Sun. Actor—*The Americanization of Emily*, *The Rockford Files*.)

Aries, 3rd Decan

IMAGE: *An ancient Greek explorer, holding a polished bronze shield, enters the crazily angled corridors of a foreign temple. He comes upon an altar marked with strange hieroglyphs, in front of which stands a priestess, whose image is reflected in a pool of water.*

In the decan image, we see a person from a fairly advanced civilization confronting a person from a much older civilization. The explorer carries the shield of Athena, which represents *reason*. This shield reflects things as they are, and shields the mind against superstitious fear. The priestess, by contrast, is a lunar being who dwells in the realm of dreams and imaginings, perhaps shamanic trance. The pool beneath her has a reflective surface that connects her to the wisdom of the subconscious. In its waters, she can see dimly into the past and the future, though its rippling surface distorts and exaggerates what it reflects, even as our dreams distort and exaggerate our waking experience. These two forms of consciousness—reason and imagination—work in tandem in Aries 3 individuals. Their minds weave back and forth between analytical reason and the symbolic language of the unconscious, between the left brain and the right brain. Through this process, they are able to create a more integrated, multidimensional picture of reality.

The adventurer of the decan image is exploring a foreign world and trying to make sense of its strange language and peculiar culture. Like the explorer, Aries 3 individuals are attracted to new horizons and foreign territories—both physical and mental. They want to discover some trove of arcane knowledge, and through focused study, decipher its meaning. Many students of foreign languages have planets here—people who study Greek, Latin, or Sanskrit. But we also find people who are analyzing and translating other kinds of languages. We find physicists who study the mathematical language of nature, anthropologists who study the stories of foreign tribes, and Tarot readers and astrologers who decipher occult symbols.

Among the examples, we also find people who have invented *new* languages—languages well suited to their foreign subject matter, yet still comprehensible to the public. In the realm of art, we find bold pioneers with innovative artistic vocabularies. Composers of this decan include Béla Bartók, Aram Khatchiturian, Charles Ives, and Gustave von Holst. The music of these people may be discordant and alien, but it has also been extremely influential. The visual artists of this decan are equally innovative, as we see from Georg Grosz, Fernand Léger, and Joan Miró. In film, we have Lilly Wachowski (*The Matrix*), Richard Elfman (*The Forbidden Zone*), Spike Jonze (*Her*), and Darren Aronofsky (*Pi*). Some scientists with planets here have also created new languages and new worldviews, as we see from Galileo, Nikola Tesla, and Francis Crick (who decoded DNA). Gary Goldschneider calls this zodiacal segment "the pioneer," and on an artistic and intellectual level, this is certainly accurate. Aries 3 individuals are seeking out new ideas and new cultural forms in order to revitalize their society. In their travels, they are therefore always on the lookout for vital new concepts to bring back to their communities.

While people of this decan can often be found studying foreign cultures, they may also consider their *own* society bizarre enough to merit serious study. Like foreign anthropologists, Aries 3 individuals carefully study their society and try to decipher its "grammar" of meaning—its mythology and style of thought. Through this ongoing analysis, they eventually get to know their society very well. Unfortunately, understanding one's culture doesn't automatically give one any power to change it. Even when the dominant culture appears completely delusional, one still has to navigate it as if it were real, much as one might navigate a lucid dream. It is never entirely possible to escape the dreamscape of one's own culture, for we are all, to some degree, prisoners of its cultural assumptions and the *vocabulary* within which these cultural assumptions are articulated.

Because Aries 3 individuals have a naturally surrealistic perspective, they have a very open, exploratory approach to the world. Many are interested in science fiction, which, after all, is not all that different from the way they experience their own lives. All the following people have planets here: H. Rider Haggard (*She*), Diana Rigg (*The Avengers*), Sophie Aldred (*Dr. Who*), Don Adams and Barbara Feldon (*Get Smart*), Robert Morse (*The Loved One*), Robert Zemeckis (*Back to the Future*), Clifford

Simak (sci-fi writer), Audrey Hepburn (*Charade*), James Franciscus (*Beneath the Planet of the Apes*), Richard Chamberlain (*The Last Wave*), Tobey Maguire (*Pleasantville*), Terry Southern (*The Magic Christian*), and Peter Weiss (*Marat/Sade*). The strange fantasies referenced above show people entering into realities so foreign and bizarre that on first viewing they are difficult to interpret.

Aries 3 individuals experience themselves as "strangers in a strange land." They approach life in a raw way, which is unusually independent of the assumptions of the dominant culture. To some degree, they are *creating* a new world through their fresh observations and conceptualizations. Their own visions of reality can act as a door to the future, if they are only brave enough to step through it.

Aries 3 individuals are turning their mind's eyes inward to investigate compelling visions of the future. They impatiently await the future to make itself known—to proclaim itself in some arcane or foreign tongue. Once they've tuned in to this vision, they set about deciphering these raw and unfamiliar ideas. If they can get a handle on one key idea—one "runic" symbol—the rest of the message may follow. To better receive this channeled information, these people must wall out the external world, for their visions are tenuous enough to require focused concentration. Sometimes they set up an inviolable space in which to do their inner work. This could be a writing room, an artist's studio, or a religious shrine. It could be a peaceful garden in which to meditate. In this space, they commune with their private "gods" and try to decipher their visions.

Like the priestess in the decan symbol, these people are very receptive to the symbols of the unconscious. The priestess stands one step behind material reality. She inhabits the astral plane, where symbols and archetypes have their own reality. Within this realm, the future is still fluid and open to manipulation. Thus, the priestess is not just channeling messages from the subconscious; she is also an active shaman, who changes the future of society through the introduction of new images and ideas. People of this decan are aware that the future is still open—that both dystopian and utopian futures are possible. They realize that it is sometimes necessary to *fight* for the future—to prevent something from happening, or alternatively, to *make* something happen. Such changes are affected most easily at the level of ideas and symbols, since by the time something has become physical, it has lost most of its effective force.

 The Egyptian god Ptah sometimes appears in this decan. Ptah is a creator god, who gave birth to the world through his thought. He *conceived* of the world in a certain way, and these ideas became reality. Ptah is associated with artisans and especially workers in metal. In ancient times, metalworkers were almost always considered shamans and magicians, for they could change one thing into something completely different. Nowadays, people may use the "language of metals" to indicate successive stages of civilization. There is the Bronze Age, followed by the Iron Age. Ptah, as the primeval alchemist, presides over these epic transformations, creating new visions that work their strange magic upon human thought and culture.

EXAMPLES

Ed Steinbrecher (Venus. Astrologer, occultist—*Inner Guide Meditations.*)
Robert Darnton (Mercury, Saturn. Historian—*The Great Cat Massacre, Forbidden Best-Sellers of Pre-Revolutionary France.*)
Daniel Perkins (Venus. Surrealistic political cartoonist—*Tom Tomorrow.*)
Gillian Anderson (Saturn, stationary. Actress—*The X-Files.*)
Tobey Maguire (Mars, Jupiter, Chiron. Actor—*Pleasantville, Spider-Man.*)
Florian von Donnersmarck (Mercury. German screenwriter and film director—*The Lives of Others.*)
Lucien Lévy-Bruhl (Sun conjunct Jupiter. Early anthropologist, ethnologist—*How Natives Think.*)
David Frost (Saturn. Host of *That Was the Week That Was.*)
Peter Bergman (Saturn. Surrealist comic with the Firesign Theatre.)
Martin Luther (North Node. Protestant reformer; translated the Bible into German.)
Audrey Hepburn (Venus. Actress—*Charade.*)
Lilly Wachowski (North Node. Filmmaker—*The Matrix.*)
Martin Goldsmith (Moon. Symbolic astrologer.)
Kurt Russell (Venus. Actor—*Stargate.*)
Sam Rockwell (Saturn. Actor—*Moon*—about a man who discovers that he's a clone.)
Jacques Derrida (North Node. Deconstructivist philosopher and theorist.)
A. E. Van Vogt (North Node. Sci-fi writer—*Slan.*)

A. Cy Twombly (Mercury, Jupiter. Artist whose work looks like scribbled graffiti.)

Alfred Butts (Sun, Mercury. Invented the game "Scrabble.")

Erwin Panofsky (Mercury. Art historian who deciphered the symbolism in the work of Albrecht Dürer.)

Joseph Campbell (Mars. Expert on world mythology—*The Masks of God*.)

Jean Houston (Mercury, Saturn. Psychologist—*Varieties of Psychedelic Experience*.)

Margot Adler (Sun. Wiccan priestess—*Drawing Down the Moon*.)

Thomas Dolby (South Node. Innovative musician—"She Blinded Me with Science," *Aliens Ate My Buick*.)

Lauren Bacall (Moon, Chiron. Vampy actress in noir movies—*Dark Passage*.)

Sigmund Freud (Venus, North Node. Founder of psychoanalysis; used dream analysis.)

Carl Jung (Chiron. Archetypal psychologist.)

Sir Thomas More (Jupiter. Catholic martyr; wrote *Utopia*.)

Barbara Watterson (Saturn. Egyptologist.)

Harlan Ellison (Venus, Uranus. Sci-fi writer—*Dangerous Visions*)

Alexander Graham Bell (Pluto. Invented the telephone.)

Alice Bailey (Saturn. Leading Theosophist; most of her writings are based on channelings from "The Tibetan.")

Helen Keller (Saturn. Blind and deaf, yet learned to speak and to decipher her world; socialist stump speaker.)

Taurus, 1st Decan

People of this decan are attractive, good-natured, and practically minded. In the decan symbol, we see a man building an addition to his house and his pregnant wife tending a garden. They are looking after their basic needs—the shelter of a house and food from their garden. They will also need money, so at least one of them will have to get a job. While people of this decan begin by attending to their basic needs, they are also committed to realizing their romantic and aesthetic dreams. They want to create a life for themselves that is pleasurable and fulfilling, and are willing to work hard to get it. These people have a buoyant, optimistic attitude. They feel that if they put in enough time and energy, any reasonable goal is within their grasp—a good marriage, a beautiful home, well-behaved children.

Taurus 1 individuals are eminently practical in attaining their goals. First, they map out a detailed plan of action; then, through patient application, they carry it out. Even when they're thrown off their stride by unforeseen obstacles, they never lose sight of their goals. They accept the fact that obstacles will arise and will have to be dealt with. If, for instance, they unearth a huge boulder in the midst of their gardening, they interrupt their work and remove it. Taurus 1 individuals are willing to tackle any problem that comes up—either in a do-it-yourself project or in a relationship. This stubborn, resourceful approach allows them to finish difficult projects that would stymie most people. It also allows them to sustain harmonious marriages, for instead of ignoring emotional problems, they talk them through until they have reestablished a positive emotional flow.

Taurus is the first of the earth signs, so it's no surprise that these people are good at making things and fixing things. Among the examples, one finds many talented carpenters, farmers, mechanics, and cooks. These people are handy with tools and enjoy taking things apart and putting them back together again. Austin Coppock, in *36 Faces*, calls this decan "The Plow." This accords well with my own decan image, which also emphasizes tools. The pregnant woman is working with a trowel, and her husband is working with a hammer. People of this decan are not just interested in tools; they are also interested in materials. They assess what materials are available, and what can be *made* out of these things. They are good problem solvers because they break down problems into their simplest parts and figure out how all these pieces are related to one another. They start by asking obvious questions: Why is this machine not working? What part needs to be replaced or retooled? What will I need to buy before getting started? Is this something I can do by myself? If Taurus 1 individuals decide they need help, they are not shy about asking for it. They gather together the necessary materials, the necessary people, and the necessary information to successfully complete their projects.

The first decan of Taurus begins in late April, when the earth is bursting with new growth. As the first decan in an earth sign, Taurus 1 has a strong connection to agriculture. These people work toward a bountiful harvest by carrying through on well-conceived, long-range plans. The woman in the decan image is tending a garden and also "building" a baby in her womb. Like the Empress card of the Tarot, she is a symbol of fertility. She prepares the soil at the right time and plants the seeds at the right time. She deals with insect attacks and waters the plants when they get dry. She understands all the steps involved in a typical growing season but adapts her efforts to unexpected problems, carrying out each task without hesitation or complaint. If she has to get her hands dirty, she doesn't mind. She is not fastidious about the temporary messes that accompany her creative projects. When she prepares a meal, she expects the kitchen to get messy. When she prepares the soil of the garden, she expects to handle manure. She is perfectly comfortable with the coarser aspects of physical existence and accepts the fact that creative activity is inherently messy.

This decan is associated with the physical body, and all of its various parts and functions. The house in the decan image is in fact a symbol of the body, since the body is "where we live" throughout our lives. The alimentary tract and the process of digestion are especially important here, as is fitting for a strongly lunar decan. The body breaks down foodstuffs through the sequential application of saliva, stomach acids, bile, and peptic enzymes. Once the food has been digested enough to be absorbed into the bloodstream, it is reorganized to build up new components of the body. The same sorts of processes are seen, in more dramatic form, in the sequential development of a baby in the womb. Many different nutrients from the mother's body are brought together to build up the physical body of the baby.

The thought processes of Taurus 1 individuals follow a similar pattern. They digest information slowly, like a cow chewing its cud. They read books slowly and think them over while they're reading, separating out what is relevant to their lives and what is not. To make ideas their own, they reframe them in their own language. They try to fully *digest* important information, however long that may take.

The dominant planets of this decan are Venus and the moon. Venus has generally been equated with beauty, love, and romance. People of this decan are, in fact, very amorous and require a regular diet of affection and appreciation. They are also susceptible to beauty and may be quite beautiful themselves. Moreover, as Venusians, they tend to favor the formal, aesthetic aspects of courtship—dating, flowers, music, poetry—the whole package. These people may be romantic, but they are also practical. When they contemplate a possible romance, they try to imagine how that relationship might play out—what kinds of benefits and problems it would include, given the two people involved. In their relationships, Taureans retain a sense of economy. They keep track of how much time and energy they can legitimately spare, and what they are actually getting for their efforts. Since the decan is closely tied to the principle of fertility, marriage and children are always at the back of their minds.

Venus is an acquisitive planet. Venusians are always judging whether they want something in their personal space or not—whether they want to add a new piece of furniture, a new book, or a new husband to their homes. Venus is a planet of discrimination, and Venusians judge potential mates not only by their attractiveness, but by their character, their reliability, and their earning power, and by how comfortable they are to be around. Sexual attraction certainly figures into the mix, but it is not given first place in their more serious relationships. Having seen too many relationships fall apart when they were based on sexual attraction, these people are looking at more solid criteria. Taureans are generally very relaxed about their sexuality, even when their desires do not follow the norm. This is one reason they are so sexy; they are at one with their bodies and at one with their sexual emotions. Often rather shy when they meet new people, once trust is established, they become remarkably honest and direct.

Curiously, people of this decan often make their homes in places that are rather uncivilized. Some make it their mission to bring a higher consciousness and a higher level of civilization to their neighborhood. Thus, they may upgrade their house as a model for the general upgrading of their community. These people make good neighbors, for they are helpful and friendly, yet they are also territorial and may protect their little Garden of Eden with a solid fence.

Taurus 1 individuals have a good grasp of what really matters in a community. They recognize that society must address people's basic needs—food, water, safety, and rules of orderly conduct. Only then can the higher aspects of civilization be cultivated. Since they are generally very aware of what's going on in their local communities (and intolerant of incompetence and dishonesty), they often involve themselves in local politics. Confident that they know what needs doing, they feel perfectly justified in moving in and pushing through their agenda. Taurus 1 individuals are continually developing and improving their environment, whether through the improvement of their home, their government, or their personal relationships. Harnessing natural forces of growth and fertility, they slowly transform their world into a beautiful garden.

While the Egyptian decan lists that have come down to us do not place Hathor in this decan, as the goddess of love, fertility, and higher civilization, she seems an appropriate fit. Moreover, she is associated with cattle and is often pictured with the head of a cow.

EXAMPLES

Mary Tyler Moore (Uranus. Actress—"America's Sweetheart," who starred in *The Mary Tyler Moore Show*.)
Henry Fonda (Mercury. Actor—*The Grapes of Wrath*.)
Gary Cooper (Mercury. Actor with a quiet, laconic style—*High Noon, Desire*.)
Sophia Loren (Uranus. Sensual Italian actress—*Yesterday, Today and Tomorrow*.)
Andy Griffith (Chiron. Played a rural sheriff on *The Andy Griffith Show*.)
Eddie Albert (Sun. Starred in the TV series *Green Acres*; environmentalist.)
Queen Latifah (Mars, Saturn. Rap star, actress—*Beauty Shop*.)

Ice Cube (Venus, Saturn. Rap star, actor—*Barbershop*.)

Ozzie Nelson (Mars. Bandleader; played himself on *Ozzie and Harriet*.)

Woody Allen (Uranus. Film director—*Radio Days*, *Hannah and Her Sisters*.)

Willie Nelson (Sun. "Outlaw" country singer; activist for the legalization of marijuana.)

Joan Baez (Jupiter, Saturn. Folk singer, activist; love songs and protest songs.)

Burt Bacharach (Venus, Chiron. Composer of many great pop hits—"Alfie," "What the World Needs Now.")

Richard Benjamin (Mercury. Actor—*Goodbye, Columbus*.)

Michael Landon (Uranus. Actor—*Little House on the Prairie*; three marriages, nine children.)

Theodor Herzl (Pluto. Father of Zionism; promoted a Jewish homeland in Palestine.)

Gerrard Winstanley (Pluto. Founder of the protocommunist Diggers in seventeenth-century England.)

Gary Snyder (North Node. Beat poet, environmental activist, Buddhist—*Mountains and Rivers without End*.)

Jacques Cousteau (Venus, Saturn. Oceanographer, environmentalist.)

Geena Davis (Moon. Actress—*Beetlejuice*, *A League of Their Own*.)

Edward O'Neill (Venus. Actor—*Married with Children*.)

Leonard Cohen (Uranus. Singer/songwriter—"Suzanne," *Songs of Love and Hate*.)

Rex Harrison (Mars. Actor—*My Fair Lady*; many disastrous relationships.)

Miles Davis (Chiron. Meditative jazz trumpeter—*Kind of Blue*.)

Jan Cremer (Sun, Saturn. Shocking gay diarist.)

King Henry VIII (Chiron. Married many times, rejecting Catholicism for England in order to legally divorce his first wife.)

Jeanne Moreau (Chiron. French actress—*La Reine Margot*, *Jules et Jim*; friend of several leading intellectuals.)

Anna Magnani (Mars. Earth-mother actress—*Big Deal on Madonna Street*.)

Walt Whitman (Venus. Gay poet—*Leaves of Grass*.)

Jean Auel (Uranus. Novelist—*Clan of the Cave Bear*.)

Christopher Isherwood (Jupiter. Novelist—*A Meeting by the River*; wrote the novel upon which *Cabaret* was based; gay romantic.)

Rosa Bonheur (Jupiter. French artist famous for her paintings of animals; openly gay.)

Gilbert Shelton (Jupiter, Saturn. Underground cartoonist—*The Fabulous Furry Freak Brothers*.)

Richard Pryor (Jupiter, Saturn. Vulgar stand-up comic; treated racial and political issues.)

Paul Mazursky (Sun, North Node. Film director—*Bob & Carol & Ted & Alice*, *An Unmarried Woman*.)

Roy Rogers (Moon, North Node. Television and film star; singing cowboy who began on the rodeo circuit; raised nine natural-born and adopted children with Dale Evans.)

Taurus, 2nd Decan

IMAGE: *In a whispered conversation, political prisoners discuss their situation and study an old map that seems to indicate an escape tunnel. At the barred door down the hall, a guard is seated, a large key on his belt.*

People of this decan are tackling major problems, and fortunately, have enough courage and determination to successfully take them on. These people recognize when they are "in a hole" and use all of their intelligence and resolve to get out of it. This hole could be a bad psychological state, a bad living situation, a bad job, a bad habit, a bad political situation, or a bad financial situation. To effectively escape these problems, these people need to identify the nature of the problem, verbalize it, and get feedback about it from people they trust. Conversations with people who are dealing with similar problems are particularly helpful, since these people can supply them with relevant new information and help them identify their blind spots.

Once Taurus 2 individuals have gathered the relevant facts and discussed them, they can then map out a method to solve the problem. If it is a big problem, they may have to break it down into smaller sub-problems before they can figure out what to do. It is important, however, for these people to advance quickly beyond mere analysis. They need to "take the bull by the horns" and act on what they know, since action will change the situation and also clarify it.

In the decan image we see a man leading a discussion among his fellow prisoners about methods of escape. People of this decan, similarly, are often found organizing the populace to tackle political or social problems. Highly aware of the pressures facing the average citizen, Taurus 2 individuals often become spokespeople for the unarticulated thoughts and feelings of the masses. In my first book—*Moon Phases*—the second Taurus phase was called "The Rebel" and was characterized by the individual's fight against oppressive social structures.

People with an emphasis here often feel oppressed and imprisoned by a society that does not recognize their needs and desires. As children, their parents and teachers routinely ignore their feelings, beliefs, and needs. No one really listens to them. In fact, the honest expression of their ideas sometimes leads to punishment. For years, these people may hold their tongues and submit to the rule of their "jailers." But privately they are constantly thinking about these things. They network with others who share similar rebellious ideas, and begin to piece together a realistic analysis of their situation. At best, these people cultivate honest, perceptive friends who can clarify their problems and help them escape the holes they are in. At worst, they socialize with dishonest people, or even criminals, who end up dragging them down to their own level. Thus, while the prisoners of the decan image might represent the unjustly condemned, they could also represent people whose irresponsible behavior and habits of thought have landed them in oppressive situations.

Saturn is powerful in this decan, but so is Chiron. As a "planet," Chiron bestows a radically independent perspective. People of this decan are quite skeptical of the received wisdom of society. They see society as something of a prison and prefer to stand outside its interpretive frameworks. In the decan image, we see prisoners poring over a map and deciphering its meaning. The Taurus 2 individual, as a chironic type, is alerting others to some aspect of the problem they have not considered—some new fact or perspective that changes the whole picture. This independent stance is the *key* to escaping their situation, even as the jailer's key, in the decan image, represents the way out of jail. The glyph for Chiron is a key. The Taurus 2 mind is in fact "key-like," in that it creates an intricate, sequential analysis that adheres closely to the facts—an analysis that will allow them to pass from an oppressive situation to a freer and more pleasant state of being.

As chironic figures, Taurus 2 individuals often cultivate fields of knowledge that offer alternative perspectives. These include psychology, occultism, sociology, and political theory. They are especially drawn to psychology, for they realize that society exercises its most effective control through the subconscious mind—through socially approved images of acceptable and unacceptable desire, and acceptable and unacceptable behavior. The ruling elite imposes these repressive ideas through mainstream films and books that teach people the correct emotional responses to every situation. In the decan image, the guard symbolizes the internal

TEMPLE OF THE STARS

censor, who keeps watch over taboo speech and desires and tries to confine them to the subconscious. As a jailer, he is an instrument of the ruling class, as it imposes its values and worldview on the lower classes.

To free themselves from imprisoning, preprogrammed responses, Taurus 2 individuals begin to analyze society's underlying values, images, and myths. They dig themselves out of imprisoning notions by directing the light of reason upon them and deciphering their coded messages. This decan is found in the charts of many psychologists. Freud has the Sun here, and Jung the Moon. Psychologists, after all, pay close attention to the hidden messages of dreams. They recognize that the unconscious mind, through dreams, acts to *digest* the deeper meaning of a person's experience. These workings of the subconscious mind can be seen, in the decan symbol, in the "prisoners plotting." The leader of this discussion, like the psychologist, is using the light of the conscious mind to make sense of these cryptic subconscious messages.

The middle decan of Taurus is associated with the throat chakra and is therefore involved in the task of finding one's true voice. In the decan image, the prisoners are talking among themselves. Actually, they are *whispering* among themselves. This represents the many voices that come into one's mind—some external, some internal. There are the voices of one's parents and one's peers, the voices of one's teachers and the media. Among all these voices, Taurus 2 individuals must find their own voice. They must identify what sounds right when they say it, and resonates with the people they trust. One's inner voice is easily drowned out by the internal voices of parents or teachers. This may be why many Taurus 2 individuals speak in an aggressive and even strident manner. They are ensuring that their own voice will be heard through a welter of other voices, most of them internal. Since their inner voice can be fairly faint, they need to listen closely, and not just with their ears. They have to tune in to their gut sense, their inner pendulum, to figure out which ideas are solid. They have to tune in to how they intuitively *feel* about things. In the middle of all the chatter—much of it empty noise—they may then recognize an idea that makes immediate sense—that "clicks." This idea may end up providing the *key* to their entire situation.

In ancient Egyptian tomb paintings, this decan often featured Osiris on a funeral bier. One also finds the Wadjet eye. Both symbols are lunar and refer to the process of working in the dark to put together a coherent whole—to reassemble the mutilated body of Osiris. While the decan lists that have come down to us never show Anubis here, he would certainly be appropriate. As guardian of the dead, the jackal-headed Anubis has pricked-up ears that symbolize close listening. Moreover, Anubis is often pictured holding "Isis' key"—the ankh.

EXAMPLES

Nellie Bly (Sun, Pluto. Investigative journalist who faked insanity to study a mental institution from within.)

Florian von Donnersmarck (Sun. Film director—*The Lives of Others*—a realistic film about intellectual repression in communist East Germany.)

Roberto Benigni (Jupiter. Comedian—*Life Is Beautiful*—about a father and son surviving a concentration camp.)

Franz Stangl (Venus. Concentration camp commander, mass murderer.)

Anne Frank (Chiron. Martyred diarist who hid from the Nazis.)

Paul Zindel (Venus. Author—*Confessions of a Teenage Baboon*—about his survival within a dysfunctional family.)

Steve McQueen (Chiron. Actor—*The Great Escape*.)

Bob Crane (Mars. Actor—*Hogan's Heroes*; sex addict.)

Edie Sedgwick (Mercury. Socialite model in Warhol films; died of an overdose.)

Emma Watson (Mercury. Actress—*The Perks of Being a Wallflower*—where she plays a teenager struggling to reclaim her self-esteem after prolonged sexual abuse.)

Karl Marx (Sun, moon. Communist theorist—"Workers Arise!")

Ivan Illich (Mars. Priest; radical critic of modern education—*Deschooling Society*.)

Dorothy Day (Moon. Catholic activist—founded the *Catholic Worker* magazine.)

Sigmund Freud (Sun. Founder of psychoanalysis.)

Carl Jung (Moon. Archetypal psychiatrist.)

Wilhelm Reich (Venus. Maverick psychotherapist—*The Function of the Orgasm*; died in prison.)

Marilyn Ferguson (Mars. Pioneer in consciousness studies—*Brain-Mind Bulletin*.)

Alvin Poussaint (Mars. African American psychiatrist who writes about raising Black children in a racist environment.)

James Joyce (Jupiter, Neptune, Chiron. Stream-of-consciousness novelist—*Ulysses*.)

Roseanne (Jupiter. Aggressively honest comedian.)

Amy Goodman (Mercury. Investigative reporter; hosts radio's *Democracy Now!*)

Leon Trotsky (Chiron, Neptune. Communist revolutionary.)

Al Gore (North Node. Senator, presidential aspirant; climate change activist— *An Inconvenient Truth*.)

Clarence Darrow (Mars. ACLU attorney in the Scopes trial.)

Sam Dash (Moon, Mars. Chief counsel for the Senate Watergate Committee.)

Cesar Chavez (Venus. Mexican American organizer of farmworkers.)

Pete Seeger (Sun, Mars. Folksinger and political activist.)

Rita Mae Brown (Moon. Writer—*Southern Discomfort*.)

Jean Genet (North Node. Literary author, onetime thief and gay hustler, in and out of reformatories and prisons.)

Jon Voight (Uranus. Actor—*Holes*, *Midnight Cowboy*.)

Kathy Bates (North Node. Actress—*Dolores Claiborne*.)

Ernest Callenbach (Jupiter. Utopian futurist—*Ecotopia*.)

Margaret Sanger (Chiron, Neptune. Nurse, birth control advocate—saving women from the imprisonment of too many children.)

Franz Cumont (Pluto. Archeologist; studied ancient religions.)

Milan Kundera (Jupiter. Author of *The Unbearable Lightness of Being*.)

Jaron Lanier (Sun. Computer scientist who writes on the manipulativeness of social media: *Ten Arguments for Deleting Your Social Media Accounts Right Now*.)

Taurus, 3rd Decan

IMAGE: *A controversial play, which exaggerates and satirizes human failings, is being performed before an appreciative audience. The playwright stands in the wings behind a one-way mirror and follows the script with his finger.*

Taurus 3 individuals are observant, reflective people who routinely question the nature of reality. These people are very confident of their own *reading* of events. Thus, in the decan image, the playwright is following the words of the play with his finger. That is to say, he has his finger on the situation; he knows what is going on. Most people are just trying to fit in. To that end, they accept a conventional picture of reality and then project it unconsciously onto the world. Taurus 3 individuals are not content with this kind of secondhand reality. They trust their gut reactions and have faith in their personal observations, even when they tell a story very different from the one being promoted by the media or the in-group. And like the playwright in the decan image, they have a strong desire to share these alternative interpretations with the public.

Taurus 3 individuals are more awake than most but nonetheless have a strong connection to the realm of dreams, for the moon is very powerful here. The consciousness of Taurus 3 individuals is dreamlike in that it *reflects* everyday experience in a way that is simultaneously distorting and revealing. Thus, among the examples we find a great number of artists whose work is dreamlike or surrealistic. Their visionary art shows that there is truth even in fiction—that distorted or surrealistic visions can penetrate to a deeper level of reality than purely factual accounts. Surrealistic art can also serve as a form of social criticism. It can point out the rift between society's outer facade and its underlying realities.

While the artistic works of Taurus 3 individuals may be as distorted as reflections in a fun-house mirror, they are curiously recognizable. To illustrate, the following artists have planets here: Terry Gilliam (*Brazil*), Bob Dylan, Philip K. Dick, Lily Tomlin, Sasha Cohen, George Bernard

Shaw, Frank Zappa, Scott Adams (*Dilbert*), Richard Linklater (*Slacker*), and Hunter S. Thompson. Most of these people are quite entertaining, but they are also critics of a society they consider disordered and abusive. They are not necessarily offering solutions; they are just holding up a mirror to the problem and saying, "This is how I see things, and if you really look, you'll see them that way too."

Despite their skill as communicators, people of this decan sometimes feel uncomfortably alienated from others. In the decan image, the play-wright observes his audience from behind a one-way mirror. He feels separated from others and is trying to break through this "glass wall" by making an emotional connection with his audience. Taurus 3 individuals try very hard to get their messages across. They are aided in this by their strong connection to their own subconscious, and through their personal subconscious to the *collective* subconscious. Taurus 3 individuals recognize that there is a universal side to human experience—that a lot of our thoughts and reactions are the same as everyone else's. Thus, in sharing their observations with others, they are often just telling them things they already know on a subconscious level. They are functioning as an "everyman," whose experience resonates with others, even when it is intensely personal.

Several of the degree symbols in this decan deal with effective communication between people of widely differing backgrounds. There is the Native American selling jewelry to an American tourist; there is Moses speaking to the pharaoh; there is the working-class beau serenading his aristocratic girlfriend. The common assumption behind these symbols is that communication is possible with pretty much anyone, if one frames one's ideas well—if one treats communication as a form of art and art as a form of communication.

The playwright of the decan symbol is first and foremost an artist. Many of the degree symbols in this decan deal with artistic creation. In *The Zodiac by Degrees*, we see a sculptor at 25, a singer at 26, a jewelry maker at 27, and a playwright at 21. These artists and artisans are materializing visions taken from their own imaginations. Some have even created *new* artistic forms—forms better suited to their message than traditional forms. These new artistic vocabularies, though rather peculiar on first viewing, are often more expressive than the accepted vocabulary of the artistic establishment. Not surprisingly, these groundbreaking artists often run into criticism from cultural conservatives. Consider the following Taurus 3 artists: Pablo Picasso, Yoko Ono, Marcel Duchamp, Jean Cocteau, Miles Davis, Bob Dylan, Isadora Duncan, Frida Kahlo, Kenneth Anger, Amédée Ozenfant, André Gregory, Hermann Hesse, and Salvador Dalí. Some of the decan's writers—for instance, Henry Miller, James Joyce, and D. H. Lawrence—faced battles with official censors. The realistic sexual content in their novels was wrongly interpreted as a rebellion against social norms, when its actual purpose was to reflect life as it is.

People of this decan often face the archetypal dilemma of the artist. They have to decide how much they should play into popular ideas of beauty and truth, and how much they should honor their own internal vision. Should they go after money by becoming hacks or even semi-hacks, or should they serve their muse, even if that could turn them into a starving artist? Some of these people are very uncompromising, for they know that if they compromise too much, they will lose their connection with their muse, and their creativity will dry up.

Given their naturally artistic temperament, Taurus 3 individuals are very active in creating the life they want to live. They are not content to imitate others or to submit to the burden of other people's expectations. They try to live from the inside—from their own sense of what is meaningful and what is real. They dress for themselves rather than others, behave according to their own code of conduct, and stand up for what they consider important. Many of the decan's degree symbols have to do with conflicting ideas about the true value of things. In the 29th degree, we see Moses arguing with the pharaoh. The pharaoh considers Moses a mere slave, while Moses sees himself as one of the chosen people. In the 27th degree, a Native American is haggling with a fat tourist over the price of a piece of jewelry. She knows the real worth of what she has made, and she refuses to be cheated. She also knows her own worth and refuses to internalize the demeaning racial prejudices that the tourist is projecting onto her. The 28th degree has a mature woman looking into a mirror before a date. She is compromising between what she knows to be her best features and what the average person might think about her. If she accentuates her authentic inner beauty and expresses it confidently, then other people will also find her attractive. They will be impressed by the strong aesthetic statement she is making through her clothes, her facial expression, and her grace of movement. If, instead, she chooses to imitate a conventional standard of beauty, she will become an also-ran in someone else's game.

Like all Tauruses, people of this decan are sensual and pleasure loving. They get great enjoyment from food, from nature, and from physical activity. They are also very romantic and have a strong desire for emotional intimacy. Since they are accepting of themselves—including their faults—they aren't afraid to connect with other people. Generally, these people are very attractive—not just because of their looks, but because they care. Compassion and caring are the underlying basis for every positive relationship, romantic or otherwise. For if one does not really care about people, how is it possible to love? Not surprisingly, people of this decan often enjoy intense, long-lasting relationships.

EXAMPLES

Pablo Picasso (Jupiter, Chiron, Pluto. Modern painter and sculptor; cofounder of cubism.)

Marcel Duchamp (Neptune. Dadaist artist—*Nude Descending a Staircase*, which breaks up motion into multiple perspectives.)

Jean Cocteau (Ascendant, Venus. Avant-garde artist. *The Human Voice* has a woman talking on the telephone to her lover, who is offstage.)

Arthur Rimbaud (North Node. Bohemian poet, lover of Verlaine—*A Season in Hell*.)

Alfred Jarry (Pluto. Playwright—*Ubu Roi*, precursor of the surrealist and futurist movements.)

Isadora Duncan (Pluto. Pioneer of modern dance.)

Amédée Ozenfant (Neptune. Developed principles of artistic "purism" with Le Corbusier.)

Ludwig Mies Van der Rohe (Neptune. Modern architect.)

Gaston Bachelard (Neptune. Philosophical writer—*On Poetic Imagination and Reverie*.)

Lillian Hellman (Jupiter. Playwright—*The Children's Hour*; blacklisted for refusing to testify before HUAC.)

Albert Brooks (North Node. Wrote and directed *Defending Your Life*, *The Muse*.)

Amber Tamblyn (Sun, Mercury, Mars. Star of television's *Joan of Arcadia*—where she has private conversations with God.)

Johnny Depp (Mercury, Venus. Actor in many surrealistic films—*Don Juan DeMarco*.)

S. Clay Wilson (Saturn, Uranus. Underground cartoonist—scenes of apocalyptic mayhem.)

Tama Janowitz (Moon. Novelist—*Slaves of New York*.)

Bob Dylan (Moon, Saturn, Uranus. Folk-rock musician, who emphasizes the unreality of modern life—"Maggie's Farm.")

David Byrne (Sun. Lead singer of the Talking Heads.)

Jack Bruce (Sun. Bass guitarist and songwriter for the psychedelic rock group Cream.)

Brian Eno (Sun. Musician—Roxy Music, "ambient music," collaborations with David Bowie, Freddie Mercury, and Roger Fripp.)

Roger Fripp (Sun. Visionary rock musician—*In the Court of the Crimson King.*)

Paul Simon and Art Garfunkel (Saturn and Uranus [both]. Folk singers—"The Dangling Conversation.")

Walt Whitman (Sun. Poet—*Leaves of Grass.*)

Hermann Hesse (Pluto. Novelist—*Steppenwolf.*)

André Gregory (Sun. Experimental-theater director—*My Dinner with Andre.*)

Tim Burton (Mars. Film director—*Edward Scissorhands.*)

John Irving (Saturn, Uranus. Writer—*The World According to Garp.*)

Martha Graham (Sun. Pioneer in modern dance.)

Josef Albers (Neptune. Cubist artist.)

Henry Miller (North Node. Novelist—*Tropic of Cancer.*)

Ryūnosuke Akutagawa (North Node. Short-story writer—"Rashomon"— with its multiple points of view.)

Wyndham Lewis (Saturn, Pluto. Painter and writer, protopunk; edited the vorticist magazine *BLAST.*)

Harry Crosby (Mercury. Libertine poet, founder of *Black Sun Press*, which published T. S. Eliot, James Joyce, and Ezra Pound.)

Richard Linklater (Mars. Filmmaker—*Slacker*, *A Scanner Darkly.*)

Paul Goodman (Saturn. Novelist—*Growing Up Absurd*, leftist activist, cofounded gestalt therapy.)

Gemini, 1st Decan

IMAGE: *A woman at a loom weaves a dress patterned with astrological figures. Unobserved, her pet cat has gotten tangled up in some yarn.*

The planet Mercury has a strong presence in the first decan of Gemini. Traditional astrologers associate Mercury with speech and everyday mental processes. They may also connect Mercury with craftsmanship and writing, yet somehow Mercury is almost never thought of as a particularly *creative* planet. This is an error. Not only are many of the degree symbols in Gemini associated with fine art, but speech itself, if one really examines it, is a highly creative act. In the process of speaking, we are taking mental images and *clothing* them in words. We are taking ideas and images from the immaterial mental realm and giving them concrete form. Fine art is similar. The artist comes up with a beautiful, interesting mental image and, through various technical skills, gives that image concrete form. Mercurial types are not just talkers, then, but can be inventors, writers, painters, architects, city planners, or fashion designers. They have great appreciation for beauty of form, and through practice, develop the skill sets required by their chosen medium. Eventually, they develop the critical eye specific to their trade. They become such masters of their craft that their creations appear to have been made by magic.

The most important creation for these people is their own unique personality. The first and last degrees of Gemini are symbolized by an insightful if distorted self-portrait, and a hall of mirrors full of beauty contestants. Both degrees deal with *self-representation*. In the first degree, there is an attempt to be honest about oneself, often by emphasizing ugliness as well as beauty. The last degree, by contrast, shows a tendency to hide behind a socially acceptable mask—to look the way people want one to look, and to say what people want one to say.

Since this is the first decan in an *air* sign, it shows the individual entering into the broader social world—the world of social interactions, culture, and politics. People of this decan have to translate who they are as spiritual beings into a workable social image. Like insecure adolescents, they must put together a persona that affords them mobility and acceptance in their social scene but doesn't feel phony or insincere. As teenagers, these people can be socially awkward, and even a bit clueless. With age and experience, however, they become skillful social maneuverers. They develop savoir faire.

Gemini 1 individuals are very observant, especially of other people. They study people and decide which personality types seem to work on a social level. They begin to imitate traits associated with social success—if they think they can pull it off—and begin to hide traits that might make them unpopular. This process results in the division of the personality into a confident, shining social persona, and a quiet, reflective shadow self. Because these people want to be liked, there is some danger that they will conform to current standards of attractiveness and end up becoming rather plastic. Most, however, create a fresh and oddly magical persona that adds something new and exciting to the social mix. In fact, they can be rather aggressive in promoting this personal aesthetic. Like the weaver of the decan image, they are actively "selling their wares in the marketplace." And they are well-aware of the competition. They know what they have that no one else has—what special art they bring to their creations.

In the creation of a social identity, one of the most basic choices is what one is going to wear. People of this decan might decide to dress as a businessperson, a farmer, a housewife, a nerd. These choices will have a big effect on how they are perceived, how they are treated, and what kinds of actions they will be allowed. Even those who put together an eccentric individualistic look still need to impress the important people in their social set; their look has to *sell* in the cultural marketplace. Questions of personal integrity are important here. These people understand that, at least to some degree, they must compromise with current tastes. They must adapt to the demands of the marketplace. Yet, as highly expressive people, they don't want to hide. Thus, they'll often put up with a low-paying job, as long as it allows them the freedom to be themselves.

Gemini 1 individuals are creating not just a social persona, but a story to go along with that persona. They are developing a personal mythology and ways of expressing that mythology—through body language, clothing, and speech. Since they visualize their internal self-portrait so clearly, even their faces begin to conform to this picture. They end up *looking* the part. And because they look the part and can convincingly *play* the part, they are fairly successful in living out their chosen story. They become the heroes or heroines in a film they create in their own minds. People of this decan are fairly committed to this personality they have created. However, they still recognize that it's something of an act, and may occasionally even pimp on themselves. They intend no dishonesty. It is their nature to perceive life as a kind of film or play, and to turn each episode of life into a story. They get a lot of pleasure out of viewing life this way. It's fun, and it's also interesting.

Weaving, in the decan image, symbolizes creativity and artistry, but it also symbolizes the working of the mind in analyzing everyday experience. Gemini 1 individuals tend to be curious about almost everything and may jump quickly from one observation to the next. Often, they follow out a number of different intellectual *threads* simultaneously. This can lead to mental confusion—a tangling of thoughts, which, in the decan image, is symbolized by the cat tangled in yarn. Patience is important here—a willingness to untangle mental knots so one can get back to one's original line of thought.

All three Gemini decans require the development of mental focus—for given the mutable nature of the sign, Geminis have a tendency to scatter their thoughts in a wide spectrum of interests. The weaving of the decan image symbolizes the difficult task of organizing one's thoughts—of weaving different lines of thought into a coherent pattern. To think in an organized way, one must be able to concentrate. And to concentrate, one must tune out the noise and distractions of the outside world. Optimally, these people find some quiet spot to think or to pursue their craft—some library or artist's studio—since quiet isolation is the best environment for pursuits that require patience and concentration.

Gemini 1 individuals must be especially disciplined when they are thinking about themselves, since the stories they repeat about themselves will become the stories they end up living. Mercury is a planet of magic, and Geminis are natural conjurors. Positively, Geminis create stories with idealistic themes and happy endings. Negatively, they create confused, pessimistic stories that attract bad events into their lives. The mind is a magician, in that it attracts events to fill in preexistent stories. When Geminis repeatedly voice a set of negative expectations—about themselves or about the human race—they wrap themselves, mummy-like, within a negative reality, much as the cat of the decan image has tangled itself up in yarn. It is no accident that ancient cultures associated weaving with ideas about *fate*. We determine our fate by the way we think. It is therefore important to employ disciplined artistry in thinking about ourselves and about the world. We need to remember that thinking is a creative act—that we are free to think any way we choose. Playfulness and whimsy are therefore important, since they remind us of our freedom to represent the world as we choose. It is in fact very difficult to create a good life for oneself without a certain amount of artistry.

So far, I have emphasized the clothing of the spirit in a social persona. Yet, the clothing of the spirit also occurs on a more internal level. Mercury, which rules this decan, represents the disincarnate intelligence or spirit. It is the immortal spirit as it travels through various incarnations, each of which has very different outward manifestations. In one incarnation one might be a man, in another a woman, in one a Russian, and in another a Turk. The Mercurial spirit, however, is antecedent to any of these manifestations. It is naked and outside the realm of time and form. In one's present life, one's first clothes are not baby bunting, but the astrological chart one was born with. This chart is not synonymous with one's identity. One need only consider people who were born on the same day as oneself. They are astral twins with most of the planets on the very same degrees, yet one finds all kinds of differences. Each individual spirit connects with their palette of astrological archetypes in a very personal way. One person might like Venus better, and another Uranus, and the self-portrait they come up with will reflect these preferences. Thus, even on an astrological level, one's identity is based on personal taste and aesthetic choices. It is a work of art.

The Egyptians often placed the cat goddess, Bastet, in this decan. Bastet was usually portrayed as a cat-headed or lion-headed woman. She was a goddess of music and merrymaking but was also a protector against diseases, evil spirits, and malevolent animals. Sometimes she was called the "Eye of Re," which is interesting, given that Aldebaran, the brightest star in the decan, was termed the "Eye of God" by the astronomer Flammarion.

EXAMPLES

Edgar Degas (Jupiter, Chiron. Painter of ballet scenes.)
Fred Astaire (Moon. Actor, dancer.)
Coco Chanel (Saturn, Chiron, Pluto. Fashion designer.)

Jan de Bont (Uranus. Filmmaker—*Twister.*)

Agatha Christie (Neptune, Pluto. Mystery writer, whose famous detective, Miss Marple, is always knitting.)

Stevie Nicks (Sun. Lead singer for Fleetwood Mac.)

Spalding Gray (Jupiter. Monologist.)

Miles Davis (Ascendant, Sun. Innovative jazz trumpeter.)

Paul Gauguin (Venus. Painter—South Seas scenes.)

Thomas Edison (Jupiter. Inventor of the lightbulb, phonograph, movie projector, etc.)

Julia Child (Ascendant, Saturn. TV chef.)

Robert DeNiro (Uranus. Talented actor—*Taxi Driver.*)

Adolf Hitler (Neptune, Pluto. Dictator, great orator.)

John F. Kennedy (Sun. President; great orator.)

John Baird (Neptune, Pluto. Inventor, early developer of television.)

Geraldo Rivera (Uranus. Self-promoting investigative journalist.)

Mae West (Pluto. Film comedienne, comedy writer.)

Prince (Mercury. Rock singer who changed his name to a Mercury-like symbol.)

Dwayne Hickman (Mercury, Chiron. Actor—*The Many Loves of Dobie Gillis*, directed television's *Designing Women.*)

Amédée Ozenfant (Pluto. Cubist artist, aesthetic theorist.)

Claude Bragdon (Mars. Architect, aesthetic theorist—*The Beautiful Necessity.*)

Bette Davis (Venus. Actress—*Dead Ringer*—about evil twins.)

Raoul Dufy (Mercury. Fauve artist.)

T. S. Eliot (Neptune, Pluto. Poet—*The Waste Land.*)

Louis XIV (Pluto. Egomaniacal king who posed for many portraits.)

Céline (Sun. Doctor and cynical novelist—*Journey to the End of Night.*)

Tina Turner (Moon. Hyperenergetic rock star.)

Frédéric-Auguste Bartholdi (Mars, Jupiter, Chiron. Sculptor—*The Statue of Liberty.*)

Dorothy Parker (Jupiter. Wisecracking short-story writer, poet, and critic; leftist activist.)

R. Crumb (Mars. Underground cartoonist—Mr. Natural and Flakey Foont.)

Edith Piaf (Moon. Chanteuse.)

Noel Fielding (Sun. Surrealist British comedian—*The Mighty Boosh.*)

Richard Ayoade (Sun. Comic actor. Wrote and directed *The Double*, a darkly comic film about a man whose place is usurped by a doppelganger.)

Arthur Conan Doyle (Sun, Uranus. Wrote the Sherlock Holmes stories, believed in fairies.)

Gemini, 2nd Decan

IMAGE: *A young Black pianist performs at Carnegie Hall. He polishes off the technically difficult finale, to enthusiastic applause. Afterward, he shakes hands with the white conductor.*

People with an emphasis in this decan are friendly, open, and talkative. Surprisingly up-front about their thoughts, their feelings, and their personal history, they "tell it like it is," even if that means breaking unspoken social rules. Two of the Sabian symbols in this decan are "a soapbox orator" and "a Black girl demands her rights from her mistress." The people depicted in these symbols have taken it upon themselves to proclaim their views without permission or social sanction. The angry Black girl is clearly breaking the rules, since she is speaking to her employer as if she were an equal. The soapbox orator has no socially sanctioned platform but has made his own platform out of a soapbox.

Gemini 2 individuals are very confident of their opinions, and eager to share them. They are always looking for a receptive audience and refuse to be either dismissed or marginalized. In the face of such behavior, they may in fact respond with anger or sarcasm. Though this uninhibited way of speaking can be somewhat rude, it has a socially beneficial effect, since it encourages others to open up and speak their minds. Through personal example, Gemini 2 individuals demonstrate that one can say whatever one wants to say and *be* whoever one wants to be—that one doesn't have to apologize for the crime of being different.

People of this decan have enough chutzpah to unabashedly express themselves in any situation. Even so, they would rather have an approved social platform from which to share their ideas and talents. In the decan image we see a Black pianist who has developed his musical skills to the point that he has been invited to play at an elite venue. Gemini 2 individuals find it easy to develop their artistic or intellectual talents, for they readily lose themselves in artistic and analytical processes. They are especially well suited to careers that rely upon verbal skills, including law, acting, singing, teaching, sales, and comedy. They do not make good politicians, however, since they refuse to sidestep thorny issues and tend to blurt out their opinions in bald pronouncements.

People of this decan are very self-aware and express themselves boldly through their speech, their behavior, and their appearance. In my book *Moon Phases*, the Gemini phase was called "The Actor." People of this decan are, in fact, rather like hammy actors, who are playing out a role on "the stage of life." They are aware of the artifice of this role but try to be as honest and authentic within it as they can. They are committed to this role, and to the story that goes along with it. By focusing on the most interesting and exciting aspects of their experience, they turn their lives into a series of episodes and adventures. Here, Mercury is acting as the Magician—as Hermes or Thoth. For like Thoth—the creator of writing—these people are "writing their own scripts." They are in a play constructed out of their own observations and mental conceptualizations.

People of this decan have very active intellects. They are forever putting together new pieces of the puzzle and get genuinely excited by their intellectual discoveries. Since they want to effectively communicate these ideas to the public, they try to express them so eloquently that they can't be misunderstood. Unfortunately, they often get so excited about their ideas that they come on too strong, dragging people into discussions about their pet concerns, even when they aren't particularly interested. Gemini 2 individuals are almost never boring, but they can be a bit exhausting, since they can run on without letting others get a word in edgewise. In fact, learning to listen is one of their chief lessons in life.

Many of the degree symbols in this decan involve the attempt to communicate across wide social barriers. There is the soapbox orator, the Black girl demanding her rights, the Chinese men in an American bar. Gemini 2 individuals may feel quite different from others but are nonetheless confident in their ability to put themselves across. They believe that good communication is possible between any two people—that one can enjoy a meeting of the minds with anyone if one has a sincere desire to do so. By extension, they see no real reason why everyone on the planet shouldn't get along.

In the decan symbol, we see a black man and a white man shaking hands. This is a symbol of the Twins; it shows two people who are aware of their common humanity beyond differences of race, class, gender, and nationality. People of this decan are interested in connecting with all kinds of people. They recognize that everyone is different and inhabits his or her own subjective world. Yet, if one really wants to understand these worlds, it can be done.

Like the "twins" of the decan image, people with an emphasis here have an underlying belief that we are all brothers and sisters under the skin. We therefore need to treat each other with respect and dignity and avoid exploiting or abusing each other by word or deed. If we share our stories honestly, people will understand us, empathize with us, and even identify with us. At least, that's the ideal. Unfortunately, a person's ego and blind spots can easily get in the way of true communication. When Gemini 2 individuals fail to make themselves understood, they may be too impatient to explain themselves more carefully; often they just raise the volume. At worst, they resort to bullying—overwhelming others with a barrage of words and a dominating personality. Underneath it all, they want to bring people together—to get them into the same world. However, their childlike naiveté may cause people to back away.

Politically, this is a very idealistic decan, with strong commitments to brotherhood, fairness, and social justice. These people are awake to social and political realities and are often found trying to alert others to the actual nature of their situation. Though Geminis are sometimes extreme and even polarizing in their opinions, the basic thrust of their politics is to make society more honest, inclusive, and democratic. To this end, they try to mobilize the populace around progressive political programs. Like soapbox orators, they stir people up and enlist them in programs of social and political reform.

The ancient Egyptians often placed the *twin* air gods, Shu and Tefnut, in this region. Note that these Egyptian twins have a completely independent origin from the Geminian twins of the Greco-Babylonian tradition. The Egyptian twins consist of a male god, Shu, who was associated with wind and clouds, and the goddess Tefnut, who was associated with moist air and rain. The Egyptians believed that these twin gods shared one soul.[41] In Renaissance images of the decan, one often finds Gemini's twins depicted as Apollo and Hercules, or alternatively, as a man playing a flute and a man holding a shovel. This last image symbolizes the polarity between the cultured man and the physical man. It alludes to the Gemini's desire to refine his or her manners and social skills, while retaining an earthy familiarity that makes them easy to approach.

EXAMPLES

Kinky Friedman (Uranus. Satirical songster—Kinky Friedman and the Texas
Jewboys; successful mystery writer; unsuccessful candidate for governor
of Texas, running on the slogan "Why the hell not?")

Julian Beck (Venus. Cofounder and director of *The Living Theater*, which
aims at shocking the audience out of complacency.)

Dr. Benjamin Spock (Venus. Influential baby doctor; activist against the war
in Vietnam.)

Dr. Ruth Westheimer (Sun. Outrageously frank sex therapist.)

Ross Perot (Mercury. Successful businessman—relentless salesman;
unsuccessful third-party candidate.)

Toni Collette (Saturn. Actress—*Mental, The Way, Way Back.*)

Eldridge Cleaver (Chiron. Cofounder of the Black Panther movement—*Soul
on Ice.*)

Aimé Cesaire (Saturn. Anticolonialist African politician; founder of the
négritude movement.)

Robert Carradine (Jupiter. Actor—*Revenge of the Nerds.*)

Camille Paglia (Uranus. Blunt, incisive cultural critic, public intellectual.)

Stephen Hawking (Jupiter. Physically handicapped theoretical physicist who
weighed in on many subjects outside his specialty; supporter of the
"many worlds" theory of quantum mechanics.)

Anaïs Nin (Pluto. Erotic diarist.)

Ron Kovic (Uranus. Wheelchair-bound antiwar activist, veteran.)

Alan Alda (Chiron. Actor—*M*A*S*H.*)

Brett Butler (Moon. Comic actress—*Grace under Fire.*)

Sally Field (North Node. Actress—*Soap Dish.*)

Garrison Keillor (Saturn. Folksy radio humorist—*A Prairie Home Companion.*)

Erica Jong (Ascendant, Mars, Jupiter. Author of *Fear of Flying.*)

Bill Moyers (Sun. TV journalist focusing on moral, spiritual, and social issues.)

Jerry Mathers (Sun. Child star of television's *Leave It to Beaver.*)

Dyan Cannon (Chiron. Actress—*Bob & Carol & Ted & Alice.*)

Bob Dylan (Venus. Brutally honest folk singer.)

Gary Brooker (Uranus. Lead singer of Procol Harum.)

Salvador Dalí (Pluto. Surrealist painter—melting watches.)

Russell Brand (Sun. Outrageous British stand-up comic, political activist.)

Buddy Holly (Moon. Oddly nerdy rock star.)

Martha Stewart (Jupiter. Public expert in all aspects of fine living;
unembarrassed by her stint in prison.)

Dolly Parton (Uranus. Country singer, actress—*9 to 5.*)

George Gershwin (Pluto. Songwriter, composer, and pianist—"Embraceable
You," *Rhapsody in Blue.*)

Jan Cremer (Venus, Mars. Gay writer—shocking autobiography.)

Steve Martin (Mars, Uranus. Aggressively loopy stand-up comic.)

Robert Reich (Uranus. Outspoken political columnist, chairman of Common Cause, secretary of labor.)

Eve Arden (Mars. Television and radio comedienne—*Our Miss Brooks*.)

Steven Vai (Sun, Venus. Heavy-metal guitar god.)

Gemini, 3rd Decan

> IMAGE: *An anthropologist lands her plane near a small village surrounded by woods. Clothed in a reflective silver suit, she climbs down among a gathering of curious residents. In her hand, she holds a sketchy, hand-drawn map.*

In the decan image, we see an anthropologist who intends to study the ways of a primitive rural village. Like the anthropologist, people with an emphasis here tend to perceive themselves as social outsiders. They are mavericks whose radically independent perspective allows them to see society in a fresh light. These people are always trying to figure out what's going on around them, especially on a social level. Thus, among the examples, one finds many sharp-eyed observers of society: comedians, cultural critics, sociologists, anthropologists, political commentators. Gemini 3 individuals do a lot of traveling. Thus, they come into contact with people who hold unusual beliefs and have different ways of life. Usually they adapt to foreign customs fairly easily. However, as outsiders, they are quick to notice the absurdity of certain customs and may comment on them in droll asides. Nor are they entirely willing to abide by the stupider rules and expectations of each country. They make some adjustments, certainly, but ultimately conduct themselves according to their own reading of the situation, even when this could land them in unknown territory without a map.

Sometimes Gemini 3 individuals feel a bit lost even in their own country. Their perspective on life may be so different from that of the "natives" that they may as well have landed in a UFO. Feeling that they don't really "know the language," they have to continually translate their thoughts into terms the natives might actually understand. These social difficulties—so typical of a "stranger in a strange land"—motivate them to get their bearings as quickly as possible. Coming down to earth and studying people at close range allows them to figure out what's going on around them. And once they're able to read their situation accurately, they are sure to make fewer mistakes.

While physical exploration is an important aspect of this decan, Gemini 3 individuals may also explore the inner world. To illustrate, William Butler Yeats, who had the Sun and Uranus in this decan, explored the world of Faerie and had a number of encounters with the Little People. Wolfgang Pauli explored the invisible world of quantum physics, whose language is mathematical. Albert Hofmann, Terence McKenna, and Paul McCartney explored worlds opened up by LSD. J. K. Rowling and L. Frank Baum explored fantasy realities, and like the Pied Piper, led millions of children into the world of the imagination. Gwyneth Paltrow, in *Sliding Doors*, simultaneously explored two parallel universes. People of this decan are very curious. They discover some unexplored cranny of reality, study it, and report back. In this way, they introduce people to different ways of seeing things—to other worlds and even other dimensions.

Gemini 3 individuals have reality conceptions that are provisional, open, and evolving. They know that they don't know, so they look at things freshly, without trying to shove their experiences into ready-made conceptual boxes. They recognize that their awareness depends on their immediate perspective, and that moving to another country, reading another book, or adopting another theory could radically alter that perspective. They also realize that no matter how old they get, they will still be connecting the dots, for as much as any one person can know, there is always infinitely more that they *don't* know. Gemini 3 individuals never stop adjusting their mental maps. They therefore live in a perpetual state of uncertainty. This doesn't particularly bother them. Misunderstandings are rarely catastrophic. One sorts them out and moves on. After all, children manage to get along, and what do they know?

Gemini 3 individuals try to enter new situations without a lot of preconceptions. However, they quickly begin to organize their observations into a rough mental map. This analysis is initially crude and cartoonlike, for like airborne pilots, they are able to make out only the most obvious features of the landscape. As they get closer to their subjects, however, the details begin to fill in, and they start to revise their original map. They begin to figure out what appeared to be there but actually wasn't, and what *was* there but was hidden from view. On occasion, they may also take a few steps back in order to regain their perspective, for they never forget the advantage of the long view. Here, the observational faculty of Mercury functions rather like a telescope, whose lenses allow one to focus in on distant realities.

The constellation of Orion occupies the entire third decan of Gemini. This constellation is made up of a number of the brightest stars in the sky. Orion has been pictured in almost every world culture as a human figure, and given its shape, it is easy to see why. This human figure, however, is an optical illusion, since Orion's stars form the figure we see *only* from the perspective of our own solar system. Everyone on Earth may see it the same way, but from the point of view of another galaxy, it would look completely different—unrecognizable, in fact.

There are many different ways of looking at things. Different cultures create different pictures for the constellations, even as different people see different forms in the same cloud formation. People of this decan do a lot of thinking in the conditional tense—in could bes and might bes. They are constantly bumping up against errors in their understanding and are therefore never particularly sure of their reality picture. Being "up in the air" can cause a certain amount of anxiety, but it is also very freeing. If objective reality is not even attainable, then one can live in any reality one can envisage. Among the examples, there are, in fact, a number of "reality artists," who create their own portrait of the world and then step into the picture. Their reality is poetic, personal, even whimsical. They make it up as they go along.

Not surprisingly, we also find a number of Gemini 3 individuals who are "space cadets." They dwell in cloud-cuckoo land—in the realm of speculation—and never come down to earth to get the real story. Admittedly, their perspective is elevated, but it is also ungrounded and even flaky. These people need to do a lot of studying—a lot of "mapmaking." Otherwise, they may end up as mere tourists in life, whose thinking never gets beyond superficial impressions and slapdash analyses.

In the decan image, we see a well-traveled aviator meeting a group of rural villagers. These rural folk, like the trees around them, have never budged from their birthplace. Admittedly, they are very close to nature, but their limited experiences render their views parochial and prejudicial. The aviator, by contrast, is an intellectual sophisticate, who reads books and newspapers and keeps up with modern ideas and theories. Internationalist in perspective, she sees past superficial differences of nationality, race, class, and gender, and almost without thinking, acts as a social leveler. People with an emphasis in this decan exhibit features of both the rural townsperson and the urban sophisticate. The educated, sophisticated side of Gemini is well known to traditional astrologers, but the instinctive, woodsy side is not. This is a fairly important omission, since even a quick look at the degree symbols (including the original Sabians)—shows many degrees with trees in them: the shaded well, the frost-covered trees, the archer in the woods, the path through virgin forests, the birds in their nest. There is a Druidic, shamanic side to Gemini that functions as their secret "home base." Gemini 3 individuals often have a very intimate relationship with nature. In quiet meditation, they are able to tune in to the inner life of the wind and the trees.

People of this decan can be somewhat clairvoyant. They catch glimpses of the divine Idea or divine light behind each person and each created thing. Certain books, films, experiences, or people speak to them more eloquently than others, for they are clearer channels of their spiritual archetypes. For people of this decan, life is a sequence of events that vary widely in their luminosity. They can only hope that the magical moments will outnumber the dull ones, and that the people they meet will have a strong connection to their spiritual archetype, or "Heavenly Twin." Geminis are always on the lookout for these "magical people," since they may be able to introduce them to interesting new ways of looking at the universe.

The ancient Egyptians pictured the constellation of Orion as the striding figure of the resurrected Osiris. This was the immortal soul of Osiris, after it had become one with the eternal light of the stars. In some decan lists, the sky god Shu appears here. He is a personification of the principles of *space* and *emptiness*. Gemini 3 is the first decan ruled by the planet Uranus, and Uranus, like Shu, is a god of the sky. Uranus is also the astrological body most closely associated with extraterrestrial space.[42]

EXAMPLES

Penny Marshall (Mars, Saturn. Actress, director: *Awakenings*, *Big*.)

Gwyneth Paltrow (Saturn. Actress—*Sliding Doors*.)

Sandra Bullock (Venus, Mars. Actress—*Miss Congeniality*, *28 Days*.)

Antoine de St. Exupéry (Neptune. Pioneering aviator, writer: *The Little Prince*.)

Günter Grass (North Node. "Magic realist" novelist—*The Tin Drum*.)

Jerzy Kosinski (Sun. Existentialist novelist—*The Painted Bird*, *Being There*.)

Salman Rushdie (Sun, Moon, Uranus. Magical-realist novelist—*The Satanic Verses*.)

Virginia Woolf (Mars. Existentialist novelist—*Orlando*, *To the Lighthouse*; nervous breakdowns and suicide.)

Tennessee Williams (Pluto. Playwright—*A Streetcar Named Desire*.)

Mary McCarthy (Venus, Pluto. Sociological writer—*The Group*.)

William Burroughs (Pluto. Beat writer—*Naked Lunch*.)

Michael Moore (Jupiter. Politically radical filmmaker—*Bowling for Columbine*.)

Abbie Hoffman (Moon, Chiron. Yippie leader, paranoid schizophrenic.)

Vicki Lawrence (Uranus. Comedienne—*Mama's Family*.)

Evelyn Waugh (Pluto. Author—*The Loved One*.)

Alice Cooper (Uranus. Shock rocker—"Caught in a Dream.")

Arlo Guthrie (Uranus. Folk singer—*Alice's Restaurant*.)

Garrison Keillor (Moon. Humorous raconteur.)

Luis Buñuel (Ascendant, Neptune. Shocking surrealistic filmmaker—*L'Age d'Or*, *The Discreet Charm of the Bourgeoisie*.)

Dustin Hoffman (Chiron. Actor in existentialist movies—*The Graduate*, *I Heart Huckabees*.)

John Waters (North Node. Director of shocking surrealist films—*Polyester*, *Multiple Maniacs*.)

Ben Stiller (Ascendant, Jupiter. Actor, director—*Reality Bites*, *Flirting with Disaster*.)

Gilda Radner (North Node. *Saturday Night Live* comic.)

James Joyce (Mars. Stream-of-consciousness novels—*Ulysses*.)

M. C. Escher (Sun, Neptune. Artist, illustrator—impossible constructions.)

John Lilly (Saturn. Research on human consciousness—isolation tanks, psychedelics.)

Marilyn Ferguson (Moon, Chiron. Published and edited the *Brain/Mind Bulletin*, cofounder of the Association of Humanistic Psychology; wrote *The Aquarian Conspiracy*.)

Jean Paul Sartre (Sun, Mercury, Pluto. Existentialist philosopher.)

Colin Wilson (Mercury. Outsider intellectual—wrote penetrating works on existentialism and the occult.)

Stephen Jay Gould (Jupiter. Evolutionary biologist; attacked racist biology—*The Mismeasure of Man*.)

Luis Alvarez (Sun, Pluto. Physicist—"wild idea man.")

Bill Cooper (Venus. Conspiracy theorist—UFOs, the Illuminati, AIDS as a manufactured disease.)

L. Ron Hubbard (Pluto. Sci-fi writer, founder of Scientology.)

Eric Hoffer (Neptune. Sociological author—*The True Believer*—which examines the belief structure of irrational mass movements.)

Roswell crash (July 4, 1947. Venus, Uranus. Was it a military weather balloon or a UFO?)

William Butler Yeats (Sun, Uranus. Metaphysical poet, leading light in the Golden Dawn.)

Cancer, 1st Decan

IMAGE: *A group of friends hang out on a riverbank, chatting and watching the boats go by. A couple of pet dogs jump in for a swim, and some of the gang strips down and jumps in after them.*

In ancient Egypt, this decan was almost always depicted as Isis in a boat,[43] pouring water out of a vase. The Egyptians associated this decan with the annual flooding of the Nile, which was brought about through the loving intercession of Isis. This beloved goddess embodied the universal life force—the rainwater that brings life not only to people, but to plants and animals. By pouring the living waters of the life force over the land, Isis brought about the rapid growth of the myriad forms of nature. People with an emphasis on this decan have a keen appreciation for the beauty and abundance of nature. They understand that they are part of life's complex web—that beyond their family, friends, and pets, there are also the creatures and plants that they eat. They see life as a web of relationships involving a constant interchange of energy, emotion, and ideas. Experiencing themselves as part of nature, they feel that their success ultimately depends on adapting to nature, by moving with its rhythms and going with its flow.

The first decan of Cancer introduces the element of *water* into the zodiacal circle. Water represents emotion and acts to dissolve the boundaries between living things. In a similar manner, people of this decan dissolve interpersonal barriers by listening empathetically to others and learning about their inner thoughts and feelings. In the decan image, we see people hanging out, talking, eating snacks, and watching the boats go by. Some people in the group are family members, while others have joined the group because of its easygoing, fun-loving ways. Early Cancers are very sociable. They tend to get along with all kinds of people, since on an emotional level they look upon humanity as an extended family. As tolerant people, Cancer 1 individuals don't expect people to be any different than they are. They realize that people come in all shapes and sizes and can't be expected to conform to their own standards of thought or behavior. This tolerant attitude can be compared to the passage of water over a rocky streambed. Water doesn't fight the rocks but flows over and around them. Similarly, in the face of argument and emotional disharmony, Cancer 1 individuals often stand back and wait for the problem to sort itself out. And if they *do* get involved in an argument, they often end up making most of the concessions, for they are more interested in restoring harmony than in scoring points.

People of this decan develop social scenes very naturally. As emotionally supportive individuals, they find it easy to collect a group of sympathetic souls. This group may include a few people who are problematical; some might even be called losers. But life isn't a contest, and as long as these individuals respect the basic rules of the group, they are accepted. Cancerians are compassionate and accepting, but they do have their limits. People who are dangerous or disruptive are kept out of the group. The boundaries of who belongs and who doesn't may be fairly porous, but they are still boundaries. The Moon is very powerful in this decan, and one of the Moon's main functions is to establish and maintain the behavioral rules of a social group—be it a family, a workplace, or a community. While people of this decan are very aware of these boundaries, they don't get upset by minor disruptions and changes. As lunar individuals, they are fairly comfortable with ambiguity, complexity, and change, and feel little need to control their environment, outside of their personal homes. Within any group, people will come and go. One person might move to another town, while another might introduce a new boyfriend or girlfriend to the group. One person leaves and another comes to fill their place. Water behaves in much the same way, for whenever it encounters a low spot, it fills it up. When Cancerians see someone who is lonely, they often reach out. When they see someone who is sad, they try to make them laugh.

In the decan image, we see some people sitting and watching the boats go by, while others strip and frolic in the water. Cancer 1 individuals long to dive into life, to immerse themselves in some beautiful emotional or sexual experience. They want to surrender to their feelings in a romantic relationship, in communing with nature, or in listening to music. At the same time, they realize that being too open can be dangerous, since there are a lot of predatory people out there. As emotionally sensitive individuals, Cancers can be rather fearful and will at times withdraw into safe, comfortable life patterns. Yet, among the examples one also finds hearty souls, who dive into various relationships until they have become "good swimmers"—until they have learned how to maneuver through all kinds of complicated emotional situations. This alternating, tide-like motion—out into the world and back into one's shell—is basic to the sign of Cancer. Most astrologers picture Cancers as dyed-in-the-wool homebodies, but a periodic quest for excitement and romantic adventure is also basic to their nature. Thus, in the decan image, we see some people who have undertaken an exciting voyage on a boat, while others are observing life from the safety of a pier.

The presence of pets in the decan image is also important. These people have very strong relationships with their pets. They understand that cats and dogs have very different psychologies from their own yet still enjoy many of the same things and can make loving allies and friends. Several of the Sabian symbols in the first decan of Cancer refer to animals. There is a goldfish, a reindeer, and a cat. People of this decan are in tune with their animal instincts, including their instinct for self-preservation, their territorial instincts, and their sexual instincts. Leaving behind the Geminian preoccupation with society and culture, Cancers are returning to a more primitive, instinctual relationship with the natural world. As sensitive and rather poetic individuals, they love to lose themselves in the beauties of the landscape. They find it easy to tune in to the secret soul of nature—to the dreams and magic that lie hidden within all natural forms. One of the degree symbols in this decan is "elves dancing in a moonlit forest glade." This alludes to mysterious processes of nature that go on below the surface—outside the scope of the conscious mind.

Intellectually, Cancer 1 individuals are quick to see the underlying connections between things, but slow to organize these insights into a coherent analysis. They spend a long time gathering all the relevant facts and then brood over them, like a hen over an egg. Rather than making snap judgments, they "sleep on a problem" until some organizing insight emerges from the subconscious. Even then, they consider their analysis provisional; as new information and new interpretations "come around the bend," their understanding may change dramatically. Once they have discovered a number of facts that don't fit into their present worldview, they may abandon their current interpretive framework entirely, much as a crab will occasionally shed its shell. In this way, they mature as thinkers, progressing from simplistic, childish notions into more complex, evolved understandings. People of this decan have a high learning curve because, like children, they have intrinsic faith in the growth process. They accept the fact that this process will occasionally require them to abandon comfortable situations and boldly step into some new phase of life—some phase of life that is unfamiliar and possibly dangerous. They accept the fact that their world tomorrow will probably look very different than it does today.

Cancer 1 individuals recognize that life involves constant changes: some major and some minor. Like the moon, they see their lives as a series of phases, punctuated by major events such as marriage, job changes, health crises, and physical relocations. Generally, these people aren't too upset by life's ups and downs, for they have great faith in the life force. If something doesn't work out, they don't try to force it but allow events to develop in their own way. At times, they are overly passive, adapting, with minor grumblings, to every vexing situation that comes along. Some give in too easily to the wishes and demands of their family and friends, their boss, and their country. Giving freely of themselves, they end up neglecting their own needs.

Since Cancer 1 individuals have a naturally adaptable, disorganized sort of personality, they often seek out the stability and protection of well-defined organizations or groups. Having a job to go to at fixed hours gives structure to their lives and forces them to be productive. Getting married gives structure to the emotional and sexual side of their lives. Cancer 1 individuals can become quite dependent on their mates, looking to them for support and guidance. At the same time, they fulfill their family roles admirably—whether as a mother, father, sister, or grandparent. When it comes to sensitive family matters, their canny emotional intelligence seems to tell them exactly what to do.

Cancer 1 individuals have a strong impulse to help others, since they are compassionate individuals who think that we are ultimately all "in the same boat." People of this decan are often associated with organizations that serve humanity, especially the less fortunate. Some act as inspirational leaders in these organizations, articulating and strengthening the ideals around which these groups were founded. They also act to unify the group on an emotional level, for they understand that the smooth functioning of any group depends on communication and adaptation. Thus, within their family and within their workplace, they never cease to promote understanding and cooperation.

EXAMPLES

Margaret Mead (Neptune. Cultural anthropologist—*Coming of Age in Samoa.*)
Mary McCarthy (Sun, Mercury. Novelist—*The Group.*)
Max Shulman (Jupiter, Pluto. Novelist—*The Many Loves of Dobie Gillis.*)
Henry Winkler (North Node. "The Fonz" on *Happy Days.*)
Cindy Williams (Mars. Actress—*Laverne and Shirley.*)
Richard Rodgers (Sun, Neptune. Broadway composer—"Some Enchanted Evening," "Getting to Know You.")
Debbie Harry (Saturn. Pop singer—"Heart of Glass," "Call Me.")
Rupert Sheldrake (Sun, Jupiter. Psi researcher—*The Presence of the Past*—telepathic communication between organisms.)
John Cusack (Sun. Star of romantic comedies—*Say Anything.*)
Lena Horne (Sun, Pluto. Black singer, civil rights activist—"Stormy Weather.")
William Penn (Mars. Settled Pennsylvania.)
Richard Bach (Sun. Novelist—*Jonathan Livingston Seagull.*)
Jeff Bridges (Uranus. Actor—*The Big Lebowski.*)
Erma Bombeck (North Node. Comic writer.)
Joan Blondell (Saturn, Pluto. Actress—*Gold Diggers of '33.*)
Katharine Hepburn (Jupiter. Actress—*The African Queen, On Golden Pond.*)
Morris Berman (Saturn. Ecological writer—*The Reenchantment of the World, Coming to Our Senses.*)
Tobey Maguire (Sun. Actor—*Pleasantville, Spiderman.*)
Juliette Binoche (Ascendant, North Node. Actress—*Chocolat, Family Life.*)
Paul Gauguin (Mercury. Colorful painter of South Seas subjects.)
Arlo Guthrie (Venus. Folk singer—*Alice's Restaurant.*)
Alex Haley (Venus, Pluto. Author of *Roots, The Autobiography of Malcolm X.*)
Barbara Woodhouse (Mars. Dog trainer—*No Bad Dogs.*)
Malvina Reynolds (Mars. Folk singer—"Little Boxes on a Hilltop," "What Have They Done to the Rain?")

Aubrey Plaza (Sun, Mercury, Venus. Actress, comedienne.)

Leon Uris (Venus. Jewish-American author of *Exodus*.)

Henry Dunant (Venus. Established the International Red Cross.)

Princess Diana (Sun. Beloved royal, land-mine activist.)

Roger McGuinn (Mercury, Jupiter. Folk-rock singer for the Byrds—"Turn, Turn, Turn," "Mr. Tambourine Man.")

Patch Adams (Saturn, North Node. Physician and clown, utopian-community organizer.)

Gérard d'Aboville (North Node. Crossed the Pacific in a rowboat.)

Gary Larson (Uranus. Cartoonist who often takes the side of animals against humans.)

Beatrix Potter (Uranus. Wrote *The Tale of Peter Rabbit*.)

Pearl Buck (Sun. Novelist—*The Good Earth*.)

John Fogerty (Saturn, North Node. Rock star, leader of the Creedence Clearwater Revival.)

Federico Fellini (Pluto. Surrealistic filmmaker—*Nights of Cabiria*, *Juliet of the Spirits*.)

Cancer, 2nd Decan

IMAGE: *In the ornate chapel of the family mansion, a woman discovers a secret door leading into a beautiful garden, where magical rites were once performed. At the center is a circular pond, and above it a faceted glass roof through which the stars can be seen.*

People of this decan have highly developed imaginations and a vivid fantasy life. The middle decan of each sign often has a "fixed" nature, and the fixed water of this decan has a strong connection to the astral plane. Images and symbols are created and retained very easily here. These imaginative images can be used in a number of ways. First, they can be materialized in works of art. Thus, the beautiful chapel and gardens of the decan image were materialized from images in the minds of their designers. The architect came up with an imaginative vision and translated this vision into blueprints, which were then used as a template for the construction of the chapel. The gardener thought out an arrangement of beautiful plants and turned this vision into a beautiful garden.

The materialization of mental images can also be facilitated by magic, since the intense visualization of mental images can attract the things being envisaged. This principle is often used in the design of churches and temples, since religious statuary, stained glass, and the like are employed to channel the energy and consciousness of the sacred things being symbolized. Cancer 2 individuals are very aware of the power of symbols and make use of them, in various ways, in their lives.

People of this decan are often involved in an earnest exploration of the inner world. They are seekers after metaphysical, religious, and existential truths. Since this is a fairly lunar decan, these people's belief-structures are initially inherited from their families. Thus, in the decan image, the family chapel represents the overarching beliefs by which a person's parents and grandparents made sense of the world. Cancer 2 individuals view life through the lens of their core beliefs. As they mature, these beliefs are modified by their experiences in life, and by their exposure to the books and traditions of other cultures. In the decan symbol, the young woman has decided that her inherited worldview is too confining. She feels that she has been hypnotized by a narrow set of beliefs imposed upon her by her family and her family's church. If she is to evolve as a conscious being, she must break through this rigid shell of beliefs, even as a crab must occasionally shed its shell. Stepping through a "secret door" that leads beyond her inherited beliefs, she finds books on the spiritual teachings of other lands, including shamanism and magic. In this way, she progresses from ritual-bound, exoteric religion to a life of reflection and meditation. She learns to receive spiritual wisdom *directly* from its inmost sources. This transition is exciting and transformative, but it can also be quite upsetting, for it can turn one's whole worldview upside down.

As explorers of new metaphysical realities, Cancer 2 individuals have more questions than answers, for it is not their habit to wall off strange realities. They want to decide for themselves the boundaries of what is real. Is there such a thing as ESP, aliens, reincarnation? Is there a God, and if so, can we communicate with this Being? What happens when we die? In the decan symbol, we see a hidden door leading into a garden devoted to magical rites. If one believes that something is impossible, an impenetrable wall is formed in one's mind, and one becomes unreceptive to that realm of reality. If, however, one fully opens oneself to another belief system, a door opens in one's mind. One can then step through that door and begin to examine the realities of this other realm. Using the lantern of one's consciousness, one can shine a light on this new set of beliefs. One can discover for oneself which of these ideas shine with the light of truth, and which have become outdated or irrelevant to one's needs. Not surprisingly, one finds a large number of spiritual teachers with planets in this decan, including Marianne Williamson, Swami Muktananda, Ed Steinbrecher, Marc Edmund Jones, Colin Wilson (*The Occult*), Alan Vaughn (*Patterns of Prophecy*), the Dalai Lama, Margot Adler (*Drawing Down the Moon*), and Robert Amadou (*Great Mediums*).

People of this decan are especially interested in knowledge that doesn't fit into the conventional worldview. They collect this anomalous knowledge and then begin to organize it into a coherent analytical framework. Because they are constantly discovering new truths, they go through a number of distinct phases in the development of their worldview. During their lifetime, they progress through a number of these intellectual "shells," as their worldview becomes more sophisticated and comprehensive. After each major revelation, a period of readjustment and rapid mental growth follows, wherein they bring their external life into conformity with the altered internal architecture of their new belief-system.

Although Cancer 2 individuals often embrace unorthodox ideas, they may hide these ideas for much of their lives. They know that they have important insights and will freely share these ideas when asked, but in the face of an unsupportive audience, they often hide their views. This allows them to explore and develop new areas of consciousness—new rooms of the mind—without a lot of criticism or interference. People of this decan recognize the importance of creating some "sacred space" in their home, devoted to the contemplation of life's deeper questions. In this space, they cultivate their connection to the divine, and their appreciation for the holiness of life. As they evolve, Cancer 2 individuals become sure enough of their beliefs that they step out of the shadows and begin to teach. Some become lighthouses to the public—illuminating people's minds and inspiring them toward spiritual growth. Like the Hermit of the Tarot, with his lantern, they send their light out into the world.

Cancer 2 individuals can be a bit preachy, but they are also good listeners. Through far-ranging conversations with other people, they learn about their values and beliefs. If these people are undervaluing some truths or overvaluing others, they confront them on these issues. Should they succeed in getting them to accept even one new piece of the puzzle, their entire world picture might undergo a transformation. Subsidiary ideas would start to crystallize around the new insight, and a reordering of knowledge would begin to take place. A new mental architecture would materialize, characterized by a precise internal geometry.

So far, I have emphasized the progressive side of the decan, but this placement can also be very conservative. Most Cancer 2 individuals are trying to deepen their spiritual understanding by stepping outside their usual way of framing reality. Yet, among the examples, one also finds people who are determined to preserve the status quo—to buttress the walls of conventional belief in order to "protect the family mansion." Examples include Ronald Reagan, George W. Bush, Senator Joe McCarthy, Billy Graham, Hilaire Belloc, Charles IX, and Jesse Helms. These people look upon new ideas as a betrayal of the values of the family, the church, and the nation. Most of the people listed above were active in politics, but it should be noted that political views form an important part of most people's belief-systems. As for the religious conservatives, these are people who embrace their family's religion wholeheartedly. They confer great authority on their preacher and the doctrines of their church, in the belief that through them they will be able to connect to higher spiritual truths.

The strong visual imagination of this decan can be turned to questions of religion and magic, but the imagination can also serve as a source of pleasurable fantasies. These include clearly visualized sexual and romantic fantasies. However, the examples also show a liking for fantasies involving adventure and magic. The following films, for instance, are associated with actors and directors with planets in this decan: *The Seventh Voyage of Sinbad, Men in Black, Juliet of the Spirits, Rosemary's Baby, Robin Hood, Tomb Raider, Charlie's Angels, Ben Hur, Planet of the Apes, Stargate, 20,000 Leagues under the Sea, The Rocky Horror Picture Show, Big*, and *King Solomon's Mines*. All these movies are embodiments of symbol-rich visions that have been worked out in great detail. Most of these lurid adventure movies trade in magic, but they are meant to entertain and show little genuine belief in the occult.

The ancient Egyptians sometimes placed the goddess Seshat in this decan. Seshat was a form of Isis, a goddess closely associated with Sirius—the brightest star of this decan. Seshat laid the foundations of temples by sighting off a star, in a ritual called "the stretching of the cord." She was a patron of architecture, libraries, surveying, and *astrology*. People of this decan are very receptive to astrology. In the decan image, one sees the stars through a faceted glass roof. This is a symbol of the astrological archetypes, as they descend through the astral plane into the reflective pool of the human soul and crystallize to form the template of one's personality. Astrologers of this decan often have a special interest in astrological timing, since two time-sensitive "planets"—the moon and Saturn—are quite powerful here. The moon has a period of 29.5 days and Saturn has a period of 29.5 years. Thus, the decan underlines the natural harmony between the macrocosm and the microcosm—between the movements of the heavens and the events of everyday life. This astrological clock tends to mark out distinct phases of one's life, marked by critical junctures such as marriages, deaths, changes of residence or career, and even spiritual revelations. People of this decan tend to believe that there is a preordained order to these major life events—that in some mysterious way their fate is in the hands of a higher power.

EXAMPLES

Jean Cocteau (Sun, Chiron, North Node. Avant-garde artist, writer.)

Bob Shaye (Established New Line Cinema; directed *The Last Mimzy*.)

Ken Russell (Sun, Pluto. Filmmaker—*Altered States, Lair of the White Worm*.)

Elisabeth Kübler-Ross (Sun, Pluto, North Node. Wrote *On Death and Dying*.)

Jacques Derrida (Pluto. Deconstructionist theorist.)

Albert Brooks (Mercury, Venus. Filmmaker—*Defending Your Life*.)

Dietrich Fischer-Dieskau (Mars, Pluto. Sublime singer of lieder and Bach—*Kreuzstab Kantate*.)

Elaine Pagels (Jupiter. "Heretical" historian—*The Gnostic Gospels, The Origin of Satan*.)

Gabriele Amorth (Pluto. Catholic exorcist.)

Marianne Williamson (Sun, Venus, Uranus. *Course in Miracles* teacher.)

John Frankenheimer and Angela Lansbury (Pluto. Director and lead actress in *The Manchurian Candidate*—about the hypnotic programming of a spy.)

James Garner (Pluto. Bamboozled prisoner of war in *36 Hours*.)

Philip K. Dick (Pluto. Sci-fi writer—*Ubik*.)

Bruce Willis (Jupiter. Actor—*The Sixth Sense*.)

Joan Allen (Venus. Actress—*Pleasantville*.)

Jan Assmann (Sun. Leading Egyptologist; wrote on the violence and intolerance intrinsic to monotheism.)

Alan Vaughn (Moon. Psychic—*Patterns of Prophecy*.)

Jules Verne (Saturn. Author—*20,000 Leagues under the Sea*.)

Hermann Hesse (Sun. Occult author—*Steppenwolf, Siddhartha*.)

Frank Buchman (Mars. Lutheran pastor—founded Moral Rearmament.)

Richard Kelly (Saturn. Director and screenwriter—*Donnie Darko*.)

Robert Heinlein (Sun, Neptune. Sci-fi writer—*Stranger in a Strange Land*.)

Amy Tan (Uranus. Novelist—*The Hundred Secret Senses*.)

Voltaire (Chiron. Enlightenment philosopher, essayist, deist.)

Immanuel Velikovsky (Mercury, Jupiter. Psychoanalyst; wrote *Worlds in Collision*.)

Marc Edmund Jones (Chiron. Astrologer, facilitated the channeling of the Sabian symbols.)

Aleksandr Solzhenitsyn (Jupiter. Novelist, critic of Stalinist oppression—*The Gulag Archipelago*.)

Werner Herzog (Jupiter. Filmmaker—*Cave of Forgotten Dreams*.)

Katharine Ross (Chiron. Actress—*The Stepford Wives, Donnie Darko*.)

Amy Adams (Saturn. Actress—*Arrival*.)

Robert Duvall (Jupiter. Actor; scriptwriter and star of *The Apostle*.)

Raymond Chandler (Mercury. Detective stories—*The Big Sleep*.)

Cancer, 3rd Decan

IMAGE: *A member of a shipwrecked community of Englishmen marries a native girl in a nontraditional ceremony. Behind them, the long neck of a brontosaurus rises over the forest.*

This decan is concerned with intimate relationships, and especially marriage. The man and woman in the decan image come from radically different cultures. They have different assumptions about what makes a good marriage, and what can be expected of a good husband and a good wife. Both may fantasize about walking into a "dream wedding" and sharing a perfect life together. The woman may picture an idyllic home next to a rippling stream, with her children playing under the willow trees. She has no doubt that these romantic dreams can be realized, at least in some form. She's a loving and lovable person, so why shouldn't she be able to put together a supportive, harmonious household?

If a relationship is based on love and understanding, people will find some way to work through any problems that arise. At the same time, they must accept the fact that on certain issues, they will never come to an agreement. In such cases, it is better to "agree to disagree" instead of muddying the waters in pointless arguments. In a good marriage, people find areas of life where their separate worlds can join in a single reality. But they also respect their partner's individuality and accept the fact that complete unity is neither possible nor desirable. People need to have some space of their own.

Relationships come in all colors, and almost any type of relationship can work if the two parties can come to an agreement. There may be a different valuation of sexual intimacy or emotional intimacy. There may be a different valuation of family life. Relationships require the bridging of many opposites. There are the differences between male and female psychology—differences that are hardwired into people's genes. There are also differences of class, race, and nationality. These differences must be ironed out through honest discussion. People of this decan must be sensitive to their significant other's emotional and cultural expectations, and, more importantly, they must be willing to compromise. A good marriage comes about only when two people can join their separate worlds into a single reality that they can both comfortably inhabit. This melting of boundaries is facilitated by the planet Neptune, which has a strong influence in this decan.

Especially important to Cancer 3 individuals is the pledge of sexual fidelity—a pledge that figures strongly in most societies' ideas about marriage. This is a declaration of loyalty not only to the spouse, but to his or her family and friends. Issues of loyalty are very important here. Cancer 3 individuals often have divided loyalties, even as the Englishman of the decan image feels loyalty to his English friends, but also to his new wife. People of this decan may have to placate others who suspect them of treachery. They must convince them of the purity of their motives.[44] Should they fail, important people in the other "tribe" could close ranks to defend the boundaries of their group.

Social inclusion versus social exclusion is a major issue here. Every group has its own ethos, its own myths, and its own rules. These rules define who is included in the group and who is excluded from the group. In the decan image, the two "tribes" are actively negotiating these matters. They are trying to reorder society along lines that will be satisfactory to both groups. In this process, they must determine which rules *must* be obeyed if the groups are to get along, and which rules can be ignored. They needn't agree on every point, but they do have to agree on the basics.

Cancer 3 individuals realize that most important decisions involve *groups* of people. To effect real change, one must therefore change the consensus of opinion. Cancer 3 individuals are very persuasive. They are skilled in argument and have a lot of charm. In their campaigns to influence people's thinking, they can be forceful and direct, or subtle and manipulative. In either case, they are remarkably tenacious in promoting their emotional, sexual, or political agendas. Generally, they are fairly confident they can win people over, and given their magnetism and personal warmth, they often can. In fact, their confidence that their views *will* be accepted is one of the main reasons that they *are* accepted.

One of the more important obstacles to the formation of a harmonious partnership is the presence both of civilized and savage impulses within each of the partners. The brontosaurus of the decan symbol refers to savage impulses that have entered unbidden onto the scene. These impulses have to be both controlled and integrated if the relationship is to work. In the decan image, the "shipwreck on the tropical isle" represents the individual's relationship to nature in the raw, and especially his or her relationship to sex. The Englishman represents civilization and intellectual attainment, but also an estrangement from nature and from primal emotions. The island girl represents a healthy, balanced physical identity, and an easy familiarity with the natural world. The marriage shows an attempt to integrate or "marry" these two personality components—the primitive and the civilized.

The brontosaurus of the decan symbol symbolizes our primitive animal instincts—particularly our survival instincts. The dinosaur harkens back to symbols assigned to this decan in ancient Egypt and ancient Greece. The Greeks regularly placed the evil water serpent, Hydra, in this area of the zodiac, while the ancient Egyptians often associated this decan with "the two turtles," which, like the brontosaurus, are long-necked reptiles.[45] The turtle is a very ancient animal, going back 157 million years. It is one of nature's true *survivors*, whose canny wisdom about the animal world has helped it persist through the ages. The long neck of the turtle suggests the human brain stem, which controls many of our more primitive physical functions, including respiration, heartbeat, eating, and the cycle of wakefulness and sleep. In other words, the brain stem controls the "sleeping" or unconscious part of our behavior. It stands in contrast to the wakeful, conscious, *human* side of our behavior. Every person contains within his or her personality both evolved human characteristics and base animal instincts. Human love, for example, contains an element of primitive sexual desire, and with it an instinct to reproduce the species. Such instincts serve the race, but only if they are kept in check by the institutions of higher civilization, and especially the institution of marriage. Human society emerged from a primitive, quasi-bestial level, but even in the most advanced civilizations, destructive passions lie just below the surface. There is an ever-present danger of reversion to savagery, as is evident from the fact that some plane crashes and shipwrecks have ended in cannibalism.

Intellectually oriented people of this decan are often students of human behavior and culture. Thus, among the examples one finds many important anthropologists, sociologists, and political analysts. At best, these people help unite the different tribes of humanity, for they explain not only the differences between human cultures, but their underlying similarities. Cancer 3 individuals are always trying to figure out how other people think, and what rules they follow within their group. This knowledge is very useful, since it helps them successfully maneuver within various groups.

This decan is a particularly watery one, even for Cancer, due to the strong influence of the watery planet Neptune. Neptune is like the sea of love that supports all life and dissolves barriers between separate groups, and even between life forms. The jungle of the decan image symbolizes the complex web of life, at its most primitive level. Some relationships within nature are mutually beneficial; some are destructive. Love may underlie all existence, but nature is also a tangled jungle of desire and mutual use. The natural order is characterized by food chains of animals eating each other to survive. Everyone knows that people can be selfish and competitive—that they may try to dominate, manipulate, or use each other. Nature has its placid, Edenic side, but like the brontosaurus of the decan image, ugly passions may rear their head at any time. The maintenance of civilization therefore depends upon social pressures that serve to maintain healthy emotional relationships, not only between individuals but between the national and racial divisions of the larger human tribe.

EXAMPLES

Jean Auel (Pluto. Novelist—*Clan of the Cave Bear*.)
Mary McCarthy (Neptune. Feminist author—*The Group, The Company She Keeps, Cannibals and Missionaries*.)
Joseph Conrad (Saturn. Novelist—*Heart of Darkness*.)
Cecil Rhodes (Venus. Imperialist, established Rhodesia.)
Frantz Fanon (Sun. Black psychiatrist; wrote on the inevitability of violence in struggles of decolonization.)
William Shatner and Leonard Nimoy (Mars. Actors—*Star Trek*, with its voyages to primitive "tribes" on other planets, and its message of racial harmony.)
Armistead Maupin (Mars. Wrote *Tales of the City*, about the sexually diverse San Francisco scene.)
Norman Lear (Mercury. Television writer, producer—*All in the Family, The Jeffersons*.)
Tama Janowitz (Uranus. Novelist—*Slaves of New York*—with its relationships based on mutual use.)
Paul Gauguin (Jupiter. French painter of Polynesian natives.)

Ned Beatty (Pluto. Actor—*Deliverance.*)

Karl May (Chiron. German novelist focused on American Indians.)

Katharine Hepburn (North Node. Romantic actress—*The African Queen.*)

Rita Mae Brown (North Node. Feminist writer—*Rubyfruit Jungle.*)

Alfred Adler (North Node. Psychologist emphasizing power dynamics, community life, and democratic family dynamics.)

Francis Ford Coppola (Pluto. Filmmaker—*Peggy Sue Got Married.*)

William Shakespeare (Saturn. Playwright—*Romeo and Juliet.*)

Joan Blondell (Neptune. Heartthrob actress—*Gold Diggers of '33*—with its marriage of opposites—Boston plutocrat and Brooklyn chorus girl.)

Danny Aiello (Mercury, Pluto. Actor—*Do the Right Thing.*)

Jean Marsh (Mercury, Pluto. Actress—*Upstairs, Downstairs.*)

S. I. Hayakawa (Sun, Mars. Academic and conservative politician; tried to establish English as the national language.)

Edward O'Neill (Mars. Actor—*Married with Children*—with its cynical ideas about family relationships.)

Émile Durkheim (Saturn. Sociology as a scientific study of institutions.)

Franz Boas (Saturn. Established modern scientific anthropology.)

Alfred Kroeber (Venus. Cultural anthropologist; studied Ishi, the last of the Yahi Indians.)

Baron George Cuvier (Saturn. First paleontologist—reconstructed animals from bones.)

Ruth Benedict (Venus, Saturn. Relativist anthropologist who wrote *The Chrysanthemum and the Sword*, about Japan.)

Thorstein Veblen (Mars, Saturn. Sociologist—*Theory of the Leisure Class.*)

C. Wright Mills (Venus, Saturn. Sociologist who wrote *The Power Elite.*)

Studs Terkel (Mars, Neptune. Wrote *Hard Times: An Oral History of the Great Depression*, *The Great Divide: Second Thoughts on the American Dream.*)

Angela Merkel (Sun, Uranus. Chancellor of Germany, crucial in managing Europe's financial crisis, behind many international pacts.)

Sonia Sotomayor (Uranus. Hispanic Supreme Court justice.)

Vita Sackville-West (Moon. Poet, gardener, who lived in a ménage à trois with a lesbian lover and her gay husband.)

Leo, 1st Decan

IMAGE: *A circus parade, led by a beaming child driving a horse-drawn chariot. Behind him come elephants, lions, and giraffes, and a swaying brass band of saxophones, tubas, and trombones.*

The sign of Leo is associated with confident self-expression, and this is certainly borne out by this decan. Leo 1 individuals are fun-loving people who experience life as an entertaining spectacle. Their main challenge is to muster up the courage to join the parade of life and go after what they want. Short of this, they could end up as mere spectators, watching from the sidelines as life's fun, drama, and adventure pass them by.

People of this decan tend to hop from one energizing event to another. They go to concerts, lectures, restaurants, sporting events, and the theater. Within their own social set, they often function as leaders—suggesting entertaining things to do, and encouraging their friends to join in. They are constantly prodding others to get involved in life—to find something fun to do, or, short of that, to bring some energy and fun to whatever they're already doing. Always on the prowl for entertaining activities, Leo 1 individuals get exasperated when nothing seems to be happening. They want to participate wholeheartedly in life and hate it when they feel alienated, stranded, or left out.

The main challenge for Leo 1 individuals is to summon the courage to participate fully in life. At a school dance, one always finds wallflowers who sit by the side and watch. But there are also those who pluck up the courage to get out there and dance, even when they have to start dancing by themselves. Because Leo 1 individuals enjoy expressing themselves, they make a concerted effort to participate. They want to live passionately, courageously. Thus, among the examples, we find many devotees of "the high life," including George Bernard Shaw, Zelda Fitzgerald, Mick Jagger, Cameron Crowe, Sally Field, Spike Lee, David Bowie, Anna Magnani, Shelley Winters, Jim Carroll, Sandra Bullock, and Bette Midler. The Beatles all have planets in this decan. They were exemplars of the sixties' lifestyle—fun, courageous, and unconcerned with convention. As young men, their lives were freewheeling, adventurous, even madcap. They were willing to take chances, to risk failure, and to strive for success. It takes a lot of courage to set one's sights on becoming a rock musician. Pursuing *any* of one's grander dreams takes a lot of courage.

Even as children, Leo 1 individuals know that they are special. This confidence is rooted in the intuitive knowledge that they are expressions of the light force and are smiled upon by God. As youngsters, these people are playful and uninhibited. They resist any attempt by their parents or teachers to control or repress them. When it comes to getting their own way, they have a lot of fight in them. They are audacious, impudent, and even a little *bratty*. Their basic attitude toward authority is "Who's going to stop me?"

Leo 1 individuals can be very ambitious. They want to rise in their field—like the morning sun as it rises in the sky. They want to develop their talents to such a height that they become visible to everyone. Picking up new skills is easy for these people, for they approach the problem with the enthusiasm of a child. And like children, they don't mind starting as rank beginners. They don't even mind being *bad* at what they are doing. One of the best things about the Leo's self-absorption is that they are good at turning off their internal critic. They are too intent on their own "act" to care whether people regard them as amateurs or also-rans. As far as they're concerned, they're *great*.

Leo 1 individuals are very self-aware. They know their own strengths and their own weaknesses and try to develop their strengths and shore up their weaknesses. Though there is a great deal of innate strength here, these people often suffer some handicap—small size, odd looks, or being from a minority race or foreign nationality. Since these traits are part of who they are, they need to own them emotionally and turn them into an integral part of a confident social persona. One of the degree symbols in this decan has a funny-looking waiter standing under a moose head. People with this degree in their charts include Barbra Streisand, John Turturro, and Frank Zappa. These are people who have turned their physical oddities into assets. Mick Jagger, who has the Sun in this decan, made his outsized lips a key element of his act. Instead of being shamed by comments about his lips, he turned them into an element of his swaggering stage persona. Part of the Leo's charm is that they are natural even when they are angling for people's approval. They can't help but be themselves, and though that self may be a bit awkward, it is endearing in its childlike innocence and bravery.

This decan is very visually oriented. This is clear from the decan image, which has a colorful parade featuring all kinds of strange profiles. There are clowns on stilts, people playing saxophones and trombones, and curiously shaped animals such as giraffes, rhinoceroses, and hippopotami. Leo 1 individuals can cut quite a figure. They are very aware of how they look, and how to best present themselves. Like teenagers going to the big dance, they put on their best act. They express their personal style in the way they dress, move, talk, and act. It is especially important that they establish a good relationship with their body. They need to have enough confidence to participate in dancing, sex, and sports. This doesn't mean they have to look perfect. Frank Zappa didn't look perfect. What's important is that they celebrate what their appearance says about who they are.

As extroverts, or at least would-be extroverts, Leo 1 individuals can get a bit outrageous. The artists of this decan are the show-offs of the art world. They make strong visual statements that are impossible to ignore, as we see from Andy Warhol, Christo, Le Corbusier, Frida Kahlo, Marcel Duchamp, Robert Mapplethorpe, and Antoni Gaudí. This outrageousness is also evident in the intellectual and literary fields, as we see from the following: Camille Paglia, Gore Vidal, George Bernard Shaw, Lina Wertmüller, William Blake, Oliver Stone, and Bob Dylan. These people have forceful, well-defined ideas, which they champion in the ongoing culture wars. Their candor sometimes frightens the faint of heart, but this doesn't particularly bother them. They are not going to repress the innate forcefulness of their personality just because they might intimidate somebody. The Sabian symbol for the first degree of Leo shows a lion roaring. People with an emphasis here will not be silenced, even if their angry "roaring" makes some people uncomfortable. These people often have fiery tempers that on occasion may really erupt. At such times, they may yell at people and push them around. Fortunately, most of the time they take a gentler approach, for they recognize that confrontations are rarely profitable.

If one looks at the examples above, one finds many people with an extremely liberated attitude toward sex. Leo is one of the most animal of all the signs. Leos have a strong physical presence and can be dominating and even intimidating. Since these people are at one with their desires, they know what they want and go out and get it. They also realize that the brave way—the *direct* way—is often the most effective way to get what one wants. Positively, people of this decan channel their abundant sexual energy into worthwhile goals, and like the sun, spread light, love, and fun to everyone around them. Negatively, their crude, animal nature is never brought under control and occasionally bursts forth in spasms of anger or lust. In the decan image we see a beautiful child reining the horses that are pulling his chariot. This symbolizes the noble, solar part of one's being asserting control over animal desires. In the absence of such control, conflicting desires would pull one in different directions and prevent one from getting anywhere, or accomplishing anything. Leo 1 individuals have to pursue their goals *wholeheartedly*, because if they are unable to discipline their conflicting desires, they will unconsciously sabotage their own efforts.

The child in the chariot is the shining archetype of the divine child. Not surprisingly, people of this decan have a great love for children. They appreciate their energy, playfulness, and creativity and are aware, at least subconsciously, that children are closely connected to God. Leo 1 individuals generally make good parents, for they enjoy spending time with their children and making them happy.

The ancient Egyptians sometimes placed Anhur in this decan. Anhur was a war god, generally represented as a bearded huntsman driving a horse-drawn chariot. He holds a bow and arrow or, on occasion, a lance. Sometimes, he is represented with the head of a lion. While I don't generally think that the decans are accurately represented by gods, the three Leo decans have clear associations with Apollo, Hercules, and Dionysus. Thus, in the first decan, the child in the chariot is related to the sun god, Apollo, as he crosses the heavens in his chariot.

EXAMPLES

Zelda Fitzgerald (Sun. Wife of F. Scott Fitzgerald, flapper, writer.)
George Bernard Shaw (Sun, Venus. Outrageous playwright—*Man and Superman*.)
Countess Dorothy diFrasso (Saturn, North Node. Roaring Twenties socialite and heiress, famous for her Hollywood parties.)
Ed Sanders (Pluto. Leader of the Fugs; poet and writer—*Tales of Beatnik Glory*.)
Goldie Hawn (Mars. Comic actress—*Shampoo*, *The Banger Sisters*.)

Nia Vardalos (North Node. Writer, director, actress—*My Big Fat Greek Wedding*.)

Norman Lear (Sun. Television writer, producer—*Maude, All in the Family, Mary Hartman*.)

William Powell (Sun. Debonair comic actor—*The Thin Man*.)

Jim Carroll (Sun. Writer, rock musician, former heroin addict—*The Basketball Diaries*.)

Jaime Pressly (Sun. Comic actress—*My Name Is Earl*.)

Armistead Maupin (Pluto, North Node. Gay writer—*Tales of the City*.)

Doug Tracht (Sun. DJ and radio comic—"The Greaseman.")

Colin Higgins (Sun, Chiron, Pluto. Film director—*Harold and Maude, 9 to 5*.)

Cameron Crowe (Mercury, Uranus. Writer, director—*Fast Times at Ridgemont High, Almost Famous*.)

Nat Hiken (Venus. Writer and director of *The Phil Silvers Show, Car 54 Where Are You?*)

Mick Jagger (Sun, Jupiter, Pluto. Lead singer of the Rolling Stones, libertine.)

Ringo Starr (Mercury, Moon, Mars, Pluto. Consummate drummer—the Beatles.)

Charles Bukowski (Mercury. Seedy writer—*Barfly*.)

Bella Abzug (Sun, Mercury, Venus. Flamboyant leftist politico.)

Antoni Gaudí (Venus. Architect of whimsical, imaginative buildings.)

Bette Midler (Mars. Singer, actress and comedienne—*Ruthless People*.)

Patti Smith (Saturn. Protopunk singer and poet.)

Susan Sarandon (Saturn. Actress and activist—*The Rocky Horror Picture Show, The Banger Sisters*.)

Geena Davis (Uranus. Actress—*Earth Girls Are Easy, Beetlejuice*.)

Sally Field (Saturn. Actress—*Norma Rae, Soap Dish*.)

René Cassin (Saturn. President of UN Human Rights Commission.)

Robyn Astaire (Pluto. Female jockey.)

Adam Sandler (Mars. Comic actor and director—*The Waterboy, The Wedding Singer*.)

Amelia Earhart (Sun. Pioneering aviator.)

Frank Buck (Mars. Hunter, writer, actor—*Bring 'Em Back Alive*.)

National Geographic Society established (Saturn, North Node. January 27, 1888.)

Bill Gates (Uranus. Microsoft pioneer, socially conscious billionaire.)

Duke Ellington (Mars. Band leader, composer—"Take the A Train.")

Robert Louis Stevenson (North Node. Adventure writer—*Treasure Island*.)

Jerry Garcia (Sun, Mercury, Pluto. Leader of the Grateful Dead.)

Pamela Anderson (Jupiter. *Baywatch* babe, animal rights activist.)

Simon Dee (Sun. Sixties' DJ on the English pirate-radio ship, Caroline.)

Leo, 2nd Decan

IMAGE: *Hercules, dressed in a lion skin and surrounded by a circle of zodiacal animals, is dancing with upraised arms. Behind him, a dragon winds up the trunk of the Tree of Life, whose golden apples arc across the top of the tree.*

People with an emphasis here are forceful, self-confident, and strong in both body and spirit. They enjoy displaying their talents and, attractive or not, like to strut their stuff. Leo 2 individuals have a good sense of humor but actually take themselves very seriously. They have great spiritual dignity, for inwardly they feel that they are tuned in to the divine—that they contain a spark of divinity, even as Hercules had one parent who was a god.

In Greek and Roman mythology, Hercules was famous for having completed twelve astrological labors. By succeeding in these twelve tasks, Hercules mastered each of the zodiacal animals and the powers they represent. Hercules is highly solar, for the sun, in astrology, is the center of the personality and as such must integrate the energies of the whole zodiac and all the planets. It accomplishes this task through the imposition of the central spiritual will upon every other aspect of the personality.

With the "king of the jungle" as their totem animal, Leo 2 individuals try to face every life situation both honestly and courageously. These people often have a lot of *physical* courage. They stand up to the threats of bad people and bad institutions. They fight for what is right. Leo's "kingship," however, is also spiritual—a willingness to fight for the ascendancy of the divine Order. This aspect of Leo finds a fitting symbol in Aslan, the heroic lion of the Narnia books. As solar individuals, people of this decan have a rather heroic self-image. Conceiving of themselves in mythic terms, they are fully committed to their fantasy about who they are, and live out this romantic identity in everyday life. This audacity of self-expression is in fact one of the most obvious manifestations of their bravery.

The strong personal myths that characterize this decan are well illustrated by the following examples: Louis Armstrong, Madonna, David Byrne, Carl Jung, Oscar Wilde, Yul Brynner, Stephen King, Divine, Danny DeVito, Judy Garland, Jacques Cousteau, Lucille Ball, Arnold Schwarzenegger, and Elvira. Many of these people are actors, but they all live within a world of their own making. They create some delightful fantasy and then invite the public to share in the experience.

Leo 2 individuals have great strength of heart. Many talented singers have planets here, and all of them sing from the heart. Examples include Carole King, Johnny Cash, Ian Anderson, Cher, David Byrne, Bruce Springsteen, Patti Smith, Linda Ronstadt, Diana Ross, Anne Wilson, Billy Joel, Jerry Garcia, Cass Elliot, Bette Midler, Barbra Streisand, and Robin, Maurice, and Barry Gibb. These performers are easy to relate to, because they're often singing about our common struggles to find love and happiness.

Leo 2 individuals exhibit an admirable "everyman" or "everywoman" quality. On an inner level, they know that we are all one—that we are all children of God. They recognize the universal nature of most human experience and find it easy to connect with all kinds of different people. As solar types, these people have a fairly good relationship with all the planetary energies; once they have established a good internal relationship with the lunar or Martian aspects of their own personality, they will find it fairly easy to relate to people who are predominantly lunar or Martian. They will not be afraid of these people, because they have already mastered these principles within themselves.

Like Hercules, Leo 2 individuals often conceive of life as a series of tests. They face life challenges that have strong archetypal, zodiacal, or planetary overtones. They may face a Mercurial challenge (an exam, for instance) followed by a Jupiterian challenge (running for office, perhaps). While some of these tests can be truly daunting, these people have nowhere to go but forward. If they prevail in these tests, they end up mastering planetary powers within themselves and are then able to use and express these energies in everyday life. The planets become faithful vassals of the central solar will, even as a knight of old would place himself in service to a king. Throughout their lives, Leo 2 individuals develop an ever-wider range of "planetary" talents and skills. Moreover, they learn to move fluidly between one planetary modality and another, even as an accomplished dancer moves easily from one style of dancing to another.

Should Leo 2 individuals fail one of these planetary tests, they can either try again or move on. Unfortunately, if they lose a number of battles, they could end up losing their confidence and ceasing to move at all. Leo 2 individuals have a lot of innate courage, but considering how high the stakes are, they have no alternative but to face up to life's challenges. They should remember that even a partial victory counts for something and can serve as a first step toward a more decisive victory.

Probably the most difficult of this decan's "Herculean" labors is the integration of the spirit and the body. Hercules is often depicted wearing a lion skin. The lion is a symbol of courage, but it is also a symbol of lust. Hercules's lion skin therefore symbolizes his mastery over his own animal nature, and especially his sexual desires. *Self-mastery* is in fact a keynote of this decan. Leo 2 individuals have a great deal of raw sexual energy—an animal vitality that if uncontrolled could take the form of angry outbursts or bingeing on sex or drugs. Since animal passion can be dangerous, these people must learn to direct it into positive channels. This involves a struggle between their higher spiritual nature and their base desires, which, in the decan image, are symbolized by the dragon. The dragon, as it winds up the Tree of Life, represents the kundalini energy winding up the spine and sublimating sexual energies into higher spheres of consciousness—especially the heart and crown chakras. Psychologically speaking, an important part of this process is the development of romantic idealism out of bestial sexual desire. It involves the cultivation of the finer emotions of the heart, and the ability to express these finer emotions, both in public and in intimate relationships.

Leo 2 individuals often sublimate their abundant life energies in some form of creative self-expression. This could be dance, sports, comedy, visual art, music, or acting. It is important for their development, in fact, that they complete at least one ambitious creative project. Since such a project involves a wide range of problems, successfully completing it requires that they prevail over each of them. In the process, they prove to themselves the all-important virtue of *perseverance*. Writing a book or recording an album involves a great number of challenges, and many hours of lonely, solitary work. Throughout this process, these people must have faith that they will eventually finish. Even as the sun disappears under the earth at nightfall, these people have periods when they feel hemmed in by darkness. During such times, they must hold firm to their inner light. They must have faith that their creative efforts are destined to see the light of day, even as the sun is destined to defeat the "dragon" of darkness every morning. They must remember that they are connected to the light force, which is the strongest force in the universe.

Many people of this decan become teachers, especially spiritual teachers. Much of what they have to teach comes from the example of their own lives and from what they have learned in their various trials. The ultimate purpose of their teachings is to *align* their pupils with the greater reality. The sign of Leo is concerned with spiritual alignment. This can be seen in a number of Sabian symbols in the sign: the Oak Tree degree, the Zuni Sun Dance degree, the Pyramid degree, the Sunrise degree. All these symbols deal with orientation, especially the fixed relationship of the sun to the earth—the basic north-south-east-west coordinates that define every map. Leos look upon the spiritual *fixity* of their nature as a major virtue. To their minds, all the major spiritual truths are eternal. They are summed up in the individual's obedience to God—their willingness to align themselves with the light force. These people see no need to go anywhere outside the Self. They need only be themselves, develop themselves, prevail as themselves. Spiritually aligned existence needs no justification outside of itself. Like metallic gold, it is resistant to corrosion and adulteration. Like the Tree of Life, it is fixed, immovable, eternal.

The ancient Egyptians often associated this decan with the god Shu, who holds up the heavens with his arms. This physical posture is reminiscent of Atlas, who was condemned to hold up the heavens. In fact, the ancient Greeks identified the Egyptian Shu with their own Atlas. Shu was a god of the atmosphere. He was considered a peacemaker because he separated the heavens and the earth, which would otherwise have fought one another.

EXAMPLES

Arnold Schwarzenegger (Pluto. Weightlifter,
    actor, politician—*Conan the Barbarian.*)

Sigourney Weaver (Mars, Pluto. Actress—*Alien, Ghostbusters*.)

Ron Kovic (Venus, Pluto. Paralyzed antiwar activist.)

Sophia Loren (Mars. Actress—*Two Women*.)

Sylvester Stallone (Mercury, Pluto. Actor—*Rocky, Rambo*.)

Harrison Ford (Mars. Actor—*Star Wars*.)

Edward James Olmos (Pluto. Actor—*Stand and Deliver*, activist for the Hispanic community.)

Tom Laughlin (Sun. Filmmaker—*Billy Jack*.)

Robin Williams (Pluto. Comedian, actor—*Jumanji*.)

Edgar Rice Burroughs (Uranus. Wrote the *Tarzan* books.)

Richard Dreyfuss (Mars, Pluto. Actor—*Jaws*.)

Muhammad Ali (Ascendant, Chiron. Champion boxer.)

Amelia Earhart (Mercury. First woman to fly solo over the Atlantic.)

Chay Blyth (Moon. Yachtsman—sailed around the world.)

Neil Armstrong (Sun. Astronaut—first man on the moon.)

Charlton Heston (Neptune. Actor—*Ben Hur*, *Planet of the Apes*, NRA leader.)

Jeff Jawer (Mars. Astrologer, pioneer of Astrodrama.)

Carl Jung (Uranus. Psychiatrist who emphasizes the importance of archetypes.)

Steven Forrest (Pluto. Astrologer—*The Inner Sky*.)

Alfred Lord Tennyson (Sun. Poet—*Idylls of the King*.)

Judy Garland (Neptune. Singer, actress, in the archetypal musical—*The Wizard of Oz*.)

Barry, Robin, and Maurice Gibb (Pluto. The Bee Gees—"How Deep Is Your Love?")

Cher (Mars. Singer, actress.)

Brigitte Bardot (Mars. Sex-kitten actress, animal rights advocate.)

Albert Schweitzer (Uranus. Theologian, physician; ran a hospital in Africa.)

Roberto Rossellini (North Node. Highly political neorealist Italian filmmaker—*Rome, Open City*.)

Lech Walesa (Jupiter, North Node. Polish labor leader, founder of Solidarity.)

Alexander Dubcek (Neptune. Liberal leader of Czechoslovakia under Communist rule.)

Óscar Arias Sánchez (Chiron. President of Costa Rica, author of the Central American Peace Plan.)

René Cassin (North Node. President of the UN Human Rights Commission.)

T. E. Lawrence (Mercury, Saturn. "Lawrence of Arabia," archeologist, writer, and military officer participating in the Arab Revolt.)

Jim Carroll (Mercury, Pluto. Onetime heroin addict, author of *The Basketball Diaries*, rock musician.)

Ann Landers (Saturn. Advice columnist with lots of chutzpah.)

Sally Field (Pluto. Actress—*Norma Rae*.)

Leo, 3rd Decan

IMAGE: *At an awards ceremony, a rock musician is presented with a circular gold medal bearing a caricature of his own face. His band joins him, and they perform a wild rendition of their signature hit.*

As children of the sun, Leo 3 individuals want to shine—to be recognized and admired for their unique contributions. They also want to be admired for who they *are*. These people are very self-aware. They have a clear internal vision of who they are and an almost irresistible impulse to express themselves. They want to demonstrate their personal archetype in their words, their actions, their home, their clothes, their spiritual beliefs, and their political activities. The question is whether they have the chutzpah to carry it off.

The rock musicians of the decan image may be wild onstage, but offstage they are sober, mature, and disciplined. They practice their songs, take care of business matters, and try to get along emotionally and creatively with their band members. People of this decan try to find a good balance between work and play—and they take both pretty seriously. When they're playing, they're *really* playing, and when they're working, they're really working. Leo 3 individuals know how to concentrate. They can bring their focus and energy to a point and keep it there for extended periods of time. This allows them to master almost anything they set their mind to—music, dance, politics, sports, or academic subjects. They are particularly gifted in the arts, for they are blessed with a strong visual imagination.

Many of the more famous people of this decan have gained the spotlight through the disciplined development of some artistic talent. They have cultivated some innate talent to the nth degree. Often this talent is something unique to them; it is intrinsic to their spiritual identity. Many famous actors, rock musicians, and dancers have planets here. For example: Edith Piaf, Harpo Marx, Mae West, Walt Whitman, William Blake,

Janis Joplin, Jimi Hendrix, Edward Gorey, Isadora Duncan, Thelonious Monk, Robin Williams, Jim Morrison, Madonna, and Mick Jagger. All these people are masters of their craft—whether that craft is rock music, poetry, comedy, or dance. Even so, they are known less for their skill than for their unmistakable personal *style*. Conceiving of themselves as actors on the stage of life, they develop a stylish dramatic role and live it out in a full-bodied way, radiating their individuality in so concentrated a beam that they are practically cartoons of themselves. Note that the *faces* of the people mentioned above are extremely recognizable. This follows from the fact that the face, as the most expressive part of the body, is ruled by the sun.

The Sun, Mars, and Jupiter all are strong in this decan. These are fiery astrological bodies in the fire sign of Leo. Fire is the element most closely associated with the imagination, and Leo 3 individuals are, in fact, extremely imaginative. Among the examples, one finds quite a number of people who have created popular works of fantasy, including J. K. Rowling, Gene Roddenberry (*Star Trek*), Alfred Hitchcock, Sylvester Stallone, Tom Hanks, Jim Carrey, Matt Groening (*The Simpsons*), Rick Moranis, Bruce Willis, Tobey Maguire, Penny Marshall, Werner Herzog, Martin Scorsese, and Sandra Bullock. These people are very aware of the myths and dreams that lie at the heart of their culture. They know what people *want* to be true, and the stories that will satisfy these desires. In this way, they become active participants in the imaginative life of the public. Since their fantasies can become quite culturally influential, it's important that they be healthy and life-affirming. They need to take responsibility for their creative choices.

People of this decan are energetic and ambitious and therefore tend to rise in life. Yet, this is also a decan fraught with temptations: the temptations of fame, power, money, sex, and high living. The worst obstacle, however, is egotism. At least subconsciously, people of this decan think that their efforts are favored by heaven—that their plans in life have been approved by God. This is basically wishful thinking. The central test for these people is whether they are willing to do the gritty, unpleasant work necessary to succeed. Many people with an emphasis here are never more than "legends in their own minds." They wait for success to fall upon them like a rainbow from the sky, all the while harboring a sulky resentment against those who have achieved success—especially those talentless people who have received exalted positions that by rights should be theirs! Brilliance of self-expression comes only through practice, and people of this decan must break through their creative inhibitions to develop their talents, even if their first efforts come off badly. They must learn to stand up to criticism, both external and internal, and cultivate their innate creativity.

Leo 3 individuals have a lot of animal vitality—a wild, untamed quality, reminiscent of a lion on the prowl. This gives them a great deal of sexual charisma, and with it a lot of opportunities for sex. Leo 3 individuals can be gluttons for pleasure and need to develop self-discipline lest this become a problem. That said, it's an inescapable part of the Leonine nature to occasionally "go wild." Some go in for scandalous behavior, flaunting all the rules to see how much they can get away with. Others make their outrageous behavior a kind of political statement, in the hope that they will inspire others to throw off their inhibitions. Leo 3 individuals understand the link between the battle for sexual freedom and the battle for political freedom. People who refuse to repress their sexual impulses are not likely to tolerate political repression. Or, stated the other way around, people who give in to repression on a sexual level are more likely to submit to repression on a political level. Among the examples, one finds many champions of freedom—especially sexual freedom. These include Lenny Bruce, Alan Dershowitz (*The New Sexual McCarthyism*), Robert Bly (men's-movement leader), Geena Davis (*A League of Their Own*), Hugh Hefner, Dr. Ruth, William Masters and Virginia Johnson (Masters and Johnson sex research), and R. D. Laing (*Politics of the Family*).

Due to the strong solar force of this decan, Leo 3 individuals have a clear sense of the way things should be, and are particularly sensitive to social injustice and political misrule. They recognize which ideas are given pride of place within the system, and whether these ideas and policies actually serve the people. Some of the more ambitious members of this decan enter the political arena. They want to have a say in which ideas, myths, and values are given the highest standing within society. They want to make sure that the ideas that have been *enthroned* in the public imagination are the right ideas, and not ideas that have crept in by treachery or by accident. Regrettably, many Leo 3 politicians are too egotistical to make particularly good leaders. They encourage a cult of personality and try to rule like little kings. Examples include Bill Clinton, Barack Obama, and Napoleon—all of whom have the Sun in this decan. Donald Trump, who has Mars and the Ascendant here, is a more extreme example.

This decan demands a serious approach to spiritual issues. Self-development should not be a pastime for these people, but a mission, for they have valuable gifts to present to humanity. Negatively, Leo 3 individuals are dreamers and dilettantes. They fail to commit to their more ambitious goals and never materialize their visions in a form that can be presented to the world. These people certainly have what it takes. But it's important that however much pleasure and fun they seek from life, they balance it with an equal measure of disciplined effort.

EXAMPLES

Terry Gilliam (Moon. Animator with Monty Python; directed *Brazil*.)
Gene Roddenberry (Sun, Mercury. Created *Star Trek*.)
Diana Rigg (Mercury. Actress in *The Avengers* and *Game of Thrones*.)
Mae West (Sun, Chiron. Comic actress, playwright.)
Shirley Temple (Neptune. Child star, singer and dancer.)
Janis Joplin (Chiron, North Node. Hard-living blues-rock diva—"Piece of My Heart.")
Madonna (Sun. Outrageous pop singer, dancer.)
Michael J. Fox (Uranus. Actor—*Back to the Future*.)
Allen Ginsberg (Neptune. Openly gay beatnik poet—"Howl.")
Ed Sanders (Sun. Leader of the Fugs, irrepressible hippie.)
Dr. Ruth Westheimer (Neptune. Outrageously frank sex therapist.)
Joni Mitchell (Jupiter. Singer-songwriter—"Woodstock," "Both Sides Now.")
Dennis Rodman (Uranus. Basketball superstar—*Bad as I Want to Be*.)
Steve Martin (Sun. Comedian, actor—"wild and crazy guy.")
Burt Bacharach (Neptune. Pop songwriter—"Alfie.")
Jim Morrison (Jupiter. Lead singer of the Doors.)
Julia Child (Sun. Droll and uninhibited television chef.)
Alfred Hitchcock (Sun. Iconic film director—*The 39 Steps*, *Frenzy*; Hitchcock always appeared in a cameo role in his movies.)
Miles Davis (Neptune. Innovative jazz trumpeter.)
Bill Clinton (Sun. Oversexed US president.)
Napoleon Bonaparte (Sun. General and conqueror.)
Maria Callas (Neptune. Tempestuous operatic diva.)
RuPaul (Uranus. Successful Black drag queen.)
Jacqueline Susann (Sun. Writer of vulgar potboilers—*Valley of the Dolls*.)
Bhagwan Shree Rajneesh (Jupiter. Spiritual teacher who emphasized sexual liberation.)

Jimmy Page and Robert Plant (Jupiter, Sun for Page; Saturn for Plant. Led Zeppelin.)

Terry Southern (North Node. Screenwriter for *Doctor Strangelove* and *The Magic Christian.*)

Haile Selassie (Mercury. Ethiopian king, worshiped as God by Rastafarians.)

Rudolf Steiner (Jupiter. Mystic, clairvoyant; founded Waldorf Schools.)

Charles Reich (Neptune. Wrote *The Greening of America.*)

Walt Whitman (Moon. Poet—*Leaves of Grass.*)

Claude Debussy (Sun. Classical composer.)

Isadora Duncan (Uranus. Innovative modern dancer.)

Jim Henson (Mars. Puppeteer—the Muppets; directed *The Dark Crystal.*)

Paul Foster Case (Venus, Jupiter. Mystic, expert on the Tarot.)

Tom Hanks (Pluto. Actor—*Big, Sleepless in Seattle.*)

Geena Davis (Jupiter. Actress—*Beetlejuice, Earth Girls Are Easy.*)

Bill Maher (Jupiter, Pluto. Political talk-show host.)

Elizabeth I (North Node. Idolized English queen. Promoter of Renaissance culture, including theater.)

Virgo, 1st Decan

IMAGE: *A junior high school girl with pink hair stands in front of the class and reads a composition criticizing the educational methods of the school. The teacher tries to silence her, but she continues to read, undeterred.*

The zodiacal sign of Virgo is often symbolized by a spike of wheat.[46] Wheat refers to agriculture, but it also refers to the archetypal seed and particularly the *seed self.* Even as children, people with planets here have a strong sense of self. They know that they're special, that they're different, and that they're even a bit weird. Yet, they stick to their guns. They remain true to themselves and expect others to take them as they are. These people have an unusual degree of self-confidence—a confidence based on the inner assurance that they are *at core* good people—that they are smiled upon by God. Though they sometimes appear immune to external criticism, they are actually fairly hard on themselves, especially if they feel they aren't living up to their own standards. They are perfectly aware that they are being evaluated by others but also understand that self-evaluation is more important than external evaluation. After all, who understands them better than they do? Centered within their self-knowledge, these people remain oddly untouched by external criticism and praise. They are neither boastful nor falsely modest. They know their accomplishments and their failures and are proud of their accomplishments and ashamed of their failures.

This decan unites two contrasting states of consciousness—the consciousness of an adult and the consciousness of a child. The teacher, representing adult consciousness, is trying to get the girl to conform to the school's rules and expectations, so that she will be able to succeed at school and, later on, in the workplace. As a respected adult, the teacher passes on the values and morals of respectable society. She reins in the child's wild side and imparts the behavioral and intellectual skills that will allow her to become a useful and accepted member of society. Though the teacher's conscious goal is to educate the child, her conception of education includes a hefty dose of socialization. The child, by contrast, experiences much of her education as regimentation and repression. As an embodiment of the mercurial principle, she is a penetrating observer with the courage to tell it like it is—to explain the current situation as she perceives it. She sees through much of what the teacher is trying to tell her. She is skeptical of rules concerning behavior, dress, and acceptable opinion, for she sees little merit in rules dictated solely by convention. The fact that she has pink hair shows that she is willing to stand out in order to be herself. She is willing to brave the criticism of her parents, her teachers, and even her peers. Her attitude is one of irrepressibility and mischievous wit. Confident of the validity of her own viewpoint, she refuses to emotionally internalize rules that she has neither thought about nor agreed to.

The girl of the decan image is a good writer but has developed this skill on her own. She places more value on extracurricular interests than school-mandated subjects, since she knows that her own interests are innate and therefore valid in a way that school subjects usually aren't. People with planets in this decan may experience a conflict between self-education and formal education throughout their lives. Generally, as they get older, they become more receptive to advice, for they learn to identify authorities whose perspectives are compatible with their own. Moreover, having worked out their own perspective in some detail, they feel less threatened by competing points of view. Virgos have a lot of faith in their own natural growth processes—not just in the realm of physical and sexual maturation, but in the mental realm as well. At the job or in their field of study, they often develop original ways of handling problems and simply ignore the "accepted wisdom." In the development of these methods, they are guided by instinct. Like bees hunting for flowers, they rely upon some mysterious inner compass to tell them how to proceed.

When people of this decan decide to learn something, nothing can stand in their way, for they have enough analytical intelligence and problem-solving ability to get past every obstacle. If they're tackling a complex problem, they divide it up into manageable units, figure out each step, and complete each task in sequence. In the process, they gain a clear, detailed understanding of their subject. Once they've reached this point, they can start teaching this material to others. Virgo 1 individuals generally make excellent teachers, for they are able to explain even complicated subjects in a way that can be understood.

One of the chief challenges for early Virgos is time management. Since Virgo is a mutable sign, Virgos tend to scatter their energies in a welter of different activities. It is therefore important that they learn to prioritize. In order to develop a unique talent, one has to give it enough time, and one can't give it enough time if one's life is so disorganized that one can't even keep up with daily chores. These people mustn't let their "to-do" lists get out of hand, nor can they indulge in perfectionism, especially in the performance of lesser tasks. To successfully develop their unique talents, they must limit the time they spend on other commitments and activities.

Virgo 1 individuals must learn to organize their time, but they must also learn to organize *information*. As Mercury-ruled individuals, these people are always processing large amounts of information. This information comes from the physical senses, from other people, and from books. They reflect upon and analyze this information and then file it away in memory. Should their thinking become sloppy or lazy, their minds will become disorganized, which will lead, in turn, to disorganization and error in everyday life.

In the decan symbol, a small girl is standing up to her teacher. In most societies, women and children occupy subordinate positions in the social hierarchy. Women tend to get ordered around by their husbands, and children tend to get ordered around by pretty much everybody. People of this decan must learn to maintain their dignity, their integrity, and their personal agenda in the face of more powerful people and more powerful institutions. In the workplace, they may face ongoing battles with management over proper work methods or over the morality of company policies. In the home, they must stand up to oppressive familial expectations. The weight of family expectations falls particularly heavily on women. The "virtuous woman," praised in most societies, is expected to perform a wide range of domestic duties, including cooking, cleaning, sewing, gardening, and taking care of the children. Since women of this decan are well aware of these expectations, they may choose to remain single and "virginal" for a long time. However, their strong maternal instincts will often end up prevailing.

In their personal relationships, Virgo 1 individuals don't like to waste time. They avoid putting a lot of energy into relationships that are not headed toward commitment and marriage. These people are serious about romance. In relationships, they are honest and forthright about who they are, what they think, and how they feel. Since people of this decan are connected to their child-self, they look for innocence and purity of feeling in relationships and are not too concerned with conventional criteria about what is fitting, attractive, or socially valued in a mate. In fact, by conventional standards, their choice of partners often seems quite odd.

In the Egyptian decan systems (which are extremely varied), this decan is sometimes symbolized by Isis seated in a temple, holding the child Horus on her lap. The child represents the young sun, fed on the milk of the stars, who, though small and vulnerable, promises to bring some magical new quality into the world. Isis represents the good mother, who protects and nurtures her child's unusual potentials.

EXAMPLES

Lily Tomlin (Venus. Comedienne—*All of Me, 9 to 5*.)
Jerry Mathers (Mars. Child actor—*Leave It to Beaver*.)
Carl "Alfalfa" Switzer (Mars. Child actor—*The Little Rascals*.)
Mervyn LeRoy (Venus. Directed *The Bad Seed, The Wizard of Oz*.)
Charles Dickens (North Node. Novelist—*Oliver Twist*.)
Maria Montessori (Sun. Innovative educator—Montessori schools.)
Juliette Binoche (Uranus. French actress—*Chocolat*.)
Dennis Rodman (Pluto, North Node. Bizarre-looking basketball superstar.)
Alice Cooper (Mars. Shock rocker—*School's Out*.)
Rocky Dennis (Uranus. Child with serious facial deformity—the subject of *Mask*.)
David Sedaris (Pluto. Gay humorist, writer.)
R. Crumb (Sun, Chiron. Taboo-breaking underground cartoonist.)
Ruth Duskin (Ascendant, Neptune. Quiz Kid prodigy.)
Richard Wright (Mars. Black author of the autobiographical book *Black Boy*.)
Camille Paglia (Moon. Impudent deflator of feminist and deconstructionist prattle.)
Stephen Colbert (Uranus, stationary. Political satirist.)
Jon Stewart (Uranus. Political satirist.)
Mike Judge (Uranus. Comic filmmaker—*Idiocracy, Beavis and Butthead*.)
Carol Burnett (Neptune. Subtly subversive comedienne.)
Jimmy Kimmel (Mercury, Jupiter. Television personality—*The Man Show, Jimmy Kimmel Live!*)
Will Rogers (Uranus. Cowboy comedian, homespun philosopher.)

Shirley MacLaine (Moon, Neptune. New Age seeker, actress—*The Apartment, The Children's Hour*.)

Enid Hoffman (Sun. Wrote *Develop Your Psychic Skills*.)

Casey Affleck (Mercury. Actor—*Good Will Hunting*.)

Temple Grandin (Mercury, Venus. Animal science professor, autism advocate.)

Ray Harryhausen (Saturn. Pioneer in stop-motion film animation—*Jason and the Argonauts*.)

Buckminster Fuller (Venus. Architect, inventor, systems theorist.)

Julia Child (Mercury, Venus. Maverick TV chef.)

Antoni Gaudí (Mars. Highly imaginative architect.)

Albert Einstein (Uranus. Maverick physicist, genius.)

Elliott Gould (Sun, Mercury. Actor—*M*A*S*H*.)

Willie Nelson (Mars, Neptune. Folk and country singer.)

Pete Townshend (Moon. Rock star, composer—*Tommy*.)

Colin Wilson (Mars, Neptune. Novelist, occultist—*The Outsider*.)

S. I. Hayakawa (Venus. Conservative Republican congressman, pushed English as *the* national language.)

Chris Columbus (Venus, Pluto. Director who gets great performances from child actors—*Harry Potter and the Sorcerer's Stone*, *Adventures in Babysitting*, *Home Alone*.)

Virgo, 2nd Decan

IMAGE: *At the dinner table, a teenage girl argues with her parents about her boyfriend. She gets up, puts on a sexy dress, and stalks out of the front door. Standing on the portico, she pauses momentarily to collect herself.*

People of this decan are feisty, sexually attractive individuals who have the courage to live life as they see it. They demand to be taken on their own terms and stand up well to social criticism. The girl in the decan image has a lot of family feeling and identifies with many of her parents' values. She may even see herself as an exemplar of her parents' ethnic heritage, religious values, and political beliefs. Yet, she also recognizes that her parents are stuck in another generation's worldview—a worldview that hasn't been updated for years.

The girl of the decan image has been arguing with her parents about dating. In reality, the argument was about sex. The girl has hit puberty. She has become aware of her own sexual feelings, as well as the sexual undercurrents in her everyday interactions. Sex is very much on her mind. Her parents, however, still see her as a sexless child. They want her to conform to rules that are no longer appropriate either to her age or her individuality. The girl argues passionately, for she sees no point in a life of empty conformity. As a highly Venusian individual, with a naturally earthy personality, she takes her romantic and sexual impulses seriously. Eager to enter into an honest, passionate relationship, she may even be open to a messy or unstable relationship, as long as it feels real. Not surprisingly, her parents consider this dangerous. They fear that once their daughter deviates from the rules, she will find herself in a sexual no-man's-land.

The teenager of the decan image sees something desirable in her boyfriend that her parents do not. She may be attracted to his sexy looks, or to the type of person he aspires to be, but she may also be attracted to his sense of humor, his ideas, his interesting friends, or his access to a car. Venus—which is the strongest influence in this decan—does not limit its focus to beauty and sexual desire; it is concerned with *anything* one might value or desire—anything one might want to bring into one's world. The girl has begun to reflect on what she likes and dislikes: in other people, in her parents, and in herself. Unlike the courtesan-like Venus of traditional astrology, she is a strong-minded individual. She knows what she values, what she wants, and what kind of person she wants to be. Since her parents have no real understanding of her world, she has "shut the door" on their criticism, at least internally, for she has no intention of becoming a prisoner of her parents' mental and spiritual ruts. Already, she has begun to step away from the safety of her home and is in the process of putting together a new family of friends and intimates—people who have similar values, who share similar interests, and who treat her seriously.

Virgo 2 individuals begin to differentiate their ideals and beliefs from those of their parents at an early age. They don't worship in the "family chapel" but have their own "altars" and their own objects of veneration. These may include posters of people they admire, recorded music they know by heart, books they've read over and over, and religious images and stories they hold dear. On an inner level, these people have pledged to remain faithful to these ideals. This may not be easy. Other people may not recognize the importance of these ideals, or even their reality. As they mature, Virgo 2 individuals often develop new values, but the ideals that defined them in their youth will still figure strongly in what they expect from themselves.

Virgo 2 individuals want to make it clear who they are and even who they would *like* to be. They display these ideals and values in the way they look, the clothes they wear, the things they say, and the way they behave. As Venusians, they spend a lot of time developing a social persona that showcases their best qualities yet still feels authentic and even fun. This social persona will have a big effect on whom they attract—and whom they repel. Thus, in the decan image, we see a girl pausing atop a pedestal-like portico and deciding upon what image will work best with her new friends. The men of this decan are also very concerned with their social image. They may not be that focused on their clothing and hair but will still develop a persona that showcases whatever makes them cool, attractive, interesting, or authoritative. People of this decan understand that their social persona is something of a construct, and therefore retain some sense of humor about themselves and the image they have created. On occasion, they may even take up a new look, for they understand that changing their appearance will change the way they are perceived, the way they are treated, and what behaviors will be expected and allowed.

While Venus is a strong influence in this decan, the lunar influence is also strong. The moon presides over social groups bound together by strong emotions. The most important of these is the family. The moon connects family members through affection and mutual aid, through conversations and group activities. But the moon is also responsible for establishing the behavioral *rules* of the group—what is expected of a parent or a child—according to their role within the family. These rules determine who is a member in good standing within the group, and who might get expelled for breaking the rules. The parents in the decan image are acting as if their daughter was still a child, over whom they have complete authority. The girl already sees herself as an adult, capable of managing her own affairs. She is beginning to figure out her *own* set of moral and behavioral rules, and she is determined to abide by them. She is perfectly willing to discuss this code of behavior with others. However, she feels no need to get anyone's *permission* to act as she sees fit.

Among the examples, one finds a lot of actors involved in family-centered television dramas. These shows often deal with negotiations between parents and children over rules of behavior. They show how dissension within the family can be healed and a comfortable order restored. While some of these TV shows promote images of the perfect family, with its perfect wife, perfect husband, and perfect children, others make fun of these roles or provide a sociological commentary on bourgeois expectations. All the following actors have planets in this decan: Florence Henderson and Robert Reed (*The Brady Bunch*); Shirley Jones, Danny Bonaduce, and David Cassidy (*The Partridge Family*); Lauren Chapin (*Father Knows Best*); Bill Cosby and Phylicia Rashad (*The Cosby Show*); Mary Tyler Moore; Carol Burnett (*Mama's Family*); Candice Bergen (*Murphy Brown*); and Edward O'Neill (*Married with Children, Modern Family*). Most of the abovementioned television shows were fairly conservative. Yet, whether they promoted loose or rigid family roles, they still helped define what constituted a good family— either through the promotion of social norms or through their rejection. Ironically, many of the actors in these shows were hardly conformists in real life. Some were involved in scandalous behavior—especially scandalous sexual behavior. People of this decan definitely have a wild side. They have a very strong appetite for pleasure and need to develop enough self-discipline to avoid overindulging in food, alcohol, drugs, or sex—at least not that often.

When people of this decan become parents themselves, they favor family rules that are reasonable, relaxed, and comfortable. They listen to their children and try to keep tabs on the realities of their social world. Nonetheless, they often find themselves playing out the same scenes they endured with their own parents. Quite a number of people with an emphasis here choose not to have children, for they are unwilling to give up the freedom and independence they worked so hard to acquire.

One of the main dilemmas facing Virgo 2 individuals is whether they should comply with unspoken social rules. If they lose track of their personal ideals and passively yield to social expectations, they could become plastic conformists who negate their true feelings to play out conventional social roles. A number of books and films created by Virgo 2 individuals deal with soulless conformism. Jack Finney wrote *Invasion of the Body Snatchers*, Fritz Lang directed *Metropolis*, and Lana Wachowski cowrote and directed *The Matrix*. All these movies express a fear of robotic regimentation or, in less dramatic terms, the danger of losing oneself in the habitual, mechanical activities of daily life. Virgo 2 individuals can be very competent in dealing with the demands of work, finance, the home, and even personal relations. But in the midst of these activities, they need to pause and remember their spiritual identity.

Self-employment is probably the best choice for these people, since it allows them to utilize methods they come up with on their own. Even when they are working for other people, Virgo 2 individuals often insist on doing things their own way. Being logical and organized themselves, they may expect their workplace to be similarly well-organized. Some try to rise in the hierarchy, so they can gain enough power to put things to rights. More commonly, they accept their situation and try to gain as much freedom as possible within their sphere of responsibility. This decan is not usually associated with power. Virgo 2 individuals often find themselves in situations where they have to adapt to other people's scenes. In the home they have to compromise with the agendas of other family members, and in the workplace they have to meet their employer's expectations. Fortunately, their bosses usually give them a lot of slack, in deference to their competence and diligence, for despite their independent nature, these people take their responsibilities very seriously.

EXAMPLES

D. H. Lawrence (Sun, Jupiter. Novelist—*Lady Chatterley's Lover*.)

Erica Jong (North Node. Novelist—*Fear of Flying*.)

Philip Roth (Jupiter. Novelist—*Portnoy's Complaint*.)

James Joyce (Uranus. Stream-of-consciousness writer, very open about sex—*Ulysses*.)

Gloria Steinem and Betty Friedan (Neptune and Jupiter, respectively. Feminist spokeswomen.)

Jacqueline Susann (Mercury, stationary. Novelist—*Valley of the Dolls*, *The Love Machine*.)

Dan Savage (Uranus. Sex advice columnist, gay.)

Zach Galifianakis (Venus. Comedian, comic actor—*The Hangover*; interviewer of many famous people.)

Jesse Helms (Mars. Conservative Republican senator from North Carolina; opposed homosexuality, feminism, and access to abortions.)

Kevin Spacey (Venus. Actor—*American Beauty*; sexual scandals.)

Charlie Sheen (Sun, Uranus, Pluto. Actor—*Two and a Half Men*; onetime sex addict.)

Adam Sandler (Sun, Mercury, Uranus, Pluto. Actor, producer in comic films but also in films treating relationship problems—*Spanglish*, *Click*.)

Norman Lear (Venus. Television producer—*All in the Family*, *Mary Hartman*.)

Candice Bergen (Moon. Lead on TV's *Murphy Brown*.)

Bill Cosby (Moon, Neptune. Perfect TV dad, multiple accusations of rape.)

Brassaï (Sun, Venus. Photographer of French brothels.)

Bill Murray (Mercury, Venus. Comic actor—*Broken Flowers*, *Saint Vincent*.)

Mick Jagger (Venus. Lead singer of the Rolling Stones—"I Can't Get No Satisfaction.")

Mary Shelley (Uranus. Wrote *Frankenstein*; early feminist—*A Vindication of the Rights of Woman*.)

Sophia Loren (Venus, Neptune. Sexy actress—*Marriage Italian Style*.)

R. Crumb (Venus. Underground cartoonist who shamelessly exposes his kinky sex fantasies.)

Woody Allen (Neptune. Filmmaker—*Annie Hall*, *Manhattan*.)

Paul Goodman (Sun, Mercury. Leftist activist—*Growing Up Absurd*, *Compulsory Miseducation*.)

Randy Shilts (Venus, Mercury. Gay journalist covering the AIDS epidemic, wrote *Conduct Unbecoming: Gays and Lesbians in the US Military*.)

Paul Bindrim (Saturn. Ran nude psychotherapy groups.)

Lisa Kudrow (Pluto. Comic actress—*Friends*, *Romy and Michele's High School Reunion*.)

Nathanael West (Venus. Novelist—*The Day of the Locust*.)
George Kuchar (Mars. Underground filmmaker—*The Naked and the Nude, The Mammal Palace*.)
Pedro Almodóvar (Saturn. Gay filmmaker—*The Law of Desire*.)
Sally Rand dances nude at Chicago World's Fair (May 30, 1933—Mars in Virgo 2nd Decan.)
Upton Sinclair (Mercury, stationary. Muckraking writer—*The Jungle*—which led to the Pure Food and Drug Act.)
Adrienne Shelly (Uranus, Pluto. Actress, filmmaker, screenwriter—*Waitress, Serious Moonlight*.)
Clarence Kelley (Venus. Second director of the FBI.)
Lauren Bacall (Mercury. Vampy actress in romantic noirs.)

Virgo, 3rd Decan

IMAGE: *In court, a contract is being mediated between management and workers. The judge, sitting behind the scales of justice, jots down the pros and cons of each lawyer's argument.*

In the decan symbol, we see a judge jotting down his thoughts on a case. He represents the moral intellect, as it considers the pros and cons of an argument, and decides how much weight to give to each side. People with a Virgo 3 emphasis are trying to arrive at an accurate reading of their situation by uncovering all the relevant facts and giving them their proper weight. Generally, these people are intelligent and clearheaded. They find it easy to understand the fine points of an argument, and to clearly articulate the ins and outs of their own point of view. Their ultimate goal is to reach a final judgment or verdict. Thus, one often finds these people making authoritative pronouncements on important issues. Having examined all the facts—dispassionately, one hopes—they are sure of their opinions and deliver them to the world as the "final word" on the subject.

The decan symbol, with its legal scene, is reminiscent of an ancient Egyptian image that was often located in this area—that of the ibis-headed Thoth, standing by the giant scales of judgment and recording the weight of a dead man's soul in a ledger.[47] Virgo 3 individuals try to get to the heart of every situation. They try to discover the intentions of other people, so they can judge whether their words and actions are coming from a good place or a bad place. The ibis is a fish-eating bird that pounces on its prey as soon as it exposes itself. The lawyers in the decan image, similarly, are quick to jump on any weakness in their opponent's argument. Virgo 3 individuals do, in fact, make excellent lawyers. Given their superior analytical abilities, they are also well suited to jobs in academia, business administration, and government.

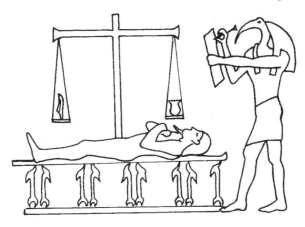

The dominant planet of this decan is Saturn. Saturn rules the inescapable law of karma as well as its earthly equivalent—the criminal justice system. Saturn, with his scythe, is also the planet of old age and death. It reminds us of our mortality and makes us think about what we have accomplished in our lives and what we have left unfinished. As Saturnian individuals, people of this decan face a number of moral crossroads in their lives. At these times, they need to take a good hard look at their options and where they are likely to lead. Some seem to think that they are morally exempt—that they are above the laws of society and entitled to act on any strong impulse or desire. They resent authority, especially anyone who might create obstacles to the fulfillment of their desires. Experience, however, soon teaches them that they'd better wise up and pay attention to the rules, since they are otherwise liable to land in trouble, or even in jail. With Saturn as the ruling planet, these people aren't given a lot of slack. Ill-planned actions and thoughtless, irresponsible behavior can bury them in a pile of unpleasant repercussions.

Due to the influence both of Saturn and the moon, Virgo 3 individuals regularly encounter rule-bound systems to which they have to adapt. Any rule-bound system might be involved: a school, a religious organization, a corporate office, the government, even one's family. Whenever an individual enters into an environment that has an established set of rules, they have to decide how far and in what ways they will acquiesce to these rules. This process begins at birth. One is born into a family with rules and a society with rules. Throughout one's life, one will continue to negotiate new sets of rules, as one enters new jobs and new social situations. Virgo is a sign of the underdog. Thus, these people may find that they have little power in the face of established institutions. Even if they have a good analytical understanding of the problems of the family, the government, or the workplace, what can they actually do about it? Do they even have a voice in the system?

The decan image features a court case in which three different points of view are represented. The strikers are ready to walk away from their jobs if working conditions don't improve. They may even be contemplating violence. The plant manager is determined to work through the situation, and the judge is detachedly examining the pros and cons of both positions. All three of these figures are present in the psychology of the Virgo 3 individual: the conservative manager, the rebel, and the judge. To some degree, people of this decan are rebellious outsiders, who can be disobedient and even rather lawless. To some degree, they are stuffy conservatives, protecting their personal interests. To some degree, they are articulate, intelligent mediators and judges. These three figures exhibit three different ways of engaging a situation. Virgo 3 individuals need to decide whether they should be in a situation or not, and their level of involvement should they decide to be in it. What position should they take in the face of problematical situations? Should they ride them out quietly? Should they have an intelligent discussion with the most problematical person? Should they set up formal negotiations? Should they try to bring down the offending institution? Should they just leave?

Saturn presides over the endings in a person's life. The strikers in the courtroom are at the *end* of their rope. They feel that they are being treated like soulless automatons and are ready to quit if things don't get better. People often bring a phase of life to an end because they are fed up. One can get fed up with a job, with a marriage, with one's family, with one's church, with one's political party, with one's country. These commitments may have been acceptable at one time, even attractive, but when they have become spiritually stifling, they need to be left behind. A common choice for people of this decan is to extricate themselves from rule-bound situations and find some undemanding social niche where they can pretty much do as they please. In this environment, they can be who they really are, rather than who they are expected to be.

Of the three figures in the courtroom scene, the most conscious is the judge. Like the judge, people of this decan are aware enough of the ins and outs of a situation that they can steer the contending parties toward a practical solution. As outsiders, they are not locked into the beliefs and assumptions of either side but have the sane, detached perspective of a person with a highly developed Mercury. Virgo 3 individuals are determined to get a firm grasp of their situation, for if they end up basing their words and actions on false readings of their situation, there are bound to be consequences. Rather than solving a problem, they could easily make it worse. If, for instance, a judge were to make a mistaken judgment in a capital case, it would have terrible consequences.

Many of the degrees in the last decan of Virgo deal with well-established scenes or institutions that have become divorced from their original spiritual values. This issue has already made its appearance in the first decan of Virgo, where we see a pink-haired girl telling her classmates that the school is not really educating them. The teaching methods of the school have remained the same but are no longer working. Social institutions need to be periodically updated and reorganized if they are to continue to serve their underlying goals and ideals. Otherwise they become empty shells. If, for instance, the national government were to lose its spiritual commitment to its citizens, justice would fall by the wayside, and society would turn into something of a prison.

Rudhyar's version of the Sabian symbol for 26 Virgo, found in *The Astrology of Personality*, is "Rapt-eyed, a boy serves in a mass read by automatons." This symbolizes an established ritual—the mass—which has become divorced from its original spiritual meaning. It has become a string of meaningless words. Virgo 3 individuals want to escape meaningless, robotic behavior patterns. When habitual ways of thinking or acting have become out of date, irrelevant, or destructive, they need to be scrapped or restructured. People of this decan are often very efficient in the management of their everyday affairs. However, there is some danger that they will lose track of their purpose in life and become immersed in a succession of competently performed chores. Awakening from this unthinking and mechanical way of life is a major issue for people of this decan. Bill Murray, who has the Sun in this decan, starred in *Groundhog Day*, where he repeats the same day over and over again. To get the girl, Murray's character makes continual adjustments to the mechanical sequence of his one day. In the process, he becomes a more authentic and emotionally decent person. Joan Allen, in the movie *Pleasantville*, plays a robotic 1950s housewife who is awakened to a more sexual and grounded existence. Alicia Silverstone, in *Clueless*, plays out a rather plastic role but awakens to a deeper, more authentic perspective on life. Janeane Garofalo, in *Romy and Michele's High School Reunion*, awakens from counterproductive habits and attitudes that she has been stuck in since high school. In the above examples, we see people who are awakening from unconscious, habit-bound ways of life. They are coming out of a robotic trance. For if one is just "going through the motions," one is essentially living in a trance.

Emotionally, Virgo 3 individuals are romantics who try to keep their intimate relationships on a high moral and aesthetic plane. In private conversation, they are unusually honest, even confessional, and may expect a similar level of honesty from their partner. Scorning cowardly evasions, and intolerant of phoniness of any kind, they are always ready to "get down to cases." This generally ends up working very well. They see honesty as the foundation of their personal relationships, and for this reason, other people come to trust them and rely upon them.

EXAMPLES

Albert Brooks (Moon. Comic, filmmaker—*Defending Your Life*.)
Katharine Ross (Neptune. Actress in *The Stepford Wives*, about upper-class men turning their wives into obedient robots.)
Scott Adams (Jupiter. Cartoonist—*Dilbert*—about the idiocies of office life.)
Giovanni Agnelli (Moon. Founder of Fiat car manufacturers.)
Óscar Arias Sánchez (Sun, Neptune, North Node. President of Costa Rica; created the Central American Peace Plan.)
John Gardner (Moon. Founder of Common Cause.)
Elizabeth I (Sun. English queen. She played many rulers off against each other, while consolidating her power.)
Martin Balsam (Venus. Played a juryman in *Twelve Angry Men*.)
Ellen Goodman (Neptune. Liberal political columnist for the *Boston Globe*.)
Michael Douglas (Chiron. Actor in many films about ill-considered courses of action—*Fatal Attraction, Wall Street*.)
Jennifer Aniston (Pluto. Actress—*The Good Girl*.)
Bill Murray (Sun, Mars. Comic actor—*Groundhog Day, Caddyshack*.)
Henry VIII (Mars. Broke with the Catholic Church in order to divorce and remarry.)
Sir Thomas More (Pluto. Refused to accept Henry VIII's renunciation of the pope and was executed for it.)
Mike Bloomberg (Neptune. Multibillionaire, onetime mayor of New York.)
Agatha Christie (Sun. Mystery writer.)
John Sayles (Venus, Saturn. Filmmaker—*Brother from Another Planet*.)
David Horowitz (Moon, Neptune. Onetime Communist, now a conservative; wrote *The Destructive Generation*.)

Bob Dylan (North Node, Neptune. Folk singer, poet—"Like a Rolling Stone.")

Judy Blume (Neptune. Sociological writer—*Wifey*, *Blubber*.)

Russell Banks (Neptune. Wrote *Affliction*, about alcoholism.)

Upton Sinclair (Sun, Mars, Ascendant. Muckraking author; exposé of the food industry that led to the Pure Food and Drug Act.)

Pietro Germi (Sun. Film director—*Divorce, Italian Style*.)

Eldridge Cleaver (Mercury. Leader of the Black Panthers—*Soul on Ice*.)

Robert McNamara (Moon. President of the World Bank, escalated the Vietnam War as secretary of defense, developed "systems analysis" in public policy.)

B. F. Skinner (Moon. Behavioral psychologist—man as machine.)

Shen Tong (Uranus, Pluto. Prodemocracy Chinese dissident, jailed.)

The assassinations of Martin Luther King Jr. and Robert F. Kennedy (April 4, 1968, and June 5, 1968. Saturn. In one of its guises, Saturn can be seen as a corpse.)

Mary Shelley (Mercury. Author of *Frankenstein*.)

William Harrah (Mercury, Venus. Established Harrah's Casino in Reno.)

Martha Stewart (Neptune, North Node. Home improvement empire; jailed for insider trading.)

René Cassin (Venus. President of the UN's Human Rights Commission.)

Ken Kesey and Jack Nicholson (Sun and Moon, respectively. Author and lead actor for *One Flew Over the Cuckoo's Nest*.)

Libra, 1st Decan

The first decan of Libra begins the second half of the zodiacal cycle and as such marks a turning point in consciousness. At the fall equinox, the light force is exactly balanced with the dark force. In the natural world, death and decay are coming to the fore, while in the interior or spiritual realm, one finds increasing clarity and luminosity. Aries, which began the cycle, initiated the cosmic outbreath, whereby the spirit began to slowly incarnate into physical forms. Libra, by contrast, initiates the cosmic *inbreath*, at which time the spirit begins to retract back into itself. Libra 1 individuals are turning toward the inner realm—toward art, poetry, mysticism, religion, psychology, and philosophy. They have begun to realize that reality is a product of consciousness as much as a physical fact—that we live within our subjective *interpretations* of reality and not just in the physical world.

The original Sabian symbol for the first degree of Libra is a white butterfly pierced by a dart of light. This symbolizes the immanence of a higher spiritual reality within the physical world, and particularly the existence of ideal beauty within the physical world. Moments of perfect grace may be experienced in a love affair, an artistic experience, or in communion with nature. In the decan image, a man is taking a picture of a beautiful moment in his relationship, in order to better commit it to memory. Later, he may look back at this picture and recall a time when he could clearly perceive his lover's divine self. This moment may come so close to the ideal realm that it seems outside of time.

Modern astrologers associate Libra with romantic love, which is the province of the sign's dominant planet, Venus. People of this decan are in fact extremely susceptible to beauty and may themselves be very beautiful. Yet as physically attractive as they may be, they identify more closely with their astral body than with their physical body. This gives them a luminous glow and an aura of mystery and enchantment. People of this decan are very sensitive to the divine beauty in other people's souls and fall in love fairly easily. As highly sexual individuals, they are also attracted to purely physical beauty. This may lead to disillusionment, since after the first bloom of love has faded, they may discover that their lover is operating on a lower spiritual and emotional level than they first imagined.

People of this decan are learning the basics of relationship. They are learning that a balance of give and take is the basis of all good relationships—that one tends to get what one gives, since there is a lot of subconscious mirroring in relationships. Often these people learn this the hard way. In their youth, they tend to be undisciplined in their behavior and may lash out at their loved ones. This leads to fights where hurtful things are said—things that can't be unsaid. After ruining a few relationships in this way, they begin to exercise more discipline and tact. They learn to discern when they need to say something and when they need to remain silent.

In my own image for the first degree of Libra, a child is trying to capture a butterfly in a butterfly net. This refers to the problem of desire, which keeps us running after people and things we want. Seeing someone we admire, we try to possess them and freeze them in time. The butterfly, pierced by a dart of light, is an unexpected gift that exists for only a moment. It is a product of *serendipity*. Libra 1 individuals need to remain open to what life throws in their path, by allowing love and beauty to unfold in their own way. John Lennon once said, "Life is what happens when you are making other plans." In other words, life occurs in the present moment—and not in plans for the future. Evolved people of this decan have an adaptable, improvisatory approach to life. This stands in stark contrast to the Martian approach found in the opposite decan. Aries 1 individuals are swordlike in their mental focus, and in their determination to realize their goals. Venusians, by contrast, are centered in the present, for they want to remain open to life's every opportunity for enjoyment and beauty.

In their intimate relationships, Libra 1 individuals play it by ear. They hold their expectations in abeyance and allow their partner the *space* to be who they are. Rather than fixating on some image they may have formed of a person, they allow them the space to change and grow.

They listen closely to what they have to say, without a lot of criticism. This encourages them to relax and open up. It promotes harmony and mutual appreciation.

Venus is above all a planet of emotional discrimination. People with Venus in earth signs, such as Taurus and Virgo, decide whether to go ahead with a relationship by predicting, through interior visualizations, the most likely course of the relationship. People with Venus in Libra, by contrast, focus more on what they want their lover to be, rather than extrapolating from their actual behavior. This can set them up for a lot of disappointment. These people understand that relationships demand compromise, but how much compromise, and what kinds of compromise? They may long for someone who appreciates the beauty of their soul, but, hungering for sex and companionship, may settle for too little. Most of the people of this decan do eventually find themselves in a satisfactory relationship. However, some end up seeking solace in a luminous fantasy world. Having experienced a lot of emotional pain, they end up preferring fantasy relationships to real relationships, since fantasy allows them to explore their most beautiful dreams.

Some Libra 1 individuals commit to their fantasy life even more fully. J. R. R. Tolkien (*Lord of the Rings*), Lewis Carroll (*Alice's Adventures in Wonderland*), and L. Frank Baum (*The Wizard of Oz*) all have planets in this decan. These people realize that fantasies have their own reality and have a lot to teach us, if we look upon them not as childish amusements but as spiritual allegories. The fantasy novels associated with this decan are, in fact, full of arcane wisdom, channeled from a higher plane.

The ancient Chinese sage Chuang Tzu spoke of a dream he had, where he experienced himself as a butterfly. Upon awakening, he wasn't sure whether he was Chuang Tzu, who had dreamed of being a butterfly, or a butterfly dreaming it was Chuang Tzu. This allegory asks us whether the waking state is more real than the world of our most beautiful dreams. It also suggests that a balance between these two states is desirable—that a friendly rapport between one's dream life and one's waking life will bring one into a more balanced and integrated state of consciousness.

People of this decan have a strong drive toward spiritual illumination. They're looking for light wherever they can find it. They may get it from spiritual teachers, from intimate relationships, from art, from philosophy, from religion, or from dreams. Staying on the track of this inner light takes a lot of focus, for its path can be as uncertain as a butterfly's wavering flight through a dappled forest. One can easily get distracted and lose one's way. Still, the goal is well worth it, for it leads to beauty and love—to heaven on earth.

If one examines the Sabian symbols of the first Libran decan, many of them show people observing something mysterious and trying to get an accurate fix on it. People of this decan are penetrating and insightful. By subtly balancing physical vision with intuitive or clairvoyant vision, they are able to accurately "capture" the gist of a situation or a person. Like the butterfly of the decan image, these people have their antennae out and pick up a lot of subtle cues from their environment. Note that a butterfly's antennae are reminiscent of the curved lines atop the Mercury symbol. Mercury does, in fact, do extremely well in this decan, due to its ability to balance spiritual and physical perception.

While this is a decan of dreamers and romantics, its high idealism is also apparent in the realm of politics. Many Libra 1 individuals are idealistic reformers, dedicated to restoring justice, fairness, and transparency to government. Convinced that the underlying ideals of their country can never die, they try to revitalize these ideals by reawakening the population to what they have lost. Libra 1 individuals also promote reform in the realm of manners. They favor refined, chivalrous behavior and discourage coarse, ugly, or abusive behavior. Libras realize that civilization depends above all on civility—on the way that people relate to one another. In a high civilization, people treat each other respectfully, even lovingly, since they are sensitive to the divine image at the core of other people's souls.

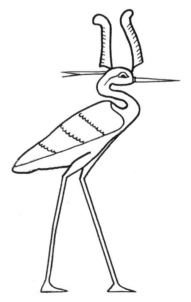

The ancient Egyptians often associated this decan with the white benben bird—a creator god identified with Venus as the morning star. In the Egyptian religion, the benben bird stood atop the primal hill as it rose from the dark ocean of formlessness, at the dawn of creation. It is an embodiment of the perfect, primal light that created the universe. The benben bird exists outside time. Like a set of nested eggs, it continually regresses back in time, to the Edenic vision that is the seed of the Creation, and the innermost hope of every love affair.

EXAMPLES

D. H. Lawrence (Uranus. Novelist—*Women in Love*, *Lady Chatterley's Lover*.)
F. Scott Fitzgerald (Sun. Novelist—*The Beautiful and the Damned*.)
Claude Bragdon (North Node. Architect, aesthetician—*The Beautiful Necessity*.)
Joni Mitchell (Neptune. Folk and jazz singer—"Both Sides Now.")
Julie Fowlis (North Node. Sublime singer of traditional Scottish music.)
Brendan Fraser (Jupiter, Uranus. Actor—*Bedazzled*, *Monkeybone*.)
Annette Funicello (Neptune. Mouseketeer, actress in beach movies.)
Nadia Boulanger (Venus. Famous piano teacher.)
Brigitte Bardot (Sun. Sexpot actress—*And God Created Woman*; her face was
   used as a model for Marianne—the symbol of the French Republic.)
Gwyneth Paltrow (Sun, Pluto. Actress—*Sliding Doors*, *Shakespeare in Love*.)
Barnet Rosset (Jupiter, Saturn, North Node. President of Grove Press; many
   legal battles against censorship.)
John Lennon (Mars. The Beatles; composed many romantic ballads.)
Drew Barrymore (Pluto. Actress—*50 First Dates*; wrote an autobiography
   titled *Little Girl Lost*.)
Vincenzo Bellini (Moon, Venus, Uranus. Composer of operas—*La
   Somnambula*.)
Marcello Mastroianni (Sun. Romantic actor in Fellini films—*8½*.)
Stephanie Meyer (Pluto. Author of teen romance novels featuring
   vampires—*Twilight*.)
Oscar Wilde (Venus. Gay playwright and aesthetic theorist.)
Ilona Staller (Mars. Porn star who later served in the Italian Parliament.)
Gary Ross (Venus. Film director, screenwriter—*Big*, *Pleasantville*.)
Donovan (Neptune. Folk singer—"Sunshine Superman," "Hurdy Gurdy Man.")
George Gershwin (Sun. Composer of pop and classical masterpieces—
   "Embraceable You.")
Jimmy Kimmel (Venus. Host of *The Man Show*; talk-show host.)
Hilly Kristal (Venus. Ran CBGB night club, promoting the Ramones, Talking
   Heads, Patti Smith, and Blondie.)
Harry Crosby (Jupiter. Heir, founded Black Sun Press and published struggling
   authors such as Hemingway, Ezra Pound, T. S. Eliot, and James Joyce.)
Amédée Ozenfant (Ascendant, Uranus. Cubist theorist.)
Tim Curry (Neptune. Gender-bending actor—*Rocky Horror*.)
T. S. Eliot (Sun. Poet—*The Waste Land*.)
Steve Allen (Saturn. Variety show host, featured many rising stars; promoted
   beat poetry and jazz.)

Norman Lear (Saturn, North Node. Liberal television producer—*All in the Family*, *Maude*; organized for liberal causes and First Amendment rights.)

Judith Crist (Jupiter, Saturn, North Node. Film critic, author of books on film.)

Renée Zellweger (Uranus. Actress—*Bridget Jones' Diary*.)

P. L. Travers (Mars. Author of the Mary Poppins books; editor of *Parabola* magazine, which treated world mythology.)

Thomas Moore (Mars. New Age author—*Care of the Soul*.)

Stanley Mouse (Mars. Artist—psychedelic posters and record albums.)

Duncan Grant (Uranus, North Node. Painter, set designer, textile manufacturer.)

George "Spanky" McFarland (Sun. Child actor—*The Little Rascals*.)

Libra, 2nd Decan

IMAGE: *Lost in a maze of paths in a starlit forest, a woman comes upon a strange tavern. Looking through a small window and then entering, she pushes past some overly eager men and asks an honest-looking man for directions.*

The woman in the decan symbol has lost her way. She has taken a wrong turn on the road of life and will, at some point, have to retrace her steps. Because she doesn't quite know where she is, she is unusually open to outside influences—some of them good and some of them bad. As a symbol of Venus, the woman of the decan image must use *spiritual discrimination* to decide whether to enter into a situation, and what to look for in that situation. There are attractive men in the bar. There is alcohol and pleasant chitchat. But she needs to keep her wits about her and remain awake to her real needs.

The main danger here is falling in with the wrong crowd—degenerates or even criminals who follow base instincts—people who seek the oblivion of alcohol, drugs, or casual sex. It is easy enough to connect with such people, since we all have these impulses. However, people of this decan need to remember their higher commitments, even when they find themselves in a corrupt crowd or a corrupt culture. As Venusians, Libra 2 individuals are generally poised and socially sophisticated. However, they aren't always in control of their appetites. They need to consider how an experience is liable to affect them, and avoid any experience that might diminish their self-respect or dim their luminous romantic ideals.

In the decan image, the woman pauses at the threshold of a bar and looks through the window to determine what she is walking into. Because it is an unfamiliar scene, she must rely on first impressions. Libra 2 individuals understand that much of life is not what it appears to be—that a lot of deception goes on in social and romantic situations. People's public personas are always somewhat dishonest. They display an attractive social mask and hide their uglier traits. Libra 2 individuals are well aware of this and are careful to sidestep people's problematic sides. They are generally tolerant people and enjoy the simple give and take of parties and get-togethers. However, they are not particularly trusting and rarely take others at face value. Through probing conversations, they figure out people's underlying psychology and revise their first impressions accordingly.

While Venus is very strong in this decan, Chiron is the most powerful influence. Chiron has generally been symbolized by a centaur. However, in my own research, it appears more often as a satyr. Both centaurs and satyrs are half human and half animal and represent the challenge of integrating human reason with one's more bestial, desirous self. People of this decan are involved in a lifelong effort to achieve psychological integration. This helps explain why these people, despite their superior social skills, are so private and inwardly directed. Outwardly, they may appear to be caught up in a pleasant social whirl, but their real focus is on their inner work.

It is the Sun's job to create a central identity around which all the other planets organize themselves. However, the Sun is weak in this decan, resulting in a personality that is not particularly unified. Libra 2 individuals have a sense of identity that is fluid and changeable, with different personality components vying for dominance. As the central decan of Libra, these people must *balance* polar opposites within the psyche. They must psychologically integrate the mind and the body, the public persona and the hidden shadow, and the masculine and feminine sides of the personality. Men of this decan acknowledge and accept their feminine side and are very interested in feminine psychology. Women, similarly, are students of male psychology. Because people of this decan are perceptive observers of the opposite sex, they know how to get along with them, but they also know how to manipulate them. It is essential, however, that they refrain from such behavior and remain honest and principled in their relationships, for anything less tends to land them in sordid, unpleasant scenes.

Given the weakness of the Sun in this decan, the task of integrating the personality falls upon Chiron. This is a difficult undertaking, for Chiron is a tricky planet, involved in illusion and misperception. Chiron governs all the projective emotions—love, desire, hate, and fear. These projective emotions cause distortions in our perceptions of reality. We may assume bad things about people because of their race. We may assume that someone is honest because they look honest. We may assume that someone who is sexually attractive will be good in bed. We may assume that someone we love is a good person, because we *want* them to be a good person. Chiron helps us get past these misperceptions. By getting to know people we are attracted to or are afraid of, we can stop projecting and learn to see them as they really are.

People of this decan are drawn to individuals who seem to embody their lusts, fears, loves, and hates. By entering into relationships with these people, they learn to distinguish their imagistic projections from reality. They overcome romantic infatuations, racial prejudices, and irrational fears, by grounding themselves in the *facts* of the situation, rather than allowing themselves to be seduced by mere *images*. These people are always trying to clarify their situations. Like the woman of the decan image—lost in a maze of paths—Libra 2 individuals are faced with too many options—too many alternate explanations. To get a better fix on what's going on, they solicit other people's opinions. If these other people are honest and perceptive, they may be able to point out one's blind spots, where one has embraced false information or prejudicial opinions. And Libra 2 individuals can help others in exactly the same way—by pointing out ill-founded opinions or mistakes in logic.

Should these people refuse to learn from their encounters, they may fall into distorted conceptions of reality. A number of prominent Nazis, Mansonites, and other extremists have planets here. Most of these people are completely obsessed with demonized visions of other races and other political persuasions. They think they are involved in a battle of good against evil, when they're actually just deluded.

People with a Libra 2 emphasis are always trying to clarify their own understanding, but as compassionate individuals, they are also trying to clarify other people's understanding. Thus, they can often be found pointing out errors in people's perceptions or offering up facts that challenge these people's cherished prejudices. Usually, they do this in a charming and humorous way, employing mischievous antics and pranks to get people to acknowledge the limitations of their viewpoint. The glyph for Chiron is a key, and in their encounters with others, Libra 2 individuals point out *key* facts that they seem to be ignoring. They try to puncture their misperceptions and, in the process, to liberate them from the prison of their delusional beliefs. As psychologically astute individuals, people of this decan can make excellent advisors and counselors. If asked for feedback on a problem, they are glad to give it. Their penetrating insights, however, are sometimes so accurate that they sting.

Libra 2 individuals are charming and persuasive conversationalists. First of all, they know a lot. They are very aware of what's going on politically, culturally, psychologically, sexually, and even spiritually, so they have a lot of interesting things to talk about. Nor do they shy away from controversy. If a truth needs to be heard, they will give voice to it. And as people who are good at reading social situations, they know when they need to say something and when they need to remain silent. They know when a conversation can go into deeper territory and when it would be better to lighten things up.

People of this decan are very interested in spiritual evolution. As with the previous decan, they have powerful imaginations and are sensitive to the archetypal and symbolic level of experience. Many talented astrologers have planets here. These are people who take the interpenetration of the spiritual and material realms as a given. They realize that there is a lot of speculation and even illusion in their art, but are nonetheless intent on getting a better fix on astrology's symbolic archetypes. Negatively, they are projecting planetary and zodiacal images onto other people, without conversing with them long enough to find out if these projections are valid. Positively, they are refining their understanding of the archetypes with every chart they cast, and passing on this superior understanding to their clients.

The Egyptians placed a number of different figures in this decan. One was a goat-legged man holding up two votive jars. With the eye of the imagination, this figure might be seen as a satyr-like bartender, holding up two mugs of beer. Perhaps this is a man trying to seduce a woman by getting her drunk. But it might also allude to the power of alcohol or other mind-altering drugs to loosen up one's conception of reality, and to allow one to see things from a different point of view.

EXAMPLES

Derek Jacobi (Moon. Actor—*I, Claudius*.)
Martin Goldsmith (Venus. Not the present author. Director and screenwriter for noir films, including *Detour*, where picking up a hitchhiker throws a man's entire life off course.)

Catherine Deneuve (Mercury. Actress—*Belle de Jour*—about a housewife who has a secret life as a prostitute.)
Margaret Lockwood (Mercury. Actress—*The Lady Vanishes*.)
Guillermo del Toro Gómez (Sun, Mercury. Filmmaker—*Pan's Labyrinth*.)
Jorge Luis Borges (Mars. Magical-realist short story writer—"The Garden of Forking Paths"—which examines life's parallel possibilities.)
Scott Bakula (Sun. Actor—*Quantum Leap*.)
Gwyneth Paltrow (Mercury, Uranus. Actress—*Sliding Doors*.)
Gerald Gardner (North Node. Founder of Wicca—*The Meaning of Witchcraft*.)
Michel Foucault (Venus. Literary critic who rejected master narratives and canonical interpretations.)
Howard Zinn (Venus, Jupiter. Leftist political science professor, historian—*A People's History of the United States*.)
George Blake (Saturn. Double agent.)
Agatha Christie (Mercury. Mystery writer—master of red herrings.)
Susanna Kaysen (Venus, Neptune. Novelist—*Girl, Interrupted*.)
Senator Joseph McCarthy (Venus. Senator, paranoid commie hunter.)
Shirley MacLaine (Jupiter. Actress, seeker—*The Trouble with Harry*, *Defending Your Life*.)
Robert van Gulik (Jupiter. Author of the intricate Judge Dee mysteries; Dutch diplomat.)
Vincent Bugliosi (Jupiter. Manson prosecutor; wrote *Helter Skelter*.)
Ursula LeGuin (Mercury. Author of fantasy books and politically informed science fiction—*The Left Hand of Darkness*.)
Susan Sarandon (Sun. Actress—*The Rocky Horror Picture Show*—where a wrong turn leads to a disastrous plunge into sexual madness.)
Michael Douglas (Mars. Actor, producer—*Fatal Attraction*, *Basic Instinct*, *Wall Street*.)
Kurt Russell (Neptune. Actor—*Stargate*.)
Liz Greene (Mars. Jungian astrologer.)
Lee Pace (Pluto. Played the Elvenking in the Hobbit movies.)
Johann Sebastian Bach (Jupiter. Prolific classical composer, improviser.)
Charles Harvey (North Node. Astrologer.)
Margot Adler (Chiron. Wiccan priestess—*Drawing Down the Moon*.)
Lindsay Crouse (Neptune. Actress—*House of Games*.)
Charlie Sheen (Venus. Actor—*Two and a Half Men*, *Anger Management*; sex addict.)
Anaïs Nin (Mars, North Node. Erotic diarist.)
Winona Ryder (Uranus. Actress—*Heathers*, *Reality Bites*.)
John Lennon (Sun, North Node. Beatle.)
Bill Moyers (Jupiter. White House press secretary; investigative reporter.)
Sidney Pollack (Jupiter. Directed *They Shoot Horses Don't They?* and *Sliding Doors*.)

Lyndon LaRouche (Jupiter. Paranoid political-cult leader.)
Patrick Fugit (Mercury. Actor—*Almost Famous*, *Wristcutters*.)
Marianne Williamson (Neptune. *Course in Miracles* teacher.)

Libra, 3rd Decan

IMAGE: *Guided by a single passenger, a hot-air balloon emerges from a bank of storm clouds into the sunlight, then drifts toward a domed, marble building on a small island.*

In this decan, the desire for mental illumination becomes stronger than the desire for physical things. With the fading of desire and the loosening of bonds to worldly concerns, the spirit is freed to soar upward toward higher planes of consciousness. People inhabit different planes of consciousness and even operate simultaneously on several different planes of consciousness. There is the dream consciousness of sleep, the ego consciousness of everyday life, and the spiritual consciousness of the higher self. The first decan of Libra emphasizes dream consciousness, the second decan emphasizes social consciousness, and the third emphasizes spiritually elevated consciousness. People of the third decan travel freely between these three levels. This *mobility of consciousness* is represented by the balloon, which can move to any altitude according to the will of the pilot.

The Egyptians pictured this decan as the hawk-headed sun god, Horus. One Sabian symbol in this decan features an eagle, another an airplane, still another a circle of angels. All of these things have wings.[48] They are navigators of the air—that is, of consciousness. In my book *Moon Phases*, the moon phase associated with the third Libran decan was called "The Angel." An angel has wings and dwells in a realm entirely above that of normal human consciousness. An angel is an intelligent form of light—even as the sun god Horus is an intelligent form of light.

People of this decan are trying to raise their consciousness, so they can live their lives from a more balanced and enlightened perspective. To maintain serenity and grace in their everyday lives, they must constantly rebalance the various areas of their existence—the physical, emotional, spiritual, cultural, financial. They must make constant adjustments to their focus of attention. This juggling act succeeds best when they approach their problems from a calm and elevated perspective, for one's state of mind has a powerful effect on the way one perceives the world. The cultivation of a serene state of mind is, in fact, probably the most important and practical of all earthly activities. In the decan image, we see clouds and wind. Wind is related to the breath. The regulation of one's breath, in meditation or in relaxing activities, is the best way to achieve the serenity and elevated perspective favored by people of this decan.

Libra 3 individuals rarely buy into the accepted worldview. They realize that most people are lost in cloudlike dreams and illusions—that they are projecting all kinds of irrelevant ideas from the past onto the future and often fail to see what's right in front of them. This confused state of consciousness leads to all kinds of problems, both for the individual and for the planet. World leaders who have no historical perspective drag their nations into destructive, unnecessary wars. Wedded to false analyses of the world situation, they are routinely blindsided by events that seem to come out of nowhere. This throws the whole world situation out of balance and plunges the population into one crisis after another.

People of this decan are trying to promote sanity, order, and balance not only in their personal lives, but in the political and cultural spheres. To this end, they often seek an official platform from which to disseminate their views. Among the examples, one finds many investigative reporters, historians, sociologists, political scientists, cultural commentators, and humorists. These people are all trying to bring a sane, balanced perspective to the general public.

To render their ideas more accessible, people of this decan often simplify these ideas by creating plays, books, and movies that are simultaneously insightful and entertaining. Through their art, they gently sweep away old ways of seeing things, even as a gentle breeze dissolves the clouds. At the same time, they introduce people to new ideas and energies that have just begun to spill over the cultural horizon.

Libra 3 individuals are very aware of changes in the cultural and political "weather." They study preexistent currents of political or cultural thought and then try to "hitch a ride," by adapting their own actions to these trends. While some remain mere observers, others try to redirect these cultural and political movements by influencing public discussion on key issues. These people can often be found at the center of some *storm* of controversy, loudly alerting the public to social or political abuses. Their articulate pronouncements often sound off the cuff, but they are actually well-rehearsed arguments carefully framed around the turning point or crux of the issue. Because Libra 3 individuals understand the subtle balances of their situation, they can be very effective in turning the tide of public opinion, for they know just where pressure can be most effectively applied.

Libra 3 individuals are trying to bring order to the global situation, but they realize that crises can also arise on a personal level, if one fails to pay attention. Many films and books created by Libra 3 individuals feature protagonists who are clueless bumblers involved in an amusing comedy of errors. Examples include Whoopi Goldberg (*Sister Act*), Woody Allen (*A Midsummer Night's Sex Comedy*), Dolly Parton (*9 to 5*), Sally Field (*Soap Dish*), Alan Arkin (*Little Miss Sunshine*), Pietro Germi (*Divorce Italian Style*), Robert Carradine (*Revenge of the Nerds*), and Kal Penn (*Harold and Kumar Go to White Castle*). These films point out the comedic craziness[49] that results when people are asleep to what's really going on, and fail to differentiate between reality and fantasy.

While Libra 3 individuals are amused by incompetence and fuzzy thinking, they themselves are clearheaded and alert. They see upcoming difficulties promptly enough to dodge them, and transient opportunities quickly enough to capitalize on them. In difficult situations, they remain calm and levelheaded. Nor do they exaggerate the difficulties of their situation. Many so-called problems are as fleeting as clouds. If one just allows them to pass, one soon finds oneself back in the sunshine. Keeping things *light* is often one's best course, since humor and a light heart allow one to pass through life's storms without losing one's emotional equilibrium.

Because Libra 3 individuals are able to rise above their problems, they are happy and relaxed. Once they have freed their minds from confusion and doubt, they begin to extricate themselves from bad scenes and petty problems. They move away from the labyrinthine complexities of city life and head for wide-open spaces: the mountains, the ocean. They free themselves from relationships that are unhealthy or unpleasant and cultivate relationships that are simple and aboveboard. Libra 3 individuals know how to relax. They take frequent trips to the countryside, where their cares and worries are softly blown away. They also take "vacations of the mind," by reading fantasy novels or losing themselves in elaborate daydreams.

When people of this decan are fully self-realized, they are exactly who they appear to be. They seem to stand within a shining image of themselves. Unburdened by petty fears and desires, they move through society unfazed by its expectations, demands, and taboos. As dispassionate observers, they don't need the truth to be one thing or another. They look at things freshly, without a burden of preconceptions. This open-mindedness enables them to communicate with even their enemies, and to walk into the highest levels of government and business unimpeded by false modesty or fear of rejection. Standing, as they do, within the light of transpersonal truth, they feel no need to fight against every falsehood. They are confident that the truth will triumph, for falsehood exists only at lower levels of consciousness, and will eventually dissipate before the bright rays of the sun.

The Egyptians often placed Horus here, as a hawk-headed man. Horus is a sun god and in this decan may symbolize the transcendence and invincibility of the light force. It is interesting to note that hawks are experts at utilizing air currents to get where they want to go.

EXAMPLES

Mary Steenburgen (Saturn, Neptune. Actress—*Joan of Arcadia*.)

Sam Rockwell (Mercury. Actor—*Galaxy Quest, The Way, Way Back*.)

Bernie Sanders (Venus. Socialist senator, presidential aspirant.)

Tony Kushner (Neptune. Playwright—*Angels in America*—about the AIDS epidemic.)

Samuel Harris (Mars. Neuroscientist, writer on religion, consciousness, and meditation.)

Eugene Roddenberry (North Node. Created the original *Star Trek* television series.)

Rudolf Hess (Saturn. Nazi official who flew solo to Scotland to negotiate a peace with England.)

Harry Truman (North Node. High-spirited president, dropped nuclear bombs on Japan.)

Scott Bakula (Neptune. Actor—*Quantum Leap*.)

Julie Hagerty (Neptune. Actress—*Airplane, Rude Awakening*.)

Will Smith (Venus, Mercury. Actor—*Men in Black*.)

Kal Penn (North Node. Actor, progressive politico—*Harold and Kumar Go to White Castle*—with its frantic hang-gliding scene.)

Ingo Swann (Venus. Worked for the US Army to see whether remote viewing, based on out-of-body travel, could be used militarily.)

Patrick Dennis (North Node. Wrote *Auntie Mame: An Irreverent Episode*.)

Timothy Leary (Sun. LSD advocate.)

Annette Funicello (Sun, Venus, Mars. Disney child star, who later on starred in beach movies.)

Bill Watterson (Jupiter, North Node. Cartoonist—*Calvin and Hobbes*.)

Nia Vardalos (Mercury, stationary. Screenwriter, director—*My Big Fat Greek Wedding*.)

Woody Allen (Venus. Comic filmmaker, cultural analyst—*Annie Hall*, *Sleeper*.)

Edmond Halley (Mars. Cartographer, named Halley's Comet.)

Sir Thomas More (Mars. Catholic martyr; author of *Utopia*.)

Oprah Winfrey (Neptune. Talk-show host, spiritual and New Age subjects.)

Jack Anderson (Sun, Moon, Jupiter. Newspaper columnist, investigative journalist.)

A. J. Cronin (Chiron. Idealist novelist—*The Citadel*.)

Edwin Muir (Jupiter. Scottish poet whose works focused on the theme of earthly paradise threatened by a fall from grace.)

John Stuart Mill (Saturn, Uranus. Nineteenth-century philosopher—*On Liberty*.)

F. Scott Fitzgerald (Mercury, Venus. Novelist of the Jazz Age—*This Side of Paradise*.)

Alistair Cooke (Venus, Mars. British-born journalist; created and narrated a thirteen-part television series titled *America: A Personal History of the United States*.)

Felix Mendelssohn (Mars. Classical composer—*For He Shall Give His Angels Charge*; *Midsummer Night's Dream*.)

Alex Haley (North Node. Wrote *Roots*.)

Keith Reid (Sun. Songwriter and lyricist for Procol Harum—"A Salty Dog.")

Lewis Mumford (Sun, Mars. Sociologist, critic of technologically driven society—*Technics and Civilization*.)

Trey Parker (Sun. Cocreated television's *South Park*.)

Johnny Carson (Sun. Talk-show host, comic.)

Caroline Casey (Sun, Neptune. Astrologer, political commentator.)

Richard Brautigan (Mars. Darkly comic novelist—*So the Wind Won't Blow It Away*.)

Dolly Parton (Jupiter. Country singer, actress—*9 to 5*.)

Satyajit Ray (North Node. Bengali filmmaker—*The Apu Trilogy*.)

Penny Marshall (Sun. Actress in *Laverne and Shirley*; directed *Big* and *A League of Their Own*.)

Barry Gibb (Venus, Jupiter. Bee Gees' lead singer—"Too Much Heaven.")

Scorpio, 1st Decan

IMAGE: *A stern, bearded judge presides over a tribunal. The prosecuting attorney finishes his argument, then picks up a religious statue and smashes it—extracting from its shards a small document, which exposes the plotting of the priests.*

In the decan image, we see a religious icon being destroyed. This symbolizes an attack on a widely held but unexamined belief. People of this decan are extremely skeptical. They are iconoclasts, who realize that popular beliefs often serve as covers for lies and misrepresentations. These people feel a responsibility to expose these lies and break their hold on the imagination of the public. They feel a responsibility to destroy what needs destroying, be it a false interpretation, a decadent artistic form, a religious belief, or even a political system.

Most people are easily deceived by anyone who can spin a good tale. They never get past the surface of reality but passively accept whatever fairy tales they are being fed by the powers that be. Scorpio 1 individuals have nothing but scorn for these fantasies. They are determined to get to the bottom of things. They investigate fishy situations and try to come up with explanations that fit all the facts, paying special attention to anomalies that betray false characterizations. The general impulse of the decan, then, is to expose falsehoods and distorted representations. This would include factual falsehoods, as well as dishonest messages hidden in television dramas and news shows, religious sermons, and government hype. People of this decan are steeled against hidden agendas and manipulative ploys. Negatively, they become so cynical that they end up seeing all higher ideals as smokescreens for the pursuit of sex, power, or money. They indulge their hatreds and become obsessed with "enemies." Luckily, most Scorpios are too wise and too empathetic to get into that headset. Scorpio is a water sign, after all—sensitive, somewhat psychic, and emotionally empathetic. As genuinely helpful people, people of this decan take a more intelligent approach to the problems they find around them.

Francisco de Goya once observed that "the sleep of reason produces monsters." As a psychic collectivity, the masses are highly unconscious, for they experience the scenes of everyday life as passively as one might observe the changing images of a dream. The majority of people are easily seduced by collective fears and desires, without ever asking themselves whether they are particularly real. Too lazy to examine the propaganda that bombards them from political and religious leaders, from corporations and the media, they are easily manipulated by unscrupulous powermongers. Scorpio 1 individuals, by contrast, take a skeptical, analytical approach to the emotionally charged images of the collective dream. They develop an intellectual and psychic shield to wall out the toxic thoughts of the group mind.

The first decan of Scorpio is ruled by Pluto. Pluto is in a sign for about twenty years and lends each generation its own zodiacal quality and its own operant myths. Most people accept these myths without questioning them. They are swallowed up in the fantasy life of their generation. When Pluto changes signs, however, these fantasies lose their attraction, for they no longer satisfy the spiritual yearnings of the incoming generation. In the movie *Pleasantville*, two modern children are beamed into a 1950s television show. They are trapped in the fantasy world of 1950s America. The generation that dominated the cultural life of the fifties had Pluto in Cancer and fell under the spell of a number of Cancerian values. They worshiped at the altar of home, marriage, and family. The Pluto in Cancer generation reacted very negatively to the early stirrings of the Pluto in the Leo generation. They pictured these youths as juvenile delinquents who disrespected their parents, the church, and their country and wasted their time in drag racing, rock and roll, and unchaperoned sex. The incoming generation, for their part, saw their parents as paranoid conformists, who were afraid to look honestly at sex, race, and politics, and worse still, had no idea how to have fun. Looking to the Stones, the Beatles, and the Jefferson Airplane as spiritual leaders, they abandoned themselves to the new myths of their generation. With Leo so powerful in their charts, they had no intention of missing the party.

While the majority of people get sucked into the prevailing myths of their generation, Scorpio 1 individuals examine cultural symbols with a critical eye. Alert to the power of symbols—for good or ill—they refuse to buy into symbols that could enslave them. Some address this issue by producing art or literature that forces people to rethink their assumptions.

Most of this art is gently satiric or mischievously humorous. At times, however, it assaults its audience with cultural bombshells powerful enough to fracture their mental defenses. These deeply disturbing visions seem to emanate from the decan's brightest star, Arcturus,[50] which opens the mind to roiling, stormy dreams. To illustrate, the following darkly imaginative visionaries have planets here: Peter Weiss (*Marat/Sade*), Kurt Vonnegut, Hunter S. Thompson, Gary Ross (*Pleasantville*), Anne Rice (*The Vampire Lestat*), Timothy Leary, Daniel Pinkwater (*Alan Mendelsohn, the Boy from Mars*), and Franz Kafka. The works of Scorpio 1 artists are often dreamlike fictions but nonetheless contain cynical, penetrating insights into social reality. Their art mirrors society's dreamlike thought-forms but arranges them in such a way that the audience is forced to ponder a number of subversive ideas. In this way, Scorpio 1 individuals help the population escape the unconscious scripts that have imprisoned them. Moreover, by blending truth and fiction in their artistic works, people of this decan promote the idea that the conventional reality-conception is bizarre, irrational, and completely open to question.

Plutonians generally have a good understanding of politics, especially its internal workings—the political in-groups, the power brokers, the bartering of favors. But power has many levels. The most powerful politicians are spokespeople for particular philosophies or points of view. They speak for a quasi-religious power group within society. The explanations they offer are coherent enough but have been slanted with the aim of maintaining their group's power. Scorpio 1 individuals are perfectly aware of these machinations. Like skilled lawyers, they draw these political spokespeople into verbal battles, where their real motives and suppositions can come to light.

Scorpio 1 individuals are especially skeptical of symbols and stories promoted by organized religion, since these stories invite people to relinquish responsibility for their own spiritual development and fall into a kind of spiritual coma. There is a strong Gnostic streak in this decan. These people want to discover for themselves the deeper nature of the spiritual world. They want to perceive for themselves the hidden or occult powers governing earthly events.

One of Pluto's functions is to keep us from waking up when some intrusive noise disturbs our sleep. Thus, if one hears a noise in the next apartment while dreaming, this noise is often worked into the dream in a plausible if deceptive way, making it unnecessary to wake up and find out what's going on. It is Pluto's responsibility to decide when it is necessary to wake up, and when one can stay within a pleasant, undemanding dream. Thus, while Pluto can act to expose false images and false narratives, it can also create them. In fact, plutonic powers are regularly used by government and religious propaganda masters, who spin facts in such a way that their false fronts won't crumble. Using the dark power of Pluto's moon, Charon, the Establishment hypnotizes the population into believing a lie. They are especially adept at using frightening imagery to scare the populace into submission.

Pluto is associated with the kundalini, or serpent power, sleeping at the base of the spine. Scorpio 1 is a decan of snakes and dragons. The star Thuban—which is located in this decan—is in fact Alpha Draconis.[51] When the Scorpionic dragon is asleep, its eyes are closed. When it awakens, its eyes slowly open, like the waxing moon as it expands through a series of phases. When Scorpio 1 individuals are fully awake, they see beyond the tattered veil of their desires and fears to what is really there. They become aware of subtle emotional and sexual undercurrents and may even display a measure of ESP and astral vision. For when the serpent power is awakened, it opens the third eye and allows one to see on the astral plane.

Scorpio 1 individuals demand a high level of honesty from others and are intuitively aware when they are lying. Since they can be very judgmental, they tend to be well-respected rather than well-liked. Some people give them a wide berth in order to avoid arguments about weighty questions they haven't thought through. Scorpio 1 individuals aren't particularly troubled by this, since it's one way of keeping spiritual lightweights at a distance. Scorpios prefer to keep company with people who enjoy discussing the deeper mysteries of life. Often, they join a kind of coven—or in Vonnegut's terminology, a "karass." Together, these people put together a penetrating analysis of society and human life. This analysis generally begins with a cynical trashing of popular narratives but in time develops into a more serious, systematic analysis.

In their more intimate relationships, Scorpio 1 individuals seek out honest people who are capable of communicating on a deep emotional and spiritual level. As soon as a sincere emotional commitment has been established, it is best for these people to tie the knot. Since Scorpios respect the concept of a vow, marriage can be a way to stabilize a relationship and make it more comfortable.

The ancient Egyptians often placed the mummified Osiris in this decan. As ruler of the underworld, Osiris is analogous to the Roman god Pluto. One of Osiris's functions is to judge the dead. Osiris examined the deceased's behavior during their lifetime, and the motivations that lay behind their actions. People of this decan, likewise, are stern judges of their own actions—especially as regards their spiritual integrity.

Pluto and Osiris link this decan to physical death. At death, the body decomposes and returns to its component parts. These parts can then be used by new life forms. The ancient Egyptians often colored Osiris green to show his connection with vegetative growth. Plants grow very well in manure and other decomposing organic matter. In the vegetative realm, life and death are closely connected, with one growing out of the other. People of this decan, similarly, have an unusually strong, deeply rooted vitality, for they are connected to the impersonal power of Pluto, which, though existing in a dimension antecedent to physical reality, acts as a hidden source of energy and power.

EXAMPLES

Jim Garrison (Mercury, Venus. New Orleans district attorney, investigated the
  Kennedy assassination.)
Salman Rushdie (Chiron. Author of *The Satanic Verses*.)
Kurt Vonnegut (Mercury, Jupiter. Atheistic sci-fi writer—*The Sirens of Titan*.)
Grace Slick (Sun. Lead singer for the Jefferson Airplane—"Crown of Creation.")
Bill Maher (Neptune. Leftist talk-show host.)
Martin Luther (Mars. Attacked the corruption of the Catholic Church.)
J. Edgar Hoover (Saturn. Director of the FBI, who knew everyone's secrets.)
Henry Miller (Uranus. Brutally honest novelist—*Tropic of Cancer*.)
Andrea Dworkin (Mars, Jupiter. Radical feminist.)
Marcel Ophuls (Sun, Mars. Documentary filmmaker—*The Harvest of My Lai*.)
Richard Pryor (Venus, Mars. Vulgar, trenchantly observant stand-up comic.)
Lillian Hellman (Mars, stationary. Playwright, blacklisted—*The Children's
  Hour*—about children who lie about being abused.)
William Marston (Uranus. Sexually oriented psychologist; invented the first
  lie detector.)

Dan Rather (Sun. Steely-eyed newscaster.)

Peter Weiss (Mercury. Playwright—*Marat/Sade.*)

Patti Smith (Chiron. Proto-punk singer and poet.)

Cardinal Richelieu (Mars, North Node. Scheming first minister to Louis XIII.)

Malcolm X (Saturn. Black Muslim leader, assassinated.)

Alexis Carrel (Mars. Surgeon—pioneer in organ transplants.)

Kinky Friedman (Sun. Satirical songwriter, mystery novelist, ran for governor of Texas.)

Michael Moore (Saturn. Muckraking filmmaker—*Bowling for Columbine, Sicko.*)

Bobby Kennedy (Mars. US attorney general who took on the mob and was assassinated.)

Brett Butler (Jupiter, Neptune. Actress—*Grace under Fire.*)

Peter Hurkos (Jupiter. Occultist—can expose photographs with his mind.)

Anne Rice (Mercury. Gothic novelist—*The Vampire Chronicles.*)

Bela Lugosi (Mercury. Celebrity vampire.)

Joseph Goebbels (Sun, Mercury. Nazi propaganda minister.)

Ernest Hemingway (Jupiter. Novelist—*The Sun Also Rises.*)

Robin Moore (Sun. Novelist—*The Green Berets.*)

Lauren Bacall (Saturn. Glamorous vamp actress—*To Have and Have Not.*)

John Cleese (Sun. Leader of the Monty Python comedy troupe—*The Life of Brian.*)

Konrad Lorenz (Mercury. Zoologist—*On Aggression.*)

Joseph Vacher (Mercury. Sadistic serial killer.)

Winona Ryder (Sun. Actress—*Heathers, Beetlejuice.*)

Oliver Stone (Venus. Political filmmaker—*JFK, Nixon, Oliver Stone's Untold History of the United States.*)

Luca Zingaretti (Mercury, Venus. Star of the *Detective Montalbano* television series.)

Scorpio, 2nd Decan

IMAGE: *Canoeing down a river under the sliver of a moon, a courting couple discusses a nasty yelling match they had a while back. When the canoe gets stuck on something, the woman leans over and looks underwater to see what is hanging them up.*

People of this decan look below the surface of reality to underlying motives and hidden agendas. The woman in the decan image is trying to see below the surface of her relationship, so she can figure out what is keeping it from blossoming. Scorpio 2 individuals tend to have rather prickly, argumentative personalities, but underneath it all, they are genuine romantics, for they are willing to go through a lot of emotional pain in order to arrive at a sensitive, caring relationship. Generally, these are sympathetic people, who are willing to listen respectfully to other people's stories. At the same time, they are alert to dishonesty and emotional manipulation and will often call it out.

Scorpio 2 individuals have a great need to communicate, and to that end, speak directly, even trenchantly, to the issue at hand. Scorning superficial chitchat, they go straight to the heart of a problem, speaking in such an articulate, focused way that their meaning is impossible to miss. To illustrate, the following aggressively candid people have planets here: Henry Miller, Roseanne, Charles Bukowski, Lenny Bruce, Sandra Bernhard, Céline, Joan Didion, and Kinky Friedman. These are people who are respected for their brutally penetrating observations. Unfortunately, this kind of raw honesty is not to everyone's taste. Most people find the deeper levels of reality too disturbing, murky, and complicated to fathom and basically don't want to be bothered. They are also leery of the Scorpio's tendency to ignore the rules of polite conversation, since this opens the discussion to all kinds of dangerous topics. People of this decan are aware that others may find them disconcerting and even rude, but certain issues, despite their unpleasantness, need to be addressed, since all forward motion will cease until they have been effectively dealt with.

Scorpio is a *fixed* water sign. People of this decan must therefore grapple with the problem of emotional stagnation. It is easy for these people to get emotionally stuck, for they tend to replay wounding emotional experiences over and over in their minds, without ever getting past them. They tend to get *hung up* on traumas that block the flow of their vital energy. Scorpio 2 individuals are learning how to process difficult emotions. This involves analytical clarification, but more importantly, it involves acceptance and forgiveness. This is a decan of purification and healing. Scorpio 2 individuals are clearing a lot of garbage out of their lives, including counterproductive habits, emotional grudges, painful memories, false ideas, unhealthy sexual fantasies, and feelings of victimization. This task goes more smoothly once they have learned to approach these problems with compassion and forgiveness. At its highest level, this decan is associated with Christ-consciousness and the Sacred Heart.[52] As sensitive souls, people of this decan suffer a lot, for they feel the thorns of betrayal and cruelty very deeply. Yet if they can connect with the compassionate and forgiving consciousness of Neptune, they are able to heal these emotional wounds. This allows them to remain openhearted toward others and enter into new relationships without burdening them with a lot of emotional baggage.

Self-forgiveness begins with emotional honesty. People of this decan are unusually candid about their own mistakes and shortcomings—the bad things they did and the good things they didn't do. Some of the decan's most famous writers are known for their confessional but unapologetic accounts of their sloppy, mistake-ridden lives. These people accept and forgive their own faults, for they recognize that we all are flawed, in one way or another. They are nonetheless proud of their commitment to living bravely and without illusions, for whatever their faults, they try to be emotionally and spiritually *authentic*.

Scorpio 2 individuals have very open reality conceptions. They acknowledge the irrational, chaotic side of life and feel no compulsion to make immediate sense of it. Scornful of people who act like they have it all figured out, they challenge these smug individuals with anomalous facts and new interpretations that cast doubts on their beliefs. They are especially interested in bringing spiritual matters back into the discussion—ESP, astral travel, astrology, and Tarot, as well as questions concerning destiny and fate.

The ancient Egyptians often pictured this decan as a baboon in a boat under a full moon. The baboon is a symbol of Thoth as a moon god. Thoth is a god of wisdom, and as a moon god bestows understanding and clarity in the emotional realm. My own image for the decan is not so different, since it features two people canoeing by the light of the moon—two people who are trying to understand each other emotionally and spiritually. In Egyptian myth, the moon, as Horus's left eye, was stolen by Set and later recovered and healed by Thoth.[53] This myth alludes to the gradual restoration of the moon's light during its waxing phases. Interpreted psychologically, it shows the gradual increase of one's understanding as one brings more *illuminating emotional intelligence* to one's situation.

Scorpio 2 individuals know that they don't have the whole picture. They know that they are traveling in the dark and slowly bringing together the pieces of some mystery. They would prefer to have a firm grasp of what's going on around them, but seem destined to spend much of their time thrashing around in dark waters, seeking further clarification. Flashes of insight come to these people in intense but disconnected fragments, which they then try to assemble into a meaningful whole. Their understanding is consequently patchy, though even their isolated insights have the power to add new light to the situation, and to heal important misunderstandings.

People of this decan do best when they accept their own confusion and ignorance and await further clarification, for when they indulge in hasty speculations, they often arrive at faulty conclusions. It takes a lot of patience to wade one's way through a series of problems—to progress from the murky ignorance of the new moon to the global understanding of the full moon. In the decan image, the courting couple is traveling down a narrow, clogged waterway. All along the way, they are removing debris—that is, erroneous beliefs—to facilitate their progress. Eventually, they leave the river and enter into a calm and beautiful lake, bathed in moonlight, whose surface *perfectly reflects* the reality of their situation. Having tackled their problems one at a time, they have arrived at a state of perfect emotional understanding.

Since this is a lunar decan, people with an emphasis here are nurturing and even motherly. Above all, they are good listeners. They take in the emotional content of what other people are saying, and respond with penetrating insights about their situation. Like emotional midwives, they are ready to help others get through difficult transitions in their lives. They try to figure out what's hanging them up, and give them feedback on how to address the problem. They may even involve themselves personally, wading into nasty, complicated situations and attempting to resolve them.

Scorpio 2 individuals are capable of close, intimate relationships. They realize that relationships are never perfect—that one has to embrace the ugly as well as the beautiful, the painful as well as the pleasurable. Emotional intimacy inevitably reveals ugly things in one's partner's nature, and these too must be embraced and forgiven. In fact, it is exactly these weaknesses that are most in need of acceptance and most responsive to the healing power of love.

EXAMPLES

Antonin Artaud (Saturn. Playwright; founded the Theatre of Cruelty.)
Brendan Behan (Jupiter. Playwright—*The Hostage*; former IRA member.)
André Malraux (Sun, Mercury, North Node. French novelist—*Man's Fate*.)
Amy Tan (Mars. Asian-American novelist—*The Hundred Secret Senses, The Opposite of Fate*.)
Glenn Frey (Sun. Lead singer of the Eagles. Composed "Lyin' Eyes.")
Charles Bukowski (Mars. Boozy writer—*Barfly*.)
Henry Miller (Moon, Mars. Confessional, sexually explicit novelist—*Tropic of Cancer*.)
Céline (Uranus. Cynical novelist—*Death on the Installment Plan*; vitriolic anti-Semite.)
Rudolf Tomaschek (Venus, Saturn. Czech parapsychologist.)
André Gide (Mercury. Novelist and playwright, defender of homosexuality—*The Immoralist*.)
Arthur Rimbaud (Mercury. Influential French poet, shot by his lover, Verlaine.)
Sandra Bernhard (Saturn. Hip stand-up comic and actress—*The King of Comedy*.)
Martin Scorsese (Mercury, Mars. Influential filmmaker—*Mean Streets, The Last Temptation of Christ*.)

Liv Ullmann (North Node. Actress in Ingmar Bergman films—*Persona*, *Cries and Whispers*.)

John Cleese (Venus. Leader of the Monty Python comedy troupe.)

Harper Lee (Moon. Novelist—*To Kill a Mockingbird*.)

Robert Altman (Ascendant, Saturn. Film director and producer—*M*A*S*H*, *Nashville*.)

William Friedkin (Mars, Saturn. Directed *Cruising*, *The Exorcist*.)

Joni Mitchell (Sun, Mercury. Reflective folk singer—"A Case of You.")

Paul Simon (Mercury. Sensitive, reflective folk singer—"The Dangling Conversation.")

Stan Freberg (Saturn. Satirist, songwriter, award-winning adman.)

Salman Rushdie (Jupiter. Magical-realist author—*The Satanic Verses*.)

Joan Didion (Jupiter. Gritty journalistic writer—*Slouching towards Bethlehem*.)

Whoopi Goldberg (Moon. Comic actress—*Monkeybone*; former heroin addict.)

William Kunstler (Moon. Radical attorney; defended the Chicago Seven.)

Lenny Bruce (Saturn. Foul-mouthed stand-up comedian who challenged the censorship laws.)

Eldridge Cleaver (Mars, Jupiter. Cofounder of the Black Panthers.)

Jules Verne (Moon, Jupiter. Fantasy writer—*20,000 Leagues under the Sea*.)

Ken Kesey (Jupiter. Novelist—*One Flew Over the Cuckoo's Nest*; leader of the Merry Pranksters.)

Richard Krafft-Ebing (Jupiter. Psychiatrist specializing in sexual deviance—*Psychopathia Sexualis*.)

Roseanne (Sun. Confrontational TV comedienne—*Roseanne*.)

Caroline Knapp (Sun, Mars. Wrote *Drinking: A Love Story*.)

Irvine Welsh (Venus, North Node. Gritty writer—*Trainspotting*, *The Acid House*.)

Patrick Fugit (Jupiter. Actor—*Wristcutters*, *Almost Famous*.)

Premiere of Rachmaninoff's Second Piano Concerto (Sun, North Node. November 9, 1901. Passionate and fluid composition dedicated to his hypnotist, who helped him break through a creative block.)

Barry Gibb (Moon. Lead singer of the Bee Gees—"How Deep Is Your Love?")

Scorpio, 3rd Decan

IMAGE: *A wise elf stands guard by a square window. He asks a difficult question of a stranger, and satisfied with the answer, lets the man climb through the window. The man soon finds himself spinning down a dark tunnel into a strange new world.*

Evolved Scorpio 3 individuals realize that the numinous, magical realm is at hand—that the border between physical reality and the astral plane is an open door, if one only has the courage to step through it. People of this decan are often deeply interested in spiritual and metaphysical questions. They look into the nature of consciousness, magic, reincarnation, and the spiritual realm. They take these matters seriously, spend a lot of time thinking about them, and try to center their lives within the spiritual truths they discover. These metaphysical questions are not merely intellectual, for Scorpio 3 individuals are regularly ambushed by strange, occult experiences that offer clues to the hidden workings of the universe. Rather than writing off these peculiar experiences, they make them the cornerstones of a new systematization of knowledge. In this *reframing* of reality, occult intuition is their guide. They trust this intuitive gift because experience has proven, time and again, that it *can* be trusted.

Scorpio 3 individuals feel that answers to even the most esoteric questions are always available to them, if they can just center themselves and tune in. Often, they do this through a kind of inner dialogue—a question and answer session with themselves. They conduct this inner dialogue in a serious and honest manner, for they realize that any form of dishonesty could weaken their relationship with their higher self or "inner teacher." In the decan image, this inner teacher is symbolized by the wise elf. As a component of the psyche, this teacher is somewhat separate from the rest of the personality—a kind of daemon, who must be dealt with on its own terms, with reverence and respect.

In the decan symbol, the elf is initiating a man into a chaotic, unstructured realm beyond his normal reality framework. He is drawing the man into unfamiliar and possibly dangerous territory. As a creature from another realm, the taunting elf challenges the man's entire worldview. People of this decan, in similar fashion, challenge the smug views of the general public by attacking basic elements in their belief-systems. Most people never examine their underlying assumptions but inhabit a false reality full of absurdities and internal contradictions. Scorpio 3 individuals force them to face these inconsistencies—at times through gentle questioning, at times through trenchant attacks. In their more aggressive moods, they counter every attempt at evasion by forcing the discussion back to the main issue. Many people find this behavior rude. They may also be annoyed by the Scorpio's assumption that they have a more penetrating and sophisticated understanding than everyone else—that they are initiates of a higher plane.

Scorpio 3 individuals are given to impish mind games. Some are even rather demonic, for they may draw others into their psychic orbit not so much to enlighten them as to disorient them within a nightmarish fantasy world. To illustrate, the following people have planets here: Terry Gilliam (*Brazil*), Roger Corman (*The Pit and the Pendulum*), Alice Cooper (*Welcome to My Nightmare*), Timothy Leary, Federico Fellini (*The Satyricon*), and Patricia Arquette (*Medium*). These people seem to enjoy their status as figures of fear and consternation. Their very presence is disturbing, for they inhabit an alternate reality and are therefore constantly eroding other people's reality-conceptions.

In my book *Moon Phases*, the phase associated with the third decan of Scorpio is linked to the Falling Tower of the Tarot—also called the Lightning-Struck Tower. There is no building in my decan image for Scorpio 3, but as with some Tarot decks, we do see a man falling, with a consequent *loss of orientation*. People of this decan can be highly subversive, for they are undermining the dominant worldview, with the hope that its collapse will allow something new to be built in its place. These people consider the conventional reality-picture an oversimplified fiction. They realize that there are many dimensions to reality, and that some of these dimensions have been systematically excluded from the conventional worldview. They are especially interested in the spiritual, occult, metaphysical, and religious dimensions and want to bring them back into the picture.

Throughout their lives, people of this decan amass a great deal of arcane knowledge. However, on some level, they feel crucified by this knowledge, for once they *know* in the gnostic sense, they feel bound to stand within their truths, live them, defend them, and proselytize them. As "heretic priests," they are often just bearing witness. They are teaching and preaching in order to clarify their belief-system to themselves. By regularly reiterating their cardinal beliefs and framing assumptions, they reinforce them in their own minds. I am reminded of the Catholic practice of circling the interior of a church and meditating on the stations of the cross. This is a centering ritual aimed at connecting one to the Christian mysteries. Scorpio 3 individuals, similarly, want to make their unorthodox ideas clear and present to their inner vision. They want to create a clearly visualized interior space—a temple of organized beliefs—and take their place within it. To further reinforce these beliefs, they befriend individuals with similar views. They may even join organizations devoted to systems of belief compatible with their own. In collaboration with these groups, Scorpio 3 individuals may develop a coherent metaphysical system and may even begin preaching their beliefs. Unfortunately, these beliefs are often so eccentric and unorthodox that they gain little traction with the public.

While Scorpio 3 individuals may seem like subversives who want to undermine the basic assumptions of established religion or of the political system, they are actually very concerned with the well-being of society. They are trying to avert a catastrophe—a kind of Falling Tower—by putting society and religion on a more solid spiritual basis. They are stabilizing the system by aligning it with undying spiritual truths. These people understand the deeper roots of political laws and cultural usages. They understand which elements of society need to be protected, and which usages are merely ceremonial and can be allowed to crumble. They also know which social beliefs need to be actively pushed over.

People of this decan have a two-sided personality. One side is conversant in the ways of the world, and the other is focused on the deeper riddles of existence. These two sides of the personality work together surprisingly well. Usually, Scorpio 3 individuals make their way through life quite successfully. They function particularly well in organizations, for they are highly sensitive to group goals and can help organize the group around these goals. As for their offbeat ideas, their coworkers are generally willing to overlook them in light of their high standards of competence and reliability.

Scorpio 3 individuals are very dependable in their deeper relationships. They uphold the marriage vows and are honest and communicative. They are also very protective of their children, whose spiritual upbringing is of great concern to them. Because of their ability to explain even complex matters, they make good teachers. However, their tendency to force their opinions on their children may be met with resistance or even outright rebellion. In fact, children sometimes bring major problems into their lives.

The ancient Egyptians often placed Tawaret, the hippo goddess, in this position. Tawaret was a fierce protector of children, who knew how to bind evil forces through magic. Often, she is pictured holding a magic knife with a chain rising upward to Ursa Minor—which, in the Egyptian view, was a constellation associated with the evil god Set. Tawaret is therefore a goddess who knows how to bind and rein in evil forces.

EXAMPLES

Gary Ross (North Node; film director—*Pleasantville, Big.*)
Jake Gyllenhaal (Uranus. Actor—*Donnie Darko.*)
Werner Heisenberg (Mercury. Physicist—"Heisenberg uncertainty principle.")
Grace Slick (Ascendant, Mercury, Venus. Lead singer for the Jefferson Airplane.)
Terence McKenna (Sun, Venus. Ethnobotanist, specializing in psychedelics and especially magic mushrooms.)
Voltaire (Sun. Cultural and religious subversive; novelist and encyclopedist.)
Darren Aronofsky (Mars, Neptune. Filmmaker—*Pi, Black Swan, The Fountain.*)
Andy/Lilly Wachowski (Venus, Neptune. Cowriter and director of *The Matrix*; transsexual.)
John Belushi (Moon. Comic actor—*Animal House.*)
Ruth Gordon (Saturn, Uranus. Actress—*Harold and Maude.*)
Timothy Leary (Mercury, Venus. Acid guru.)
Alice Cooper (Chiron. Disturbing, surrealistic rock star—*Welcome to My Nightmare.*)
Mary Martin (Mercury, Venus. Singer, actress—*Peter Pan.*)
Whoopi Goldberg (Sun, Saturn. Comic actress—*Sister Act, Monkeybone.*)
Jean-François Revel (Mars. Philosopher—*Without Marx or Jesus.*)
Bertolt Brecht (Chiron. Playwright—*The Threepenny Opera.*)
Terry Gilliam (Sun. Animator, filmmaker—*Brazil, Time Bandits.*)
Antonietta Lilly (Mercury. Wrote on communication with dolphins.)
Federico Fellini (North Node. Surrealistic filmmaker—*Juliet of the Spirits.*)
Ricki Lake (Neptune. Actress—*Hairspray.*)
Ted Danson (Chiron. Actor—*Bored to Death*; environmental activist.)

Camille Paglia (Jupiter. Intellectual gadfly—*Sexual Personae*.)
Allen Ginsberg (Saturn. Gay beatnik poet—"Howl.")
Nicolaus Copernicus (North Node. Astronomer—attacked geocentrism and put forward a heliocentric theory of the universe.)
Gershom Sholem (Venus, Chiron. Academic historian of the Kabbalah.)
Michel Foucault (Saturn. Poststructuralist philosopher.)
Pablo Picasso (Mercury. "Deconstructionist" painter.)
Patricia Arquette (Neptune. Actress—*Medium*.)
Martin Luther (Sun. Leader of the Protestant Reformation.)
Meredith Monk (Sun, Mercury, Venus. Composer of Celtic-inspired music—*Dolmen Music*.)
Carlos Castañeda (Mars, Saturn. Occultist—stories of Mexican shamanism.)
Erich von Däniken (Jupiter. Sensationalistic writer on "ancient aliens.")
Frances Yates (Jupiter. Historian of Renaissance Hermeticism—*The Rosicrucian Enlightenment*.)
Ray Bradbury (Mars. Sci-fi writer.)
Donald Weems (Venus. Black Panther who escaped from prison twice.)
Bryan Fuller (Neptune. Television writer; created *Dead Like Me*, *Pushing Daisies*, *American Gods*.)

Sagittarius, 1st Decan

IMAGE: *Amid bright, waving pennants, a prince and his advisor sit astride their horses, looking out over the side of a cliff. After listening to his mentor's advice, the prince sets off for a university town, barely visible on the horizon.*

This is a Jupiter-ruled decan, associated with both teaching and learning. The prince in the decan image is keen on his upcoming life at the university, and open to the many possibilities that lie before him. His understanding of the world will expand considerably once he has left the provincial world of his birthplace and has begun to explore the wider world before him. The prince is probably more excited by the prospect of adventure and romance than by the formal education he is about to receive. He respects formal education as a way of developing the mind and realizes that he'll need a college degree if he is to take his place among the cultural and political elite of his country. However, he's also aware that the world itself can serve as a university, with lessons enough for those who have the humility to receive them.

Experiential knowledge is central to the Sagittarian approach to life. The first *degree* of Sagittarius—the keynote degree—is symbolized by war veterans about to embark on a new adventure. It pictures people whose brave approach to life has gained them many important experiences. Sagittarius has been associated, traditionally, with both religion and philosophy, and certainly Sagittarians are broad-minded thinkers. However, they are not particularly attracted to systems of thought or belief. The most overtly religious degree of Sagittarius is the last degree, symbolized in the Sabians by "the Pope holding audience." The last degree of a sign is associated with that sign's most decadent tendencies. Dogmatism, and especially religious dogmatism, is one of the chief dangers for Sagittarians. Mental growth depends on mental flexibility. When someone gets caught up in a rigid system of thought, their worldview quickly falls out of touch with the changing modern scene. It becomes irrelevant and even wrongheaded.

Sagittarians need to keep moving in life; they need the mental stimulation of new vistas, new adventures, new books, new people, new jobs, and new places. Getting overly settled—either physically or mentally—shuts these people down. Experience is their lifeblood, and without it, they can lose their zest for life. It's especially important for these people to maintain an active mental life. They should be on the lookout for exciting ideas and then *run* with them. These ideas may end up proving wrong, but when they do, they can just discard them and move on.

One of the main themes of this decan is intellectual and physical *maturation*. The prince of the decan image is barely out of childhood. He still doesn't know what he wants to accomplish in life. Like most young college students, he has not outgrown his desire for fun and games. However, he is already on the lookout for something he can believe in—some long-range goal that will give direction to his life. This is no sure thing. Because Sagittarius is a *mutable* sign, these people tend to scatter their energies. They can easily get caught up in the petty dramas of their immediate situation and lose sight of their higher goals. Moreover, if they run across an option that is more attractive than their present course of action (or just more fun), they may be tempted to "change horses in midstream." Sagittarians encounter many distractions on their path. They run into people who have plans for them—who want them as a follower, an ally, or a drinking partner. People of this decan need to avoid these people's agendas, games, and scams until they have found their own way in life.

Many of the degree symbols in this decan deal with games and sports, including soccer and surfing. In the decan symbol, this emphasis on sports can be seen in the accomplished horsemanship of the two principal figures. The old mentor is basically Chiron—the centaur or man-horse. As a figure who is half human and half animal, Chiron teaches us how to integrate the mind and the body, the animal instincts and the higher self.

The horse is a symbol of the physical body. Developing control over one's horse therefore symbolizes the development of physical agility and sexual self-confidence. The decan's relationship to physical activity is especially clear in the fourth degree, whose Sabian symbol is "a child taking its first steps." Toddlers learn to walk by instinct, and part of that instinct is a readiness to fall and pick themselves up again. People of this decan are very resilient. They aren't afraid of the occasional failure and are therefore willing to enter new activities as rank beginners. They realize that in any skill-based activity, practice makes perfect. The occasional failure is part of the game, and it matters little as long as one is advancing toward mastery.

The development of strength and coordination is an important part of this decan. People of this decan get a lot of pleasure out of energizing physical activities. The horse is one of the primary symbols of Sagittarius, and horses are animals that run with great speed and grace. Sagittarians, likewise, take great joy in physical movement—in athletics, in dance, in sexual activity.

This decan has a special relationship to the martial arts: archery and swordsmanship, but also the more spiritually oriented martial arts of Japan and China. In old pictures of Sagittarius, the centaur figure often holds a bow and arrow. Archery is, in fact, a Sagittarian sport. To become an expert archer, one must apprentice under a master archer and practice, practice, practice. Though this decan is associated with military arts, most of the people with an emphasis here have no connection to the military. They are generally not even particularly combative. However, like soldiers, both the men and women of this decan aspire to fearlessness in facing adversity, and competence in winning life's battles. They have a lot of body awareness, and with it, physical self-confidence.

Physical maturation is one aspect of this decan; spiritual maturation is another. When they're young, Sagittarius 1 individuals are not particularly goal oriented. Energetic and adventurous, they are constantly on the lookout for fun and excitement. Life, for them, seems something of a game, with its ups and downs, its wins and losses, but basically something that goes around in circles rather than actually getting anywhere. Looking upon life as a game is not a problem for a child but represents an overly cynical attitude in an adult. Moreover, it turns one into a spectator of life rather than a wholehearted participant. Sagittarians need to think about what they want to achieve in life and come up with a game plan to reach these goals. Luckily, they are well equipped for this task, for Jupiter gives them a very good *overview* of their situation. The prince of the decan image is poised atop a cliff. He has an elevated perspective on life and the world and can therefore map out a practical route to his long-range goals. His basic impulse is to speed off on his mission, like an arrow released from a bow. Yet he checks himself and confers with his mentor, much as a professional athlete will confer with a coach before jumping into action.

The formulation of goals and strategies is a skill ruled by the planet Mars. Curiously, all six decans of the Jupiterian signs of Sagittarius and Pisces exhibit Mars's analytical, strategic approach to life. It would seem that Jupiter and Mars naturally work together. In the Sagittarian decans, this Martian influence is particularly strong. Sagittarians exhibit all of Mars's strategic intelligence: its ability to focus on the game and to plan winning strategies. In the first decan, the native is trying to learn, through practice, how to use Jupiter and Mars in a controlled, mature way. In the case of Mars, this involves developing strategic thinking, while reining in lust and anger. In the case of Jupiter, it means thinking in terms of the big picture and coming up with relevant, meaningful goals.

In deciding upon a plan of action, people of this decan play the odds. It is impossible to predict the success of any projected course of action. Choices must consequently be based on an assessment of probabilities. From the outside, people of this decan may seem quite rash in their choices. But in their own minds they are fairly confident that they have "bet on the right horse." Sagittarians are analytical, but they are also keenly intuitive. They are aware of energy currents within the larger situation and recognize that if this energy is flowing, it has to be going somewhere. Following a path that is energizing is therefore bound to lead one to a worthwhile destination. People of this decan are always trying to find a "groove" that feels right—that feels like it is moving into a positive future. They may have a lot of rational arguments for these choices, but it is ultimately their intuition that tells them where to go.

Sagittarius 1 individuals want to lead lives that are meaningful—not just for themselves, but for their community and their nation. These people have strong beliefs about where society should be heading. They are well aware of competing social values and beliefs and are willing to defend and champion their own beliefs. The decan image, modified slightly, might show an army poised on a mountaintop. Flags are flying, and cavalrymen are gearing up for battle. Because people of this decan hold up their beliefs, like flags, for all to see, and because they are will- ing to fight for these beliefs, they often emerge as leaders within their group. They are effective in this role because they understand human psychology. They know what people can and can't do, and what they will and won't do. They are therefore able to sell their goals to the group and persuade them to help out.

On a purely personal level, these people are relaxed, warm, and charming. Outgoing and socially confident, they enjoy partying and other group activities. Many are witty conversationalists and accomplished storytellers. A number of writers and filmmakers have an emphasis here. These people tell stories about life and how to live it. Their lofty perspective is often humorous—rather like Jupiter looking down from Mount Olympus and commenting upon the silly dramas of humanity. Besides being good storytellers and good speakers, these people are also good listeners, responding intelligently and helpfully to other people's remarks. In relationships, they are generally honest and communicative. However, their powerful sex drive and their taste for excitement may lead them into promiscuous behavior, at least when they're young. Since people of this decan pursue very individualistic paths in life, they get along best with people who are willing to follow them or are at least going in the same direction. Thus, they often end up with mates who are "fellow travelers" with similar tastes, interests, and goals.

EXAMPLES

Winston Churchill (Sun. Prime minister, led Britain through WWII; wrote history books.)

Woody Allen (Sun, Mercury, Jupiter. Comedian and film director—*Sleeper*.)

Bill Maher (Mars, Saturn. Political humorist—*Politically Incorrect*.)

Amber Tamblyn (Jupiter conjunct Uranus. Actress—*Joan of Arcadia*.)

Jon Stewart (Sun, Mercury. Political humorist, commentator.)

Judd Apatow (Mercury. Director, screenwriter—*Knocked Up*, *The Forty-Year-Old Virgin*.)

Herbert Marcuse (Saturn. Political theorist; he argued that capitalism and technology result in sexual repression—*Eros and Civilization*.)

Giuseppe Garibaldi (Neptune, North Node. Italian general and patriot—helped free Italy from Austria.)

Trofim Lysenko (Saturn. Russian agronomist; argued for the inheritance of acquired characteristics.)

W. E. B. Du Bois (Saturn. Civil rights activist, cofounded the NAACP.)

Cesar Chavez (Saturn. Labor leader, organized farmworkers.)

George Patton (Mercury. General—tank warfare.)

Joan Baez (Mars. Folk singer and peace activist.)

Ernest Hemingway (Chiron, Uranus. Novelist, adventurer—*The Sun Also Rises*.)

Alexandra David-Néel (Saturn. Adventurer; first Western woman in Tibet.)

Claude Levi-Strauss (Sun. Social anthropologist, "structuralist.")

Charles de Gaulle (Mercury. French general, head of the Free French, longtime prime minister.)

Joseph Scheidler (Saturn. Antiabortion leader.)

Golda Meir (Uranus. Prime minister of Israel.)

Jimmy Cagney (Uranus. Actor specializing in gangster roles.)

Gary Ross (Saturn. Film director—*Pleasantville*.)

Franklin D. Roosevelt (North Node. President who led America through the Depression and World War II.)

Jane Fonda (North Node. Actress, antiwar activist—*The China Syndrome*, *9 to 5*.)

Dale Evans (Mercury. Swing singer, horsewoman, advocate for Down's syndrome children.)

Terence McKenna (Mercury, Mars. Writer on psychedelics, especially psilocybin.)

Petra Kelly (Sun, Jupiter. Cofounder of the Green Party, human rights activist.)

William Kunstler (North Node. Lawyer for political dissidents, including the Black Panthers, Lenny Bruce, and Abbie Hoffman.)

Stonewall Rebellion (Mars. Gays in raided nightclub fight police, initiating a new phase of the gay rights movement—June 28, 1969.)

Georgette Robinson (Sun. Belgian secret service agent who ran an escape route through France.)

Pete Seeger (North Node. Folk singer and activist for civil rights, disarmament, and the environment.)

Erich Maria Remarque (Saturn, Uranus. Writer—*All Quiet on the Western Front*.)

Dick Clark (Sun, Mercury, Mars. Host of *American Bandstand*. Desegregated the audience and hosted and promoted many important Black performers.)

Jim Breslin (Venus. Political columnist.)

Sagittarius, 2nd Decan

IMAGE: *At a noisy carnival, a man walks past a Ferris wheel, a lion tamer, and a row of slot machines. He stops to watch a beautiful blonde acrobat, suspended within a ring of fire and performing an acrobatic dance.*

Jupiter is the dominant planet of this decan, as it was for the first decan. In *Jupiter's Dance*, I argue that Jupiter is associated with dance. This became clear when I examined lists of people born with a stationary Jupiter. These include Rita Hayworth, Ginger Rogers, Chuck Berry, Tina Turner, Busby Berkeley, Jim Morrison, Mae West, and Rita Moreno. Jupiterians favor a sensual type of dance—a dance of pulsating rhythms and circular motions. This is not ballet. In fact, almost no famous ballet stars were born with stationary Jupiters.

In the decan image we see a woman performing an amazing acrobatic dance. The dancer can be seen as the god Shiva, dancing in a ring of fire. This is the dance of creation and destruction, which in this decan expresses itself chiefly in the replacement of one cultural form by another. Dance crazes come and go. The Charleston became a rage because it connected people to a vital new spirit. In time, this impulse burned itself out and was replaced by a new dance. The spirit of God touches down in different cultural forms and then moves on, leaving behind outdated movements that have lost their vital energy. As expressions of the imaginative play of God, cultural crazes are by nature ephemeral. They inspire genuine enthusiasm at first but eventually lose their luster and their fire.

Among the examples, we find many people who created innovative works of *popular* culture—works that served to invigorate the imaginative life of society. Examples include Charles Dickens, Walt Disney, Ed Sullivan, Judy Blume, Louis Armstrong, Dr. Ruth Westheimer, Johnny Carson, P. L. Travers, Steven Spielberg, Ray Bradbury, Burt Bacharach, Criswell, Fred Astaire, and Whoopi Goldberg. These people are outstanding entertainers but are often known less for their artistic skills than for the mesmerizing intensity of their vital energy. There is an unmistakable *magic* here. These people create their own myths, their own scenes, their own realities. They create visionary fantasies that are worked out in such detail that they are not just exciting and energizing, but hypnotically engrossing. Actors and performers of this decan excel in fantasy. Many of these fantasies are fairly ephemeral and, with time, lose their popular appeal. Others become cultural classics. The following people, for instance, have planets in this decan: Harpo Marx, Judy Garland, Stephen King, Bela Lugosi, Mozart, and Robert Louis Stevenson.

One of the main themes of this decan is *belief.* At a carnival, fairgoers frequent palm readers and stage magicians, temporarily suspending their disbelief so they can better enjoy the show. They may understand that a trick is involved, but for the time being let themselves believe that it's magic. Of course, belief itself *is* a kind of magic, for if one believes something fervently, that belief opens a lot of doors. If one can clearly visualize oneself doing something, one often finds that one *can* do it. Not surprisingly, we find many actors and performers with planets here, for people of this decan have the ability to inhabit a dream or illusion in a convincing way. If an actor fully believes in the persona they have created, they can play that role with conviction. They can inhabit the role so thoroughly that others believe it as well.

Sagittarius 2 individuals picture themselves as the heroes and heroines of their own personal dramas. Not content to settle for the energyless, conventional scripts that most people buy into, they look for a story they can fully believe in. They want to live passionately and wholeheartedly, for if life is a stage, our lives are meaningful to the degree that we take responsibility for creating our own defining roles. People of this decan are trying to find some role, some myth, some adventure that they can throw themselves into. They want to create an exciting myth about themselves and to discover, by acting out this myth, to what degree it is supported by reality. They understand that other people have their own myths and fantasies. And they can thoroughly enjoy other people's "acts," as long as these people are aware of what they're doing. But they have nothing but scorn for people who go through life playing out roles, games, and myths they had no part in creating.

Sagittarius 2 individuals have enough faith to fully inhabit their personal myths, but they also have a cynical side. They know that much of life, like a carnival, is a scam and a cheat. Moreover, once they've been taken in a few times by life's lamer "rides," they refuse to be taken in again. Thus, while this is a decan of belief, it is also a decan of cynicism and *disbelief*. People of this decan tend to be skeptical of the established myths of their nation. They question almost everything, from the political system, to religion, to cultural icons, to conventional codes of behavior. They are especially suspicious of "sacred cow" culture that has lost its spiritual vitality, for like travelers in a foreign country, they are quick to see when a myth has lost its energy and its cultural relevance.

As children, Sagittarius 2 individuals tend to see the divine in everything; their world is full of gods. But perhaps they believe in too much—Santa Claus and the Easter Bunny, for instance. After being disillusioned a number of times, they decide that conventional myths and conventional religion are for suckers. They come to regard much of life as a carnival—a rigged show that looks a lot better than it is. They may view high school, college, their job, the church, or the government as *rackets*, which take no account of their personal goals and treat them like marks, punters, and rubes.

Many sarcastic comedians have planets in this decan. They make fun of people's cluelessness, as well as the stupidities of society. Their humorous comments are meant to entertain, but they are also meant to kill off cultural usages that are already half dead. Behind this destructive impulse lies the conviction that old customs need to be destroyed in order to make room for vital new cultural impulses. People of this decan intuitively understand the cyclical nature of life—the inevitable sequence of new beginnings and new endings, of creation and destruction.

Sagittarius 2 individuals, by deflating some cultural tendencies and inflating others, act to refresh and invigorate the cultural landscape. They puncture myths and cultural usages that are empty or overblown, and they hype up and inflate the things they want to support. Like a carnival barker, or a chanting cheerleader, they add energy and enthusiasm to whatever scene or belief they are trying to promote.

Jupiterian consciousness alternates between passionate involvement and philosophical withdrawal, between fervent belief and cynical skepticism. As Jupiterians, people of this decan maintain an active balance between the passionate participant and the amused observer, dancing confidently between one and the other. An ongoing hunger for experience draws them outward, and the need for meaning and understanding draws them inward. The centrifugal force of the senses draws them outward toward the carnival of life, while their passionate need to *understand* draws them back toward their spiritual center. People of this decan alternate between belief and disbelief. They can be pantheists who accept the spiritual reality of many gods, but they can also be utter atheists. Shiva, the dancer of the decan symbol, changes forms constantly. Shiva is now masculine, now feminine, now creative, now destructive. It is a god that takes every possible form, including the gods of every nation: past, present, and future.

While Jupiter is the strongest influence in this decan, Chiron is also very strong. Like the centaur, people of this decan have a distinctly double nature: the human and the animal. Chiron bestows very powerful animal instincts. These people must therefore learn to resist temptation—especially sexual temptation. Austin Coppock calls this decan "The Bridle" and says that these people need to "keep the body and mind in line with intention, despite contrary forces."[54] People of this decan are easily bored and are often looking around for something to throw themselves into. There is consequently some danger that they will let their animal impulses run away with them. They may be tempted to immolate themselves in sensory experience, bingeing on sex, drugs, extreme sports, or some other path to ecstasy. The higher self must rein in these impulses, since to become a prisoner of one's desires is to live like a caged animal. Strong desires, like lions, are always dangerous and are made all the more dangerous by a world that offers every opportunity to indulge them. People of this decan need to rein in their impulses and also their thoughts, for if they can learn to bridle their thoughts, they will be able to fly, like Pegasus, on the wings of fantasy into visionary spaces. Bach, Beethoven, and Mozart all have planets in this decan. These composers have seemingly "unbridled" musical imaginations. Their creativity, however, rests on a foundation of tight mental self-discipline.

People of this decan are very savvy about human desire and may use this knowledge to their advantage. They are quick to identify what they have that other people want, and eager to develop and exploit these "golden" qualities. Often, they employ a certain amount of sexual seduction in their act, since sex interests pretty much everyone. But they also appeal to other human desires. Thus, in the decan image, there's the sexy dancer appealing to human lust, slot machines appealing to human greed, as well as rides where one can lose oneself and forget one's problems. Many astrologers see this decan as the ascendant of the

United States. This would certainly fit. We are a country whose most valued commodity is entertainment, particularly fantasy films. We are also a country of hustlers and hucksters, skeptics and dream merchants. We are the country of Disneyland, Hollywood, and Las Vegas.

As we see from the slot machines, people of this decan tend to be gamblers. They know how to *play* a situation, as well as how much *play* the situation has—how much they can get away with. When they get an impulse or an idea that gives them a lucky feeling, they go with it. By contrast, if an impulse *doesn't* feel right, they hold out for that "good groove" that smells of success. At best, these people are tuned in to the swaying rhythm of the universe. They are so centered and attuned that they meet the right people at the right time and arrive in new situations just as a window of opportunity is opening. They are great believers in divinely arranged synchronous events and try to learn from these events whatever they were meant to learn. Since they are playing the odds, they may occasionally be misled or taken in. But that is part of the game, and one gets good at a game only by playing it.

The ancient Egyptians often placed a lion here, or even the twin lions known as *Aker*. These two lions, illustrated above, show the sun as the vital present, framed by two lions representing the past and the future. The lintel under the sun represents the horizon. In ancient Egypt, the horizon was considered the border between the spirit world and the physical world. It was where the gods entered most easily into the affairs of the living, and where the future spilled over into the present. This brings up the decan's prophetic side. People of this decan have an excellent overview, which allows them to experience an unusually broad swath of time. Their consciousness of the present is fluidly connected to their awareness of the past and future, and this gives them a pretty good idea of what's coming next.

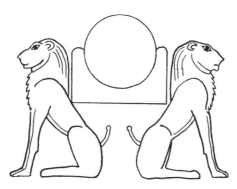

EXAMPLES

Walt Disney (Sun, Uranus. Cartoonist; created the Disneyland fantasy world.)

Larry Harvey (Jupiter. Founder of the Burning Man ephemeral-art festival.)

Harold Ramis (Mercury. Screenwriter for *Animal House*; directed *Groundhog Day*; actor and writer for *Ghostbusters*.)

Norman Lear (Mars. Producer of many TV shows, including *Maude* and *All in the Family*.)

Nathanael West (Mars. Novelist—*The Day of the Locust*—about the seamy underside of Hollywood.)

Drew Barrymore (Neptune. Actress, director—*Firestarter, Charlie's Angels*.)

Madonna (Saturn. Hyperenergetic singer, dancer.)

Robin and Maurice Gibb (Chiron. Musicians in the Bee Gees, who were at the center of the disco dance craze.)

Brenda Lee (Sun, Mars. Country singer—"Little Miss Dynamite.")

Ludwig von Beethoven (Moon. Visionary classical composer.)

Wolfgang Amadeus Mozart (Moon, Pluto. Classical composer.)

Johann Sebastian Bach (Mars. Innovative classical composer.)

Belinda Jo Carlisle (Saturn. Singer in the Go-Gos.)

Fred Astaire (Ascendant, Chiron. Singer, dancer in fantasy movies.)

Buddy Holly (Jupiter. Rockabilly pioneer.)

Neal Cassady (Moon. Beatnik; driver for the Merry Pranksters' psychedelic bus.)

Jack Nicholson (North Node. Actor—*Easy Rider, Carnal Knowledge*.)

Roseanne (Venus. Cynical comic actress—*Roseanne*.)

Frank Sinatra (Sun, Mercury. Singing idol, actor.)

Jim Morrison (Sun. Hedonistic lead singer of the Doors.)

Redd Foxx (Sun, Mercury. Vulgar Black stand-up comic, actor—*Sanford and Son*.)

Tom Lehrer (Saturn. Daring comic singer—"Poisoning Pigeons in the Park," "The Vatican Rag.")

Katherine Heigl (Mars, Neptune. Actress—*Roswell, 28 Dresses*.)

Jeff Bridges (Sun, Chiron. Actor—*The Big Lebowski*.)

Burt Bacharach (Saturn. Songwriter—"Alfie.")

Burt Reynolds (Jupiter. Actor—*Smokey and the Bandit*.)

Joseph Conrad (Sun, Mercury. Novelist—*Heart of Darkness*.)

Bob Crane (Saturn. Actor—*Hogan's Heroes*; sex addict.)

Frank Frazetta (Saturn. Famous illustrator of pulp science fiction.)

Gypsy Rose Lee (Mars. Striptease artist, comedienne.)

Maria Callas (Mercury. Tempestuous operatic diva.)

Marjoe Gortner (Venus. Youthful evangelist; played himself in *Marjoe*.)

Federico Fellini (Venus. Surrealistic filmmaker—*Juliet of the Spirits*.)

Sagittarius, 3rd Decan

IMAGE: *Sword in hand, St. George kneels over a bizarre dragon, whose gaping mouth pours out billows of smoke and flames.*

Sagittarius 3 individuals have strong beliefs, and the courage to live by them. Among the examples, we find many crusaders who grappled with *titanic* problems. Martin Luther King took on racial segregation and the powerful, ugly myths that support it. Max Theiler took on yellow fever. Mark Twain took on American religion. William F. Buckley took on liberal intellectuals. Vladimir Lenin took on capitalism, and the czar. Robert Welch, of the John Birch Society, took on the "Red Menace." Noam Chomsky took on the establishment press and the ruling-class myths it promotes. Among the examples, one also finds a number of people who opened up whole new fields of inquiry. Georges Cuvier invented modern paleontology. Max Weber established modern sociology. Frances Yates pioneered the study of Renaissance occultism. At least potentially, then, people of this decan are capable of great things.

Sagittarius 3 individuals are mentally ambitious. They want to see the big picture—and see it clearly. Like the dragon, with its gaping mouth, they want to get their teeth around the full measure of a problem. They know this won't be easy, since highly contested issues often include elements that are obscure or even purposely hidden. Getting a handle on these murky truths is difficult. People of this decan sometimes overreach themselves, extrapolating from insufficient evidence to create far-reaching theories that upon later examination appear utterly fantastic. I am reminded of the story of three blind men encountering an elephant; each describes the elephant as a different beast, because they confuse the part for the whole. In like manner, Sagittarius 3 individuals may uncover one part of a major problem and then exaggerate it in such a way that it falsifies their whole position. These people find it easy to recognize when there is something wrong with the conventional picture of reality. A few critical insights, however, are not enough to illuminate the whole picture. To fully grasp a problem, one needs to approach it from a number of angles and then consider which theory or theories have the most explanatory power.

People of this decan begin questioning things at an early age. They are skeptical of their parents' belief system and can often be found arguing over questions of religion, politics, or culture. Moreover, they argue like it matters, for they are intent on getting to the underlying truth of an issue. As children, they may begin by exposing failings in their parents' worldview, but with time they develop a belief system of their own. They come to know *what* they believe and *why* they believe it.

In analyzing major problems, these people must take the time to correctly identify their true nature; they must uncover the "head of the beast." Given their penetrating intelligence and sharp intuition, they are well suited to this task. They go after their quarry relentlessly, like a hunting dog that has caught the scent. Once they have intuitively sniffed out part of the problem, they "worry it" until they have gotten a better hold on it. Their instinct and intuition, which are essentially animal faculties, let them know when something "stinks"—when there is more to a situation than meets the eye. This helps them move straight to the heart of the problem.

In the decan image, smoke and flames encircle the dragon, making it hard to see. People of this decan may find it difficult to get their minds around a problem on account of its large scale, but they may also encounter purposeful obscuration, since evildoers often hide behind lies, exaggerations, and consciously constructed smokescreens. The power elite routinely wraps itself up in false mythologies in order to hide its true nature. Think, for instance, of John Wayne movies, which justify the slaughter of the Native population. These sorts of myths have to be exposed and directly attacked. Much as Perseus held up the head of Medusa, Sagittarius 3 individuals must hold up the ugly truth for all to see.

Sagittarius 3 individuals often picture themselves as fighters in a battle between good and evil. Unfortunately, this self-righteous stance does not guarantee the morality of their position. We find quite a number of violent fanatics with planets in this decan. Given their powerful imaginations, people of this decan can easily *project* qualities onto others that are largely products of their own minds. This is especially true of their enemies, whom they often picture as absolute monsters—dragons, in fact. Having failed to assess their opponents accurately, these people spew out the smoke of hatred and accusation. They bully their opponents intellectually and even physically, justifying their behavior on the grounds that it is "in service of the truth." One is reminded of the Crusaders, who served a noble cause but fell into cruel and barbaric behavior. Such moral failure, when it does occur, may arise from hasty, inaccurate interpretations but more commonly arises from an imbalance between the mind and the heart. In their examination of problematical people and institutions, these people need to discipline themselves to remain fair-minded. They shouldn't believe something just because they *want* it to be true.

Sagittarius 3 individuals are very attuned to the larger spiritual and mythic dimensions of their culture. They grasp what stage the global situation occupies in the evolutionary scheme, and may try to find some way that they can help—some way that they can effectively engage the larger problem. To this end, they seek some point of purchase that will allow them to effect major changes. Much as the Big Dipper, with its long handle, appears to stir the heavens, these people need to find some handle, some leverage point, that will allow them to affect the situation as a whole. A few will actually realize this goal. On a political or cultural level, they will become movers and shakers.

Jupiter rules circular motion, and in this decan Jupiter presides over cycles as fundamental as the changing of the seasons, and the changing of the astrological ages. Since the galactic center is around 27 Sagittarius, the decan is also associated with the slow rotation of the galaxy. Cycles of war and peace, of stability and turmoil, define the course of human history. These changes may be the result of foreordained cosmic cycles, but they can nonetheless be accelerated by human efforts—especially collective human efforts.

While this is often a decan of principled struggle and even violence, there is always a third position in any conflict—that of quiet withdrawal. As a planet, Jupiter is involved in both engagement and disengagement. This is already apparent in the previous two decans. In Sagittarius 2, there is a man walking through a carnival. He can choose to get involved in the various rides and games, or he can choose to walk on by. In Sagittarius 1, the prince pauses at the top of a cliff before setting off on a big adventure. Similarly, Sagittarius 3 individuals can choose to get involved in a cause, or to simply observe it from afar. In the decan image, behind St. George and the dragon, there is a peaceful cottage with smoke rising from its chimney. Many people with planets here choose to keep their distance from unprofitable battles. They recognize that they have neither the energy nor the will to take on the larger problems of existence. These people may also be skeptical of their own intellectual capacities. Is it possible to know reality in its broadest terms? Is it possible to pin reality down with nine-inch nails (or dragon's teeth)? Sagittarius 3 individuals may consider existence too huge and too mysterious to be grasped. It is not so much a dragon as a chimera—a fearful but ephemeral illusion. Rather than trying to make sense of what may be nonsense, they try to live life in accordance with their own preferred rhythm—their own inner song.

Sagittarius 3 is associated with Draco, a very large constellation that circles the North Pole. According to the ancient Egyptians, the circumpolar constellations were of evil influence. Generally, the Egyptians pictured the *first* decan of Sagittarius as Horus spearing the evil crocodile god. My own image for the *third* decan is similar, though the crocodile has been replaced by a dragon. This transposition is supported by the examples, but also by several Sabian symbols located in this decan. For instance, the Sabian symbol for 26 Sagittarius is "a flag-bearer in battle." Like St. George, this is a heroic figure attacking an enemy with a lance. The large Greco-Roman constellation of Hercules is also found in Sagittarius. Hercules is generally pictured as a kneeling figure, with one foot on the head of Draco, the dragon.

EXAMPLES

Stephen Crane (Mars. Novelist—*The Red Badge of Courage*.)
Friedrich Engels (Mercury, Uranus, Neptune. Communist theorist, analytical historian.)
Carl Sagan (Moon. Astronomer; advocate for science.)
Jane Fonda (Sun. Actress, antiwar activist.)
Silvia Baraldini (Moon. Black Panther.)
Al Gore (Jupiter. Politician, climate change activist—*An Inconvenient Truth*.)
Michel Onfray (Saturn. Philosopher promoting atheism.)
René Crevel (Saturn. Gay Dada playwright.)
Elvira (Chiron. Absurdist horror host, actress.)
Martin Luther King Jr. (Saturn. Civil rights activist, martyred.)
Ed Harris (Chiron. Actor—*The Truman Show*.)
Cameron Diaz (Jupiter. Comic actress—*Charlie's Angels*.)
Al Pacino (Moon. Actor—*Serpico*, *Cruising*.)

Abbie Hoffman (Jupiter, North Node. Yippie activist who used absurdism as a weapon.)

Kathy Bates (Jupiter. Actress—*Dolores Claiborne*.)

Peter Davis (North Node. Muckraking author—*The Selling of the Pentagon*.)

David Horowitz (Mercury. Conservative ideologue—*The Destructive Generation*.)

Robert Carradine (Mars. Actor—*Revenge of the Nerds*.)

Wilhelm Canaris (Mercury. German admiral, tried to kill Hitler.)

Rush Limbaugh (Chiron. Conservative commentator who paints false portraits of his enemies.)

William F. Buckley (Mercury. Conservative commentator—*The New Republic*.)

Maximilian Robespierre (Pluto. Fanatical leader in the French Revolution, guillotined.)

Hilaire Belloc (Saturn. Catholic historian and propagandist who attacked secularism, Protestantism, and the theory of evolution.)

Bette Midler (Mercury. Singer and comic actress.)

Billy Graham (Moon, Mars. Evangelist.)

George Washington (North Node. Leader of the American Revolution.)

Steven Spielberg (Sun. Filmmaker—*Schindler's List, Saving Private Ryan*.)

Janis Joplin (Mars. Hippie blues singer.)

Charles IX (Moon. French king, ordered a massacre of Protestants.)

Stewart Brand (Sun, Mercury. Futurist, created the *Whole Earth Catalogue*.)

Delio Cantimori (Uranus. Historian of heresy in early modern Europe.)

Bradley Manning (Sun, Mercury, Saturn, Uranus. Soldier who downloaded hundreds of classified documents for WikiLeaks; transsexual.)

Capricorn, 1st Decan

IMAGE: *A castle atop an isolated mountain peak, surrounded by a great wall. The king oversees the rebuilding of the wall, while in the valley below, the queen attends to the great mill, a dwarfish child playing by her side.*

The first decan of Capricorn makes for strong, practical people, intent on bettering their situations. Naturally ambitious, these people rise through the ranks of business or government by virtue of their problem-solving ability, their hard work, and their aptitude for office politics. Natural charisma also comes to their aid. These people emanate a natural authority that is not lost on others. Many have a commanding physical presence, and like a castle on a hilltop, are hard to ignore. Generally, the ambitions of these people run along traditional lines. They want a warm, orderly family, a beautiful home, meaningful work, and the respect of their family and their community. To get these things, they are willing to work very hard.

In the decan image, the mill can be taken as a symbol for any business or moneymaking enterprise. On a deeper level, however, the axle of the mill symbolizes *self-discipline*. Discipline is the central axle, or *backbone*, of all productive activity. It is the magic mill that grinds out all that one desires, for it is the linchpin of success in almost every sphere of activity. Because people of this decan are intelligent and disciplined, they are good at setting up and running businesses and organizations. They generally run a tight ship, demanding as much work from their employees as they demand from themselves. They fire people if they aren't carrying their weight, but they are also good at delegating authority. Practical and money minded, they keep a close eye on expenditures and profits and identify and address the most important obstacles standing in the way of their organization's success.

As Saturnians, Capricorn 1 individuals expect to encounter obstacles as a matter of course, yet they are confident that most problems can be solved, given enough thought and effort. These people are great problem-solvers. They can be as sure-footed as mountain goats, for they intuitively grasp the sequence of obstacles they must overcome in order to attain the summit of their ambition.

Occasionally, people of this decan get stuck somewhere along the line, not because they *can't* solve a problem, but because they refuse to address it. Capricorns are often rather pessimistic. In thinking over a complex project, they may imagine any number of steps where things could go wrong. In fact, unless they can come up with a plan that's practically foolproof, they may give up before they start. The king in the decan image is building a wall around his castle. This is a huge task, but nonetheless manageable if it is tackled one stone at a time. People of this decan need to divide major problems into a sequence of manageable tasks, since looking upon these tasks as gigantic or "mountainous" leads to depression and may cause them to give up.

Capricorn 1 individuals often see themselves as the most intelligent and practically-minded person in their group. Confident that they know what is best for the group, they do not hesitate to take over group projects, organizing and managing people according to their own understanding of the situation. Since this is often perceived as bossiness, it can be a source of resentment. However, people of this decan have a rather tough hide and don't take this to heart. They accept the fact that competing to win or to maintain a leadership position will involve a certain amount of unpleasantness. Not surprisingly, many forceful political leaders have planets in this decan, often of a conservative bent.

Capricorn 1 individuals want to rise in the social hierarchy but understand that any new social position comes both with new prerogatives and new responsibilities. The king and queen of the decan image may be "enthroned" in a high sociopolitical position, but they also have heavy responsibilities. The king is looking after the defenses of the castle, and the queen is looking after the financial well-being of the community. In *Moon Phases*, I called the first Capricorn moon phase "The Widowed Queen." Upon the death of a king, a queen is saddled with a heavy load of social and political duties. In a similar manner, Capricorn 1 individuals take on a great deal of responsibility in their workplaces and their homes. Bound by a sense of duty, especially to their families, they willingly accept conventional roles if they feel they are necessary to the well-being of the clan. They will become the ideal wife, the successful breadwinner, the brilliant child. They will forgo personal goals and ambitions in order to fulfill the needs of the collective. That said, these people want to be very clear about the limits of their responsibility. In the decan image, the king is strengthening the wall around his realm. He feels responsible only for those who live inside this wall. People living outside the wall he regards as irrelevant or as potential enemies. Capricorn 1 individuals are very tribal. They have a strong sense of loyalty to specific groups: to their family, first of all, but also to their nation.

People of this decan are used to running things their own way and are happiest when others acknowledge their authority. At home, they like to rule the roost. They see their home as their castle and have strict rules concerning behavior within the home. Often they assume the role of the *paterfamilias* or *materfamilias*. They preside over dinner-table discussions of family problems and suggest practical solutions. Since they are rather authoritarian, they expect their children to toe the line on a large number of issues. Predictably, their attempts to manage the lives of other people are often met by rebellion. This decan begins around Christmas, with all of its family politics and its expectations, disappointments, and fights. Grown children come back to find their parents still ordering them around. Parents discover that their child is dating someone they dislike. Capricorn 1 individuals must remember to put all this aside—to give other people some slack, and to give themselves some slack, as well. Life is not all work; it also involves relaxation and enjoyment. Capricorns must remember to get off the clock periodically and make time for the people and activities they love.

Capricorn 1 individuals have a strong sense of family. Even family relationships that are strained are very much on their minds. Still, they often avoid tackling family problems, since their own emotional insecurities make it difficult for them to address such volatile issues. They have no problem working for others or helping them with advice or advantageous introductions. But they don't seem to realize that what others really want from them are open expressions of acceptance and love—and they don't want to have to ask for it. One of the hardest lessons for Capricorn 1 individuals is learning how to let down their defenses long enough to really communicate—to let other people in.

People of this decan want to appear always strong, never weak. It's a tough world out there, and they want to be able to meet it with a kind of ruthless competence. Capricorn 1 individuals can be very armored on an emotional level. This allows them to operate well in unsupportive or hostile environments. This is a great advantage for businessmen or businesswomen working in competitive work environments, but it also helps in family situations fraught with hostility, guilt trips, or other forms of emotional manipulation. Capricorn 1 individuals wall these emotions out. They may feel loyalty and affection for the group but are nonetheless determined to maintain their independence and autonomy *within* the group, and that means knowing how to shut out unwelcome emotions.

This brings up a curious aspect of this decan. These people are naturally psychic. They tune in fairly easily to people's private thoughts, and they also pick up on the fears and desires of the general public. Often they are not too happy about this. It scares them, perhaps rightfully so. Thus, they tend to wall out their psychic perceptions. The Sabian symbols for this decan feature a fair amount of clairvoyance, magic, fatality, and synchronicity. Generally, Capricorn 1 individuals consider such matters distracting and unproductive, for life confronts us with enough problems without having to deal with questions for which there are no solid answers. Better to wall these things out of one's life and concentrate on the more practical demands of one's situation.

In the decan image we see a dwarfish child playing next to the queen. The child represents the Capricorn's fretful anxiety that things are not turning out as they should—that things are not progressing or are progressing in a deformed way. The dwarf may represent a component of their own personality that they aren't comfortable with. People of this decan may have sexual kinks or harbor negative emotions such as hate or fear. They may feel shame for having failed people in some way. Capricorn 1 individuals know their own strengths, but they also know their weaknesses. And they don't want these weaknesses to prevent them from reaching their goals. Optimally, these people take full responsibility for the development of their character. They make continual efforts to shore up their weaknesses and develop a reliably strong character. This is the most practical of tasks, for discipline and character are all that they will need to accomplish great things.

EXAMPLES

Walt Disney (Mars, Chiron. Built Disneyland, a huge moneymaking enterprise with a giant castle.)

Helena Rubinstein (Sun. Cosmetics entrepreneur—one of the world's richest women.)

Marlene Dietrich (Sun, Chiron. Actress—*Witness for the Prosecution.*)

Isambard Brunel (Jupiter, North Node. Engineering giant. Built the Great Western Railway, as well as many innovative steamships, bridges, and tunnels.)

Sir William Cecil (Pluto. Chief advisor to Elizabeth I, treasurer and secretary of state.)

Indira Gandhi (North Node. Prime minister of India who presided over a state of emergency, where for two years she ruled by decree.)

Curtis Sliwa (Moon. Crime fighter, founder of the Guardian Angels.)

Lorne Greene (Venus. Actor—*Bonanza, Battlestar Galactica.*)

Frances Galton (Uranus, Neptune. Anthropologist, head of the eugenics movement.)

Myrna Loy (Uranus. Actress—*Thin Man* series; Democratic activist.)

Humphrey Bogart (Sun, Mars. Actor—*Casablanca, To Have and Have Not.*)

Donald Regan (Venus. President of Merrill Lynch, Reagan White House chief of staff.)

Tycho Brahe (Sun, Mercury. Astronomical researcher, lived in a castle but was thrown out because he abused the local peasantry.)

Ross Perot (Saturn. Data-processing entrepreneur, independent candidate for president.)

Richard Nixon (Mercury, Jupiter. US president; paranoiac.)

Régine Zylberberg (Sun, Saturn. French singer and owner of nightclubs.)

Larry King (Mars. Talk-show host.)

Enrico Fermi (Jupiter. Developed first nuclear reactor, "architect of the atomic bomb.")

Al Gore (Moon. Senator, vice president; environmental activist.)

Mary Tyler Moore (Sun, Jupiter. Actress—*The Mary Tyler Moore Show.*)

William Harrah (Moon. Founder of Harrah's Hotel and casinos.)

Robert Schmidt (Sun. Astrologer—Project Hindsight.)

Richard Harris (Saturn. Played Dumbledore in the giant castle of Hogwarts.)

Maggie Smith (Sun, Mercury. Actress—*Macbeth, The Prime of Miss Jean Brodie,* Professor McGonagall in the Harry Potter films.)

Rush Limbaugh (Mercury. Reactionary political commentator.)

Ulysses S. Grant (Uranus, Neptune. Union general and US president; instituted Reconstruction; tried to end all slavery and guarantee Black citizenship.)

Maria Callas (Venus. Operatic diva.)

Robert Stack (Mercury. Actor—*The Untouchables, Unsolved Mysteries.*)

Margaret Mead (Chiron. Cultural anthropologist—*Coming of Age in Samoa.*)

Gustave Flaubert (Uranus, Neptune. Novelist—*Madame Bovary.*)

Maggie Kuhn (Uranus. Founder of the Gray Panthers.)

Ayn Rand (Uranus. Novelist who promoted a philosophy of selfishness— *Atlas Shrugged.*)

Robert Penn Warren (Uranus. Novelist who wrote *All the King's Men*—about Huey Long; also wrote *Who Speaks for the Negro?*)

Glenda Jackson (North Node. Actress—played Charlotte Corday in *Marat/
Sade*; elected to Parliament.)
Warren Burger (Uranus. Chief justice of the Supreme Court, supported
abortion rights and school desegregation.)
Annie Lennox (Sun, Mercury, North Node. Lead singer of the Eurhythmics.)

Capricorn, 2nd Decan

IMAGE: *Under a huge tree in the central square of an old-world town, a horned satyr suddenly appears, turning somersaults and dancing wildly. The townspeople give chase to the fleet-footed figure but succeed only in destroying a lot of property.*

People with planets here are rebelling against the sexual prudery and unimaginative thinking of conventional society. The strongest "planet" in this decan is Chiron. In my research, Chiron routinely figures as a satyr rather than a centaur, though both creatures, it should be noted, are half human and half animal. Chiron's main function is to integrate the mind and the body—human reason and animal instinct. This process begins with the establishment of a more natural, physical sense of identity. Generally, people of this decan begin life with the same repressions as everyone else. However, their robust animal nature eventually turns them against uptight social norms. They work to rid themselves of social and sexual repressions and become more natural, more integrated, and more sexually and physically self-confident.

Capricorn 2 individuals have a mischievous, disobedient nature. They regularly break the rules, not only because they don't feel any particular affinity with them, but because conventional rules are often at odds with nature. They feel a bit like primitive tribespeople, who are alienated from modern society and can't wait to take off their uncomfortable modern clothes. Shrugging off conventional codes of behavior, these people inspire others to reexamine traditional social rules. In the course of doing so, they act to destabilize society. Predictably, society's power elite look upon these people with skepticism and hostility. They try to marginalize them, and if that fails, may turn to open coercion. Capricorn 2 individuals are well aware of these repressive maneuvers and may expend a lot of energy dodging them.

People of this decan often express their social rebelliousness through humor. Some of the most famous people of this decan are comedians.

Playing the clown gives these people license to adopt an exaggerated antisocial persona. Like the king's dwarf of olden times, they feel entitled to flaunt the rules of polite society. To illustrate, the following mischievous, argumentative oddballs have planets here: Ben Stiller, Phyllis Diller, Jonathan Winters, Roseanne, Roberto Benigni, Woody Allen, Quentin Crisp, Carmen Miranda, Bob Denver, John Belushi, Soupy Sales, Laraine Newman, Dorothy Parker, RuPaul, Peter Sellers, and Danny DeVito. These people use humor to show up society's flaws, and especially the absurdity of unthinking conventional behavior. On some level they are saying, "Your so-called reality is made of cardboard. It isn't real."

Capricorn 2 individuals often have a social persona that is waggish, magical, and unexpected. They glory in their odd individuality, exaggerating their most striking personality traits until they have become almost cartoonlike. This rather artificial social persona gives them license to behave as they wish. I am reminded of Clark Kent donning his Superman outfit. The costume allows him to fully assume the role of Superman. Similarly, by adopting a persona as peculiar as, say, Dolly Parton or Marilyn Manson, people of this decan claim a great deal of psychological space, for even when they're not clowning, they are operating out of a system of rules that is entirely their own.[55]

While the basic impulse of these people is self-liberation, Capricorn 2 individuals are also breaking down repressive social rules for the benefit of the general population. These people can be profoundly subversive. They are enemies of the established order, which they see as a mazelike prison of social and political rules. In the decan image, the old-world town represents the old order—a world stuck in inherited traditions that haven't been examined for generations. Most people are caught up in this antiquated worldview and move through life as mechanically as wooden figures in a medieval clock. To wake these people up, Capricorn 2 individuals introduce foreign ideas and cultural forms that have no place in the conventional reality-conception. Often they champion some "shadowy" or hidden part of their identity. This might be a certain type of behavior (especially sexual behavior), but it could also be an unorthodox system of belief. By refusing to repress the socially illicit aspects of their personality, they force other people to examine their inherited assumptions. They puncture the old worldview, so that any false or incomplete systematization begins to fall apart. This, in turn, provides space for a new worldview to crystallize. Generally, they do this in a good-humored if pointed way. At times, however, they give vent to anarchic impulses, and even a bit of deviltry.[56] A satyr, after all, is basically a little devil.

To some degree, people of this decan are trying to *overturn* the established order. They are showing others that established morality and established belief can be utterly perverse—that bad people often end up running things, and good people often end up in jail. This theme of reversal can be seen in the ancient Roman festival of the Saturnalia— which took place when the sun was in Capricorn. This was a time of feasting, gambling, and sexual license, for in Roman times, Saturn was pictured not as the Grim Reaper, but as a god of agricultural fertility, wealth, and celebration. During the Saturnalia, men dressed as women and women as men, while patrician lords and ladies waited on their own slaves. In a medieval festival, derived from the Saturnalia, people even elected a "King of Misrule." This theme of reversal—of turning things upside down—is an important part of this decan and is represented, in the decan image, by the somersaults of the satyr. The Saturnalia was like a social safety valve, where antisocial impulses were given free rein. It also helped undermine rigidly conventional social forms that had outlived their usefulness.

Unlike people of the first decan, who may repress or dismiss their occult experiences, people of the second decan realize that paranormal events are among the most important elements missing from the conventional world picture. After all, such phenomena call into question the nature of time and causality, the primacy of matter over energy, and the existence of action at a distance. In my book *Moon Phases*, I called the phase associated with the second Capricorn decan "The Magic Realm." This is the realm of trolls, fairies, pixies, leprechauns, elves, satyrs, and goblins. People of this decan have an unlikely, magical quality to their personalities. Suspicious of the adult world from an early age, they refuse to accept the dull, distinctly *un*magical worldview of conventional society. They remain grounded in their subjective experience and never lose their childhood appreciation for the magic of nature, where every tree has an animating spirit, and every animal is a conscious being with whom one can communicate.

Capricorn 2 individuals are very open to life's mysteries—from ESP, to sexual polymorphism, to metaphysics, to the occult secrets of nature. Intellectually, they are highly analytical. They are constantly fitting together new pieces of the puzzle in order to come up with a more accurate world picture. Anomalies and incongruities are given special attention, since they reveal where the accepted worldview deviates from reality—where it has major *holes*. Much of reality is invisible to us. Human beings are blind to x-rays, UV light, and a host of other realities. Because these things are invisible, people act as if they aren't real, when they might, in fact, be central to what is actually going on.

Capricorn 2 individuals realize that they'll never fully understand the magical and invisible forces of nature, yet they refuse to consign these things to some convenient box. Instead, they try on various explanations for size to see how much explanatory power they have. On occasion, they adopt flaky theories that they must later reject, but even these false theories help free them from the imprisoning beliefs of bourgeois society. Capricorn 2 individuals refuse to let other people define their reality for them, but insist upon their right to inhabit whatever world seems real to *them*. Though on occasion they may play the fool, they are inwardly convinced that their feet are planted firmly on the ground. They may not understand the whole picture, but they have put together pieces of the puzzle about which most people are totally blind.

In some of the ancient Egyptian lists, this decan was ruled by Set, pictured as a rabbit. Set is a god of mischief, destabilization, and even evil. The rabbit is one of Set's more benign forms, but it is still a fearsome figure, more closely affiliated with the giant demonic rabbit in *Donnie Darko* than the White Rabbit of *Alice in Wonderland*. Note, however, that both of these rabbits led people into dangerous dimensional warps. They destabilized the world by introducing creatures and events that have no place in this world.

Perhaps a more fitting god would be ancient Egypt's Bes: the lion-faced dwarf. Bes is a mischief maker and a *clown*, a god of dance and celebration. Yet, he is also a master of magic. Bes was popular with the common people, since he could protect them from negative magic, both in their homes and in their dreams.[57] He was able to do this because, like the mischievous dwarves in *Time Bandits*, he was aware of dimensions of reality normally invisible to human perception.[58]

EXAMPLES

Woody Allen (North Node. Filmmaker—*Stardust Memories, Sleeper.*)

Michel Foucault (North Node. Destructive, poststructuralist philosopher.)

Umberto Eco (Sun. Novelist, semiotician—*Foucault's Pendulum.*)

Herbert Marcuse (North Node. Political theorist who argued that capitalism, materialism, entertainment culture, and modern technology were forms of social control—*One-Dimensional Man.*)

Dustin Hoffman (Ascendant, Jupiter. Oddball actor—*The Graduate, I Heart Huckabees.*)

John Kennedy Toole (Mercury. Author of *A Confederacy of Dunces.*)

Julianne Moore (Saturn. Anarchic actress—*Boogie Nights, Short Cuts.*)

Jonathan Winters (Jupiter. Crazed comic—*The Loved One.*)

Roseanne (Mars. Star of the feminist, stereotype-destroying sitcom *Roseanne.*)

Ben Stiller (Mars. Actor, director—*There's Something about Mary, Mystery Men.*)

George K. Miller (Uranus, Neptune. Outrageous YouTube comic, singer— "Filthy Frank.")

Lenny Bruce (Jupiter. Satirical stand-up comic, tried for obscenity.)

Jim Carrey (Mars. Crazed comedian—"Fire Marshal Bill.")

Kate McKinnon (Sun. *Saturday Night Live* comic.)

Abbie Hoffman (Venus. Antiwar activist, anarchist, cofounder of the Yippees.)

John Belushi (Venus, Jupiter. *Saturday Night Live* comic, *Animal House*; died of a drug overdose.)

Mel Blanc (Uranus. The voice of Bugs Bunny.)

Elvis Presley (Sun. "Elvis the Pelvis," overtly sexual rock singer— "Jailhouse Rock.")

Eric Hoffer (North Node. Sociological writer—*The True Believer*, which explained irrational mass movements such as Nazism.)

Colin Morgan (Sun. Star of *Merlin*, where he fights to legitimize sorcery.)

Anton LaVey (Saturn. Satanist leader.)

MacGregor Mathers (Sun, Chiron. Ceremonial magician—the Golden Dawn.)

Johnny Depp (Moon. Ultrahip actor—*Ed Wood*. Played the Mad Hatter in *Alice in Wonderland.*)

J. R. R. Tolkien (Sun. Fantasy novelist—*Lord of the Rings.*)

Daniel Radcliffe (Neptune. Star of the Harry Potter films.)

C. S. Lewis (North Node. Author of the Narnia books.)

Neil Gaiman (Saturn. Fantasy writer—*American Gods, Neverwhere.*)

Jean Genet (Mercury. Gay novelist—*Our Lady of the Flowers.*)

Frida Kahlo (Mars, Uranus. Mustachioed Mexican painter—religious themes.)

Oscar Wilde (Jupiter, Chiron. Playwright, poet, and wit—*The Importance of Being Earnest.*)

Hayao Miyazaki (Sun, Mercury. Filmmaker, animator—*Spirited Away.*)

Al Capp (Uranus, stationary. Cartoonist—*Li'l Abner.*)

John Malkovich (Chiron. Actor, director—*Being John Malkovich*.)

David Bowie (Sun, Mars. Androgynous rock star.)

Quentin Crisp (Uranus. Drag queen, novelist—*The Naked Civil Servant*.)

Elaine Pagels (Mars. Heretical historian of Christianity—*The Gnostic Gospels*, *The Origin of Satan*.)

Burt Reynolds (Venus, North Node. Actor—*Smokey and the Bandit*, *Boogie Nights*.)

Amy Heckerling (North Node. Directed *Fast Times at Ridgemont High*, with its antihero Spicoli.)

Toni Collette (North Node. Actress—*Mental*, *The Sixth Sense*.)

Arthur Rimbaud (Jupiter, Chiron. Libertine, protosurrealist poet.)

Laraine Newman (Chiron. Comedienne—*Saturday Night Live*.)

Peter Sellers (Jupiter. Eccentric actor—*Dr. Strangelove*, *The Magic Christian*.)

Jim Jarmusch (Chiron. Filmmaker—*Mystery Train*, *Only Lovers Left Alive*.)

Sam Phillips (Sun. Record producer who discovered "wild men" Elvis Presley, Jerry Lee Lewis, and Howlin' Wolf.)

Capricorn, 3rd Decan

IMAGE: *A man stands under a stone archway leading into a dark forest and wonders which of the many pathways he should take. A strange man appears and opens an illustrated, allegorical book. Pointing to one illustration with a slim wand, he indicates the correct path.*

People of this decan need to pause on the road of life and take stock of where they are and where they are going. They must prioritize their goals and reassess their strategy for reaching these goals. Only after they have decided on their primary goal in life can they make real progress, for they can then set aside subsidiary pursuits and go after their highest goal with energy, focus, and resolve. Should Capricorn 3 individuals fail to organize their lives around their overarching values and aims, they become confused and ineffective in the management of their affairs.

Capricorn 3 individuals are trying to find their *true path*, so they can fulfill their innate destiny. This is a tall order, for their lives are full of unexpected twists and turns that require a lot of choices. These people often feel uncertain about what they should do next. They don't think they have enough information, and they fear that it will prove difficult to retrace their steps should they choose the wrong path. Many paths in life are, in fact, dead ends; some are even dangerous. Capricorn 3 individuals would feel better if they could get a map of the terrain before setting out. Perhaps they need help. With luck, they may run into just the right person to give them counsel.

In the decan image, the traveler is receiving advice from a strange man with a magic book, which is also a kind of map. This is a guide or guru figure, who is operating on a higher level of consciousness and mental organization. He is basically a personification of the arch's keystone. Like the keystone, he is above the situation. He is not looking through a maze of trees but can see the whole forest as if from an aerial map. All relevant knowledge about the upcoming situation is laid out within his mind.

The guide represents the higher self of the individual, or perhaps some sage person that they meet on their travels. The guide may even represent God, as architect of the universe and overseer of human destiny. The guide has an overview not only of space, but of time. He can see the overall pattern of a person's destiny because he knows why he or she chose this particular incarnation in the first place. He knows why they decided to descend into the labyrinth of time and space. The wayfarer of the decan image, by contrast, is a bit lost. Having subscribed to an overly materialistic view of life, he assigns the highest reality to external circumstances and external events. He has forgotten how, before birth, he planned out this life with his spirit guides. He has forgotten how he entered into this dark, confusing dream, and doesn't know how to wake up.

The guide may know the way, but accessing his knowledge is not particularly easy. In fact, until one has passed certain moral tests, the guide may not even make an appearance. The guide can only point a person toward the path that he or she has chosen before birth—a path that renders service to the whole of humanity. If the individual is not ready to commit to this path, the guide remains hidden.[59] People who have not found their true path tend to feel inauthentic, confused, and unhappy. They can't understand why they're running into so many obstacles. People on their true path, by contrast, meet with few obstacles. Events that were mapped out with their spirit guide, before birth, fall into place as planned. Help also comes from above. Their guide may speak to them through other people—through some professor, spiritual teacher, or odd character they meet along the way.

The magical book in the decan image is first and foremost an illustrated story, and second, a kind of life map. People of this decan realize that life is composed of stories, made up in part by themselves, in part by society, and in part by a higher destiny. These stories are not simple, for beneath life's surface lies a complex tapestry of hidden influences, strange synchronicities, and unexpected encounters. Capricorn 3 individuals, at least subconsciously, are aware that the real world and the world of the imagination are not separate but interpenetrate—that there is a warp and woof to their life story that combines fact and imagination. They'd prefer it if life were simple and straightforward, but realize that it is fundamentally mysterious and can be represented just as accurately by an allegorical story as a factual description. Experientially, life's most important events are dramatic scenes of a powerfully symbolic nature, whose deepest meanings need to be unraveled through reflection. By studying these scenes, Capricorn 3 individuals can eventually figure out the overall patterns of their lives. By analyzing the interplay between destiny and willful choice, they begin to attain a clearer picture of their real *story*. This helps them identify false narratives and puts them in a better position to shape their story along positive lines.

Once people of this decan have figured out their own lives, they may take up the role of the wise teacher, for they can now look down upon life from a higher and more coherent perspective. As teachers, their chief challenge is to translate their higher understanding into terms that can be understood by less evolved minds. Often, they embed their life-wisdom in plays, novels, or films, since these artistic genres are well suited to the examination of life's deeper mysteries. Many thoughtful independent filmmakers have planets here, including Robert Altman (*Nashville, Shortcuts*), Peter Bogdanovich (*The Last Picture Show*), Woody Allen (*Annie Hall, Stardust Memories*), Rainer Fassbinder (*Ali: Fear Eats the Soul*), David Lynch (*Blue Velvet*), Jim Jarmusch (*Mystery Train*), Louis Malle (*Atlantic City*), and Federico Fellini (*8½, Amarcord*). Among the examples, one also finds a number of writers and philosophers who delve into the mysteries of life; for example, Umberto Eco, Tama Janowitz, John Milton, Robert Anton Wilson, Tennessee Williams, Jean Anouilh, Leo Tolstoy, Virginia Woolf, Paul Bowles, and William Styron.

The stories recounted by these authors often center on people who stand at a moral crossroads, where the wrong choice could lead to disaster. Often, their protagonists are morally adrift. They avoid grappling with their real problems because they aren't ready to make the decisions they need to make. The authors of these stories don't pretend that these choices are simple or clear cut. Nor do they pretend to have all the answers. Still, they provide an entry point into a conversation about the human condition and suggest a few promising lines of approach. They frame the problems of modern life in a new way and invite the reader to enter into the discussion.

The ancient Egyptians sometimes associated this decan with Thoth, pictured as an ibis-headed god, writing in a book with a stylus. This stylus can be seen as a magic wand, for Thoth is a god of magic—especially the magic of words. The words by which we make sense of our stories end up defining our lives, because whether we realize it or not, we create the dominant patterns of our lives by the way we picture our lives and the way we explain our lives to others. Until we take responsibility for this act of creative magic (and become one with the magic of Thoth),[60] we are essentially lost. We act as if we have no choice in the overall pattern of our life—as if we were pawns of fate—when it is actually our habits of thought that shape our destiny. A particularly useful practice for people of this decan is to keep a journal of their dreams and their daily experience. By committing their lives to written form, they can gain a little distance from their habits of thought and beliefs about reality.

EXAMPLES

Colin Wilson (Saturn. Metaphysical writer—*The Outsider*, *The Occult*.)

Jules Verne (Uranus. Futurist novelist—*20,000 Leagues under the Sea*.)

Gwyneth Paltrow (North Node. Actress—*Sliding Doors*.)

William Butler Yeats (Ascendant. Poet, magician.)

Thomas Burgoyne (Chiron. Occultist—*The Light of Egypt*.)

Jason Lotterhand (Mercury, Uranus. Onetime head of the B.O.T.A., with its emphasis on the deeper secrets of the Tarot.)

Susan Sarandon (Ascendant, Moon. Actress—*The Rocky Horror Picture Show*.)

Robert Anton Wilson (Sun, Saturn. Occultist, writer—*The Cosmic Trigger of the Illuminati*.)

Bo Gritz (Sun. Conspiracy theorist—UFOs, AIDS as a man-made disease.)

Patricia Neal (Sun. Actress—*The Day the Earth Stood Still*, *A Face in the Crowd*.)

David Lynch (Sun, Venus. Filmmaker—*Twin Peaks*, *Lost Highway*.)

Juliette Binoche (Moon. Actress—*Chocolat*.)

Woody Allen (Mars. Filmmaker—*Sleeper*, *Radio Days*.)

Elaine Pagels (Mercury. Historian of Christianity—*Adam, Eve, and the Serpent*.)

Jean Auel (Venus. Novelist—*Clan of the Cave Bear*.)

Robert Stack (Sun. Host of *Unsolved Mysteries*.)

Alan Vaughn (Mercury. Psychic; writes about precognition in *Patterns of Prophecy*.)

Marianne Williamson (Moon. *A Course in Miracles* teacher.)

Gustave Doré (Mercury, Neptune. Illustrated Dante's *Divine Comedy*, including the *Inferno*.)

Umberto Eco (Mars, Saturn. Semiotician, novelist—*The Name of the Rose*.)

Margaret Lockwood (North Node. Actress—*The Lady Vanishes*, where she must break free from a false narrative.)

Nicolas Cage (Mars. Actor—*National Treasure, Peggy Sue Got Married*.)

George Orwell (Chiron. Author of *1984*.)

H. G. Wells (Jupiter. Fantasy novelist—*The Time Machine, The Island of Dr. Moreau*.)

Dolores Cannon (Saturn. Hypnotherapist, past-life regressions.)

James Mason (Uranus. Actor—*20,000 Leagues under the Sea, Journey to the Center of the Earth*.)

Doug McClure (North Node. Actor—*At the Earth's Core, The Land That Time Forgot*.)

L. Ron Hubbard (Mars, Uranus. Sci-fi writer, founder of Scientology.)

Thomas H. Dyer (Saturn. Cryptographer who broke Japanese naval codes during WWII.)

Mortimer Adler (Saturn. Educator who created the Great Books program with Robert Hutchins; convert to Catholicism.)

Robert van Gulik (Uranus. Dutch diplomat to China and Japan; wrote the intricate Judge Dee mysteries.)

Bruno Ganz (Mars. Swiss actor—*Wings of Desire*.)

Richard Elfman (Jupiter. Rock musician—Oingo Boingo; directed *Forbidden Zone*, about a surrealistic trip to the underworld.)

Drew Barrymore (Mars. Actress—*Altered States, 50 First Dates, Donnie Darko, E.T., Doppelganger*.)

Gérard Depardieu (Mars. Actor—*The Return of Martin Guerre*.)

Peter Jackson (Jupiter, Saturn. Filmmaker—*Lord of the Rings*.)

Aquarius, 1st Decan

IMAGE: *The Pied Piper follows a zigzag course up a mountain path. He has a knapsack on his back and carries a single feather in his hand. Ahead of him, an eagle soars toward a distant waterfall, high on the mountain.*

People of this decan are pioneers, eager to pull up stakes and follow their intuitive promptings wherever they may lead. They follow a unique path—a path that others may consider strange and even foolish. On an intuitive level, they are certain that this path leads somewhere—that it is a door leading into the future and onto a higher plane of consciousness. Trusting themselves to Nature and to God, they abandon the safeties of bourgeois existence to explore the outer boundaries of human potential. Occasionally they lose their way, but they're not too concerned, for they trust the cosmos to redirect them, through signs and signals, back to the right path. They have faith that they are protected—that they will be taken where they need to go, and meet the people they are supposed to meet.

The Tarot card associated with this decan is the Fool. In the Rider-Waite Tarot, the Fool walks along a mountain path, looking up at the sky rather than at the chasm that lies before him. He is a fool on account of his humorous perspective and his unconventional behavior. But he is also a fool because of his cavalier attitude toward practical, earthly realities—toward money, possessions, and personal safety. Instead, he follows the winds of inspiration wherever they lead. The single feather that he carries represents knowledge from a higher level of consciousness. It is just one feather and not a set of eagle's wings, but it reminds him that at some point he will be able to fly—to soar to a higher, freer state of consciousness. Since this upward path begins with a single feather, he needs to honor this gift and follow it wherever it leads.

Aquarius 1 individuals are aware of just how little we really know. They have little faith in the conventional reality picture, which they look upon as a convenient fiction that, far from being coherent, is actually full of holes. Aquarians consider it foolish to believe that the basics of reality have been nailed down, when beliefs vary so widely among the earth's populations. Thus, they are willing to explore possibilities that others consider utterly impossible. Sometimes the naysayers are right. Sometimes Aquarian ideals *are* impossible. But on occasion, the Pied Piper will prove everyone wrong. He will walk through a door in the side of the mountain—a door that other people can't even see. Aquarius 1 individuals have a lot of spiritual intuition. They can intuitively sniff out when a path exists that can get them to their goal. And as curious people, they are willing to travel this rocky path, just to see where it leads.

When they're young, people of this decan are unsure of their goals. They are uncertain about where they want to end up, much less how to get there. Yet, even at this early age, they have their antennae out. They already feel the magnetic pull of realizable ideals, waiting somewhere in the future. They are already turning toward distant truths, glimmering beyond the horizon.

Aquarius 1 individuals do not travel a straight path through life but zigzag through a number of intermediate living places and professions. At each stage, they learn something new, then move on. To preserve their mobility, they travel light. Thus, in the decan image, the Pied Piper carries only a small bundle of worldly possessions. Freedom is very important to these people, and as Janis Joplin sang, "Freedom's just another word for nothin' left to lose." Aquarius 1 individuals realize that they can't wait for the government to free them; they have to free themselves. An important part of this process is wrenching themselves away from situations that have gotten stuck. People of this decan don't want to get stuck in bad relationships, bad towns, bad countries, bad philosophies, or bad attitudes. They understand that one actually *can* walk away from a lot of one's problems. By detaching oneself from a situation, mentally and emotionally, one gains the freedom to move on.

People of this decan look around them and see a lot of folks who are stuck—who are frozen in situations that are going nowhere. Aquarius is a cold sign, associated with midwinter, when streams have iced over and may not thaw until spring. When people of this decan feel stifled or stuck, they may abandon their possessions and commitments. They may end a relationship they've outgrown. They may move to another country. Aquarius 1 individuals have many potential selves. They must follow that component of the self that leads into the future, and leave behind the selves they have outgrown.

Aquarius 1 individuals are able to handle big changes, but they too can get stuck. Curiously, when they fail to leave a situation that they really *should* leave, fate often steps in with some unforeseen disaster. Their house may burn down; their spouse may die; they may lose their job. They are then forced to move on, into some unfamiliar new stage of life.

People of this decan often develop a rather detached attitude toward their birth family. Family members conceive of them in a rigid way, making it difficult for them to change and evolve. Anything they do, try, or espouse is met with criticism. As children, they are often pegged as oddballs and may react by trying to conform. Usually, this doesn't work, since their friends tend to be other rebels and oddballs. Through these friendships, and through their droll insights into the stupidities of human behavior, they learn to tune out the criticisms of their classmates and their family. They grow deaf to social criticism and in the process become free agents—free to think what they want, do what they want, go where they want.

As youngsters, Aquarius 1 individuals will often experiment with different looks. They may adopt a goth look or a nerd look. They may make up their own look. The message behind these external transformations is "Don't box me in." People of this decan are aware that outward social conformity makes it difficult for one to change one's mindset. In the 1960s, young men were making an important statement by letting their hair grow. Long hair told people, "I'm not bound by your rules anymore." It was not just a matter of the going fashion but facilitated internal changes of consciousness. Social personas can certainly help people fit into a particular scene, but once they have outgrown that scene, they need to put on a new set of "social clothes."

The antenna-like Uranus is very strong in this decan. People of this decan are tuned in to a new and different vibration and operate on a different wavelength than most of their peers. Since they tend to view modern society as a corrupt interlocking system, they will often set off to find a group of people tuned in to the same vibration and committed to the same social and political ideals. My own symbol for the first *degree* of Aquarius has a pioneer schoolteacher ringing a bell to summon the children to class. The bell puts out a new sound—a vibration that only a select few can hear. Once Aquarius 1 individuals have become aware of this high-frequency "buzz," they may drop everything and set out to find out what it's all about.

Aquarians are social idealists. They have a vision of the future, and a stubborn determination to materialize this vision. They realize that humanity cannot evolve *as a whole* if society has a leaky bottom—if a segment of the population is poor, is unsafe, has no political voice, and has no access to education. Any idealistic restructuring of society must address these root needs; otherwise nothing will really change. The first, or keynote, degree of Aquarius pictures a schoolhouse in a pioneer community. Utopian pioneers have to think about all the basics that make up a viable society. Where are they going to get water, food, money? How are they going to make group decisions? How are they going to educate their children? Creating an alternative community takes a lot of analysis and planning. It is a kind of Freemasonry, where abstract political models are translated into concrete social structures.

Though people of this decan generally follow their own eccentric paths in life, some end up as leaders. Through their galvanizing presence and the freedom of their being, they show others a new way of living. They become exemplars of the ideal citizen of a city of the future. Aquarius 1 individuals recognize the barriers that are keeping society from evolving. Their chief goal is to penetrate these barriers in order to facilitate their own evolution. However, in the process, they are blazing a trail that others may follow; they are building a makeshift bridge into the future. Some take this task very seriously. They see themselves as social engineers who are leading others into a clearly visualized future. They put together a plan—sometimes a detailed plan and sometimes a rough sketch—and then sell this plan to the public. Admittedly, a lot of Aquarius 1 individuals are considerably less purposive. There are wanderers here, and even drifters—people who allow themselves to be blown aimlessly through life, without ever committing themselves to anything.

In ancient Egypt, this decan often shows a group of shackled enemies of the state, about to be beheaded. Egypt's rigid, orthodox society did not tolerate antiestablishment rebels and nonconformists. Such people were considered enemies of the established order, and by extension, enemies of the pharaoh and the gods. Modern democracies are obviously much closer to the truths of Aquarius than the theocracies of the ancient world. Perhaps Maat would be a better fit for this decan. Maat is the goddess of truth and consort to the god Thoth, who appears in the previous decan. Maat represents truth, order, straightness, and correct foundation.[61] She is often depicted with wings and wears a headdress crowned by a single feather.

EXAMPLES

Ellen Burstyn (Saturn. Actress—*Alice Doesn't Live Here Anymore*.)

Jean Auel (Mercury. Author of *Clan of the Cave Bear*.)

Bill Nighy (Venus, Jupiter. Actor—*Pirate Radio*, *Still Crazy*.)

Bridget Fonda (Sun. Actress—*Rough Magic*.)

Steve Gaskin (North Node. Hippie guru.)

John Irving (Venus. Novelist—*The World According to Garp*.)

Rainn Wilson (Sun, Venus. Actor—*The Last Mimzy*, *The Rocker*.)

Lord Baden-Powell (Mercury. Founder of the Boy Scouts and Girl Guides.)

Artur Axmann (Uranus. Head of Hitler Youth.)

Bob Denver (Venus, North Node. Actor—*Gilligan's Island*, *The Many Loves of Dobie Gillis*, as Dobie's beatnik pal, "Maynard G. Krebs.")

Benjamin Spock (Saturn. Pediatrician who promoted a more flexible and affectionate style of childrearing; antiwar activist.)

Eugene McCarthy (North Node. US senator; ran for president on an antiwar ticket, with a following of eager college students.)

Christina Applegate (North Node. Comic actress—*Grand Theft Parsons*, *Don't Tell Mom the Babysitter's Dead*.)

Simon Pegg (Mercury. Comic actor—*Paul*, *The World's End*.)

John Steinbeck (Jupiter. Novelist—*The Grapes of Wrath*—which portrays a family of impoverished Okies on a trek to California.)

Emilie de Ravin (Venus. Actress—*Roswell*, *Lost*.)

Ellen Degeneres (Sun, Venus. Television comic who came out as a lesbian.)

Zoé Oldenbourg (North Node. Historian of the Cathar heresy.)

J. D. Salinger (Mars. Writer—*Catcher in the Rye*.)

Woody Harrelson (Jupiter. Actor—*Zombieland, Natural Born Killers*)

Charles Manson (Moon, North Node. Violent cult leader.)

Neal Cassady (Jupiter. Beatnik writer, car thief.)

Abba Silver (Sun. American rabbi; Zionist leader.)

Stephen Chbosky (Sun, Venus. Novelist, film director—*The Perks of Being a Wallflower*—with its gang of damaged misfits healing each others' lives.)

Caroline Myss (Mars. Medical intuitive.)

Jonas Salk (Uranus. Developed an early polio vaccine.)

Claude Steiner (North Node. Author of *Scripts People Live*.)

Raymond Buckland (North Node. Warlock; wrote a self-study course in Wiccan magic.)

Oprah Winfrey (Sun, Venus. Actress, talk-show host, promoter of New Age alternative therapies.)

Ralph Ellison (Mars, Uranus. Black writer—*Invisible Man*.)

Robert Stack (Venus. Actor—*Unsolved Mysteries*.)

Robert Anton Wilson (Mars. Author of *The Illuminatus! Trilogy*)

First successful airplane flight at Kitty Hawk (Mars. December 17, 1903.)

Eudora Welty (Mars. Writer, poet—*The Golden Apples*.)

Billy Tipton (Uranus. Female jazz musician who hid her sex and lived as a man and even raised children with another woman.)

Gay Talese (Mercury. Sociological writer—*Thy Neighbor's Wife*.)

Nick Mason (Sun. Drummer and founding member of Pink Floyd: "Set the Controls for the Heart of the Sun.")

Aquarius, 2nd Decan

IMAGE: *A puppeteer presents an allegorical puppet show from within a wooden booth. Customers line up to watch the show through a peephole. Within, they see a walled pond, under the stars, with a heron standing over a large egg.*

Aquarius 2 individuals realize that most people are not awake to their situation but are sleepwalking within a collective fantasy. The general population willingly inhabits this shared fantasy because it is coherent, manageable, and gives them a sense of belonging. Unfortunately, once they have accepted this conventional reality-conception, it becomes hard for them to escape, for they automatically rationalize away any incongruous event that doesn't fit the picture. They begin to believe that the mental walls that they have built are solid, and lose track of the fact that they are only mental constructs and are actually full of holes.

Aquarius 2 individuals refuse to commit to the conventional reality-picture because they realize that it doesn't "hold water." Their own view of reality is a lot more open-ended. They understand that there are a lot of things going on behind life's facade, including invisible and occult influences as well as powerful individuals pulling the strings from behind the scenes. They recognize that they themselves don't have the whole picture—that their ideas about reality are patchy. Positively, this motivates them to figure out *what is really going on.* Negatively, they are so unsure of their own views that they defer to the conventional worldview. They act as if this worldview were true, even if they privately suspect it is nothing more than a convenient fiction.

People of this decan recognize the difficulties of putting together an accurate internal model of reality. They are therefore not hurried in their thinking but wait patiently as new pieces of the puzzle take their place within a slowly coalescing analysis. Like the gestation of a fetal bird within an egg, this is a natural process that cannot be rushed. The new world picture must mature in its own time, even as the lens of a fetal eye is slow to coalesce and clarify. Confused ideas and images may prevail until an illuminating insight, from a higher plane, reveals a more coherent and organized way of perceiving reality. Eventually, a new vision is born, and the remaining falsehoods of the old worldview fall away, even as bits of eggshell fall away when a hatchling breaks out of its enclosing shell. Once these people have been born into this new and more focused vision of reality, they must summon the courage to live within it, however much it conflicts with the reality-conception of those around them.

While Aquarius 2 individuals know that they are still confused, at least they're not sleepwalking within some collective fantasy. They are very *interested* in the dreams and imaginings of the collective and enjoy analyzing their symbolic content. But they have no intrinsic loyalty to this shared mythology. People of this decan are like anthropologists in a foreign country. They enjoy studying the belief-systems of foreign peoples, including their dreams and guiding myths. They may consider some of these myths stupid and even destructive. They may therefore try to actively debunk these myths—to convince people that these myths are just fantasies. While we find some aggressive debunkers here, others address the problem more artfully, transforming the mythic landscape by creating subtly subversive art or films.

Modern astrologers never mention Uranus's involvement in the construction and deconstruction of myths and stories. They picture Uranus as an extremely *rational* planet, associated with science, math, and astronomy. And while they regularly associate Uranus with astrology, the central place of myth and symbol in astrology is generally attributed not to Uranus but to Neptune. This is an error. Uranus, as the "awakener," is necessarily involved in the false ideas, myths, and fantasies from which the population needs to be awakened. It can awaken people only by involving itself in the dreams that people are unconsciously inhabiting. The whole sign of Aquarius is misinterpreted along similar lines, for it is generally depicted as far more rational than it really is. Aquarius does, in fact, have a natural connection to science. However, it is also associated with astral imagery and the world of dreams.

Many important film directors have planets in this decan. And these are people who are definitely working on the astral plane. Included are Sergei Eisenstein (*Battleship Potemkin*), George Romero (*Night of the Living Dead*), Robert Altman (*Short Cuts*), Tim Burton (*Miss Peregrine's*

Home for Peculiar Children), Alejandro Jodorowsky (*The Holy Mountain*), Roman Polanski (*Rosemary's Baby*), Robert Kelly (*Donnie Darko*), D. W. Griffith (*Intolerance*), Steven Soderbergh (*Sex, Lies, and Videotape*), Florian von Donnersmarck (*The Lives of Others*), Robert Wise (*The Day the Earth Stood Still*), Sidney Pollack (*They Shoot Horses, Don't They?*), François Truffaut (*Shoot the Piano Player*), and Jim Jarmusch (*Mystery Train*). These directors often employ surrealistic or dreamlike elements in their movies, and through them, try to actively manipulate archetypes within the collective mind. One might compare them to the puppet master of the decan image, in that they are pulling strings from behind the scenes. Though their curious takes on reality are often just meant to entertain, they nonetheless remind people of the fluid nature of reality. They encourage people to create their own stories and awaken from the lockstep myths of the dominant culture.

Film directors do most of their work in complete isolation. Long before they begin filming, they come up with a story by allowing images to slowly gestate within their imaginations. They develop various themes and link them together, not through intellectual analysis but through imagistic dream-logic. Opening themselves to whatever images come to them, they trust that these images will be relevant to the current human situation, even as one's dreams always offer important insights into one's waking life. These filmmakers do not pretend to explain the world through their films. Reality is far too mysterious for that. Rather, they offer up visions of life that, while surreal, reveal hidden truths about the current situation. One might say that they are *dreaming* for the collective. They are fertilizing the group mind with new ideas and images channeled from the divine Overmind, as it makes itself known through their subconscious minds. They may even be presenting the public with a peek into the future—into what is yet unborn, or "in ovo."

Curiously, a number of Aquarius 2 individuals have had important symbolic roles thrust upon them by fate. They have become dominant characters within the collective imagination. Ed Sullivan, for instance, hosted the Beatles and Elvis Presley, even though he was no real fan of rock and roll. Lester Maddox, a mere restaurant owner, became the figurehead of diehard southern segregationism. Marion Anderson, by singing at the Met, became a national symbol of racial integration. Lance Armstrong, through his personal victories, became first an archetype of heroic courage and then an archetype of shameless cheating. Winona

Ryder became the voice of teen alienation. Shirley MacLaine became a spokesperson for New Age ideas. Aquarius 2 individuals have important messages to share, yet it is often *fate* that determines the message they promote, and even the form this message will take.

While the filmmakers of this decan are trying to give birth to a new vision of reality, one also finds comics and satirists, who are criticizing the ridiculous ideas and behaviors of the masses. Aquarians of this decan are very perceptive individuals. They see things that others miss, as well as things they would rather not see. They hold up a distorted mirror to human behavior and show how stupid much of it is—how brainless, robotic, "marionette-like." Through mischievous but pointed humor, they attack key assumptions in people's cloistered worldviews. They toss in weird observations that penetrate people's mental armor and call into question their entire perspective.

In the decan symbol, customers press their eyes against a peephole in order to see a puppet show. This tells us that Mercury is strong here, for Mercury is closely associated with the lens of the eye. In this decan, the Mercurial focus is not on the external world, but on one's internal assumptions about reality. People of this decan have an unusual lens—an unusual way of seeing things—that they are constantly trying to share with the public. The retina of the eye is also important here, since it is essentially a mirror that receives a reversed image of external reality, broken up into pixel-like dots that are sent to the brain to be interpreted. People of this decan recognize that we don't actually live in the external, physical world. We live, rather, within an interpretive *image* of the world, envisioned within our brains. We live in an imagined worldview rather than in the physical world. This realization allows these people to separate themselves from the imposed, conventional worldview, and to create a much more interesting and individualistic world picture. I am reminded of *The Lego Movie*, where the reality-building magicians have all been imprisoned, while the corporate ruling class attempts to glue down a single vision of reality and force the enslaved population to live within it. Aquarius 2 individuals are like magicians and conjurors in that they are creating strange, alternative worlds and inviting others to "take a peek." They have important points to make—points that are relevant to the current cultural and political situation. Working their quiet magic, they toss new ideas into the pond of the collective mind, in the hope that they will create interesting ripples.

Aquarius 2 individuals are often torn between the demands of their own spiritual development and their sense of duty to the rest of humanity. Generally, they opt for a highly private existence, where they can meditate on their experience without a lot of distractions. These people realize that we live in a world that we construct for ourselves—that one's real home is the *mind* and the kinds of things that are in it. For this reason, they consider a peaceful, sane state of mind the most valuable thing there is. To achieve this, they may withdraw to a rural home where their minds can become as still as a sheltered pool. In this peaceful environment, they will find it easy to receive their dreams and visions.

The Egyptians sometimes placed Gengen Wer, the goose god, in this decan. This god was associated with the king of the gods, Amun, whose name means "the hidden one" or "secret one." Amun was self-created and then created everything else, though he remained distant and separate from his creation. He was an invisible, inscrutable creator god, who operated behind the scenes. Gengen Wer is also a creator, for she laid the World Egg, which is the basis of the Creation. Note that one of the original Sabian symbols of Aquarius is "The Cosmic Egg."

EXAMPLES

Burr Tillstrom (Uranus. Puppeteer—*Kukla, Fran and Ollie.*)
Marcel Marceau (Venus. Mime.)
Philip K. Dick (Moon. Metaphysical sci-fi writer—*A Scanner Darkly.*)
John Irving (Mercury. Dyslexic novelist—*The World According to Garp.*)
Tama Janowitz (Chiron. Writer—*Slaves of New York.*)
Ransom Riggs (Sun, Mars. Author of *Miss Peregrine's Home for Peculiar Children.*)
Patrick Macnee (Sun, Venus. Actor in the often surrealist TV show, *The Avengers.*)
Sir Thomas More (Mercury. Author of *Utopia.*)
Virginia Woolf (Mercury. Visionary novelist—*Orlando, To the Lighthouse.*)
Lewis Carroll (Uranus. Author of *Through the Looking Glass.*)
Winona Ryder (North Node. Actress—*Heathers, Beetlejuice.*)
Joan Allen (Moon. Actress—*Pleasantville.*)
Chris Carter (Moon. Creator of *The X-Files.*)
Roger Corman (Jupiter. Horror and exploitation film director—*Little Shop of Horrors.*)
Judy Blume (Jupiter. Sociological writer—*Blubber, Wifey.*)
Scott Adams (Chiron. Cartoonist—*Dilbert.*)
Carol Burnett and Tim Conway (Saturn. Comic duo.)

Eric Idle and John Cleese (Mars. Comics—*Monty Python*.)
Roseanne Barr (Mean Node: Sociologically astute comic.)
Geena Davis (Mercury. Actress—*Beetlejuice*, *Earth Girls Are Easy*.)
John Lilly (Uranus. Explorer of consciousness—isolation tanks.)
Richard Tarnas (Jupiter. Professor of philosophy, cosmology, and
     consciousness; author of *Cosmos and Psyche* and *LSD Psychotherapy*.)
Ishmael Reed (Jupiter. Poet, novelist—*Mumbo Jumbo*.)
Orson Welles (Moon, Uranus. Actor, director—*The Third Man*, *The War
     of the Worlds*.)
Anthony Burgess (Mercury. Novelist—*A Clockwork Orange*.)
Leonard Wibberley (Uranus. Author of *The Mouse That Roared*.)
Piers Anthony (North Node. Sci-fi writer—*Macroscope*.)
Tom Wolfe (Mercury, Mars. Journalistic writer—*Bonfire of the Vanities*.)
René Char (Chiron. Surrealist poet.)
Umberto Eco (Venus. Writer—*The Name of the Rose*, *Foucault's Pendulum*.)
John Frankenheimer (Mars. Film director—*The Manchurian Candidate*.)
Vance Packard (Uranus. Muckraking author: *The Hidden Persuaders*, *The
     Status Seekers*.)
First Dada performance (Sun, Mercury, Uranus. February 5, 1916.)
Robert Wise (Jupiter. Film director—*The Day the Earth Stood Still*.)
Marie Louise von Franz (Uranus. Psychologist who analyzes fairy tales.)
Alice Cooper (Sun. Rock musician—*Welcome to My Nightmare*.)
Jason Behr (Venus, Jupiter. Teen alien on *Roswell*.)
André Breton (Mercury. Founded the surrealist movement.)

Aquarius, 3rd Decan

This is the least physical of the thirty-six decans. People with an emphasis here are able to forget about their bodies and fly off into extended meditations on life, death, and the meaning of existence. For these people, consciousness is the primary reality, rather than the physical world. The physical world, after all, is completely transitory. Every physical thing falls apart, comes to an end, dies. Consciousness, on the other hand, does not end at physical death but transitions to a wholly spiritual plane of existence.

People who have had near-death experiences or remember the time immediately before their birth say that from the other side, human life seems an exciting game or adventure. It's as if the spirit put on a pair of virtual-reality glasses and entered into an alternate reality. Unfortunately, this illusion is so compelling that we get hypnotized into thinking that it is the only reality. We forget our higher selves and our divine origins. Aquarius 3 individuals are trying to awaken from this dark dream. This involves a certain amount of analysis but also depends upon the ability to *remember*.

In the decan image, we see a spider weaving a web, and a caterpillar weaving a cocoon. This represents the good and bad patterns of thought that we weave around ourselves. The good patterns of thought open into a freer and more luminous state of being. They transform us, over time, from caterpillars into butterflies. The bad patterns of thought are negative vortexes that wrap us up in paranoid belief systems. Whether we weave positive or negative stories depends on whether we choose love or hate. If we hate, our worldview becomes a paranoid vortex, and

TEMPLE OF THE STARS

we are slowly transformed into ugly creatures. If we choose love, we slowly evolve into angelic beings.

Two of the *degree* symbols in this decan feature butterflies emerging from a cocoon. On a symbolic level, this shows darkness giving way to light, and ignorance giving way to enlightened understanding. Aquarius 3 individuals are interested in the nature of consciousness and the various methods by which one can achieve a higher level of consciousness. The following consciousness raisers, for instance, all have planets in this decan: Robert Anton Wilson, Timothy Leary, Marilyn Ferguson (*The Aquarian Conspiracy*), Elisabeth Kübler-Ross, John Lilly, Marianne Williamson, Colin Wilson, Marie-Louise von Franz, Alan Watts, and Martin Buber. These outspoken spiritual teachers had rather esoteric ideas but were remarkably effective in reaching a broad audience.

The struggle to free oneself from darkness and emerge into light depends, above all, upon spiritual aspiration, but it also requires the elimination of falsehoods from one's belief system. Aquarius 3 individuals are often very aware of their own habits of thought. They regularly examine their beliefs and try to identify any falsehoods that may be hiding there. They track down these negative thought forms to their original source, then search out other, related falsehoods. In this way they cut themselves free from a web of lies. We see this theme explored in *The Matrix*. In this movie, we see people hooked up to a consciousness-altering machine, which makes them think they are awake when they are actually asleep. Those who are partially awake are trying to find some way out of this imprisoning labyrinth—this false reality-conception. Aquarius 3 individuals, like the rebels of *The Matrix* or *Dark City*, are beginning to awaken from the false dreams of their culture. They are becoming aware of the power of hypnotic myths to trap people within false realities. This awareness can make them rather hostile to myth, religion, and advertising, since they all use powerful images to wrap people in dreams and illusions. Yet, because people of this decan understand the power of myths and symbols, they are also aware of the power of *magic*. Thus, even as they *dehypnotize* themselves from the ruling myths of society, they are conjuring a vision of the future—a vision that is clear enough in their mind's eye that they will eventually be able to step into it.

The ability of Aquarius 3 individuals to stand outside the accepted worldview points to the importance of the planetoid Chiron in this decan.

Chiron imparts an eccentric, alternative view of life and has a tricky ingenious quality—like the key that is its symbol. Chironic individuals are puzzle solvers par excellence. These people realize that to get from point A to point B, they will have to figure out the complex natural procedure that will make this transformation possible, even when this pathway is as jagged and complex as the edges of a key. They adhere to the natural order of this process, attending to everything in sequence and never jumping ahead of themselves. In the decan image, we see a caterpillar going through various phases in its transformation into a butterfly. Aquarius 3 people know how to focus in on the steps in any complex process. This allows them to come up with detailed, practical plans to change the direction of their own lives or the direction of society. Many people of this decan involve themselves in politics as a way of promoting the evolution of society. And because they are able to come up with accurate political analyses, they are often quite effective in promoting their agenda.

Evolutionary transformation versus rigidity and stasis is the chief polarity of this decan. In the decan symbol, the skull symbolizes the mind's tendency to rigidify into imprisoning assumptions and dogmas. This is the fate of many old people. The elderly are often unwilling to entertain new ideas. Instead, they fit every new event into a preexistent "skeleton" of reality assumptions. They act as if they have it all figured out, when they're actually just fearful and closed-minded. This rigidity eventually leads to death, since people who have lost their ability to react flexibly to their changing surroundings end up getting mowed down by one thing or another. Unable to escape bad habits of thought and behavior—either through a loss of energy or a loss of will—they become as vulnerable as blighted trees, which are blown down by the first big gust of wind.

The Tarot card associated with this decan is Death. Death's Saturnian scythe[62] mows down every living thing without exception. Every one of us is living out an endgame—symbolized here by the skull at the end of a box canyon. The elderly are very aware of death because they've already experienced the death of many friends and family members. Having lived a long time, they have also experienced the death of social scenes, cultural movements, etc. Negatively, this just scares them, causing them to clutch more firmly to their possessions, their ideas, and their routines. Positively, this makes them turn toward the life of the soul, for the soul is immortal and is not subject to the disintegration and death that is the fate of all physical things.

The butterflies of this decan are emerging into a place outside space and time; they are leaving behind the material world and moving into the luminous sphere of the afterlife. In ancient Egypt, this elevated state of consciousness was symbolized not by a butterfly, but by a bird called the *akh*. After the death of the body, the soul or *ba* of the deceased joined the sun god Re as he traveled in his boat through the netherworld. Through this unification with the light force, the soul was transformed into an immortal *akh* and entered the fields of the blessed as it rose with the sun at dawn. The *akh* was therefore a symbol of immortal life and undying consciousness.[63] From a Christian perspective, the *akh* would correspond to the immortal soul, freed from the constraints of earthly existence.

Aquarius 3 is an especially important decan, since it is the decan that we are in *now*. We have exited the Age of Pisces and entered into the Age of Aquarius. But because the precession of the equinox goes backward

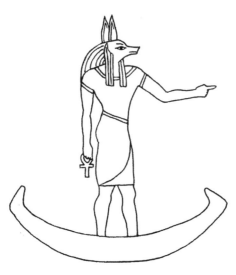

through the signs, we have entered this particular decan of Aquarius. If you reread the above description, you will see just how closely our current situation conforms to the existential issues of this decan.

The Egyptians sometimes placed the wolf-headed god, Wepwawet, in this decan. Wepwawet stood in Re's boat as it passed through the sky river of the Duat or netherworld. He was revered as the Opener of the Way and was a guide to the spirits of the dead.[64]

EXAMPLES

Elisabeth Kübler-Ross (Jupiter. Wrote *On Death and Dying*.)
John Lilly (Jupiter, North Node. Spiritual seeker—isolation tank, psychedelics.)
Philip José Farmer (Venus, Uranus. Sci-fi writer—*The Magic Labyrinth*, *Gods of Riverworld*.)
Roger Boom (Mercury. Created the first cryogenic storage unit.)

Tim LeHaye (Mars, Jupiter. Coauthor of *Left Behind* books, about "the Rapture.")

Milos Forman (Sun, Mercury, Mars. Filmmaker—*One Flew Over the Cuckoo's Nest*.)

Jack Palance (Venus, Uranus. Actor—*The Bagdad Café*, *Sudden Fear*.)

Herman Kahn (Sun, Mercury, Venus, Mars. Strategist for nuclear war, employing game theory.)

Amy Tan (Sun. Novelist—*The Bonesetter's Daughter*, *The Hundred Secret Senses*.)

Roz Chast (Mars. Loopy cartoonist who explores modern anxieties.)

James Watson (Mars. Codiscoverer of the double-helix structure of DNA; helped found the Human Genome Project.)

Rainn Wilson (Mars. Goofy actor—*The Last Mimzy*—with its funnel-like bridge to the future and its sound-controlled spiders.)

Audrey Hepburn (Ascendant. In *My Fair Lady* she is transformed from a guttersnipe to a delicate beauty in a butterfly-like white gown.)

Lilly Wachowski (Mars. Cowriter and director of *The Matrix*, with its cocoon-like human pods.)

Richard Chamberlain (Venus, Saturn. Actor—*The Last Wave*.)

Bette Davis (Chiron. Actress—*Now, Voyager*—where she emerges into a completely new life.)

David Goodis (Mercury, Venus, Uranus. Author of *Dark Passage*, where the protagonist is wrapped in bandages during a life-changing facelift.)

Marianne Williamson (North Node. Spiritual teacher—*A Course in Miracles*.)

Patrick McGoohan (Moon. Actor—*The Prisoner*.)

Charles Dederich (Ascendant, Mars. Ran the drug and alcohol rehab center Synanon.)

John Travolta (Sun. Actor—*Saturday Night Fever*—about escape from a dead-end existence.)

John Dean (Jupiter. Nixon aide who bailed and began pointing fingers.)

Sam Dash (Venus. Chief counsel for the Senate Watergate Committee.)

Winona Ryder (Mars. Actress—*Heathers*—where she must backtrack from a destructive life direction.)

Marlene Dietrich (Venus. Émigré actress—*Witness for the Prosecution*; anti-Nazi activist who helped Jews escape Germany.)

Tobey Maguire (Moon. Actor—*Pleasantville*—where he helps bring change to a culture that is totally stuck.)

Alan Vaughn (Venus. Psychic—*Patterns of Prophecy*.)

Josephine Tey (North Node. Detective writer.)

Julian Assange (Mars. Founder of WikiLeaks.)

Sid Gottlieb (Uranus. CIA agent who used LSD in mind-control experiments.)

Patricia Neal (Venus. Actress—*The Day the Earth Stood Still*, *A Face in the Crowd*—where she has to destroy the protégé she had been promoting.)

Augustus Owsley Stanley III (Saturn. Chemist who manufactured 10,000,000 doses of LSD in the sixties; soundman for the Grateful Dead.)

Shirley MacLaine (Saturn. Actress, popularizer of New Age ideas—*Out on a Limb*.)
Kim Novak (Sun, Mercury. Actress—*Vertigo*, where she assumes a new identity.)
William Holden (Uranus. Actor—*Sunset Boulevard*.)
Robert Anton Wilson (Venus. Author of *The Illuminatus! Trilogy*, radical agnostic and popularizer of discordianism.)

Pisces, 1st Decan

Pisces 1 individuals are very aware of the chaotic, unstable conditions of the world—and not just the physical world, but the mental and emotional world as well. These are unusually sensitive people, who readily pick up on the emotions, thoughts, and desires of other people, as well as confusing impressions, desires, and fears within themselves. This can be somewhat overwhelming. How are they supposed to make sense of this flood of information? Like the sea captain in the decan image, these people often find themselves in difficult situations—situations that require them to know what they are doing and where they are going—to be composed, levelheaded, and decisive.

Most people act as if they have it all figured out. They pretend they know where they are, where they're going, and how they're going to get there. Pisces 1 individuals are too psychologically astute and too *psychic* to believe it. They know that most people are "at sea" and *don't* really know what they are doing. There are major inaccuracies in their worldviews—where fantasy replaces reality—making it difficult for them to navigate their situation in an intelligent, effective way. Underneath it all, most people are just "poor fish"—bumblers, who through a lifetime of practice have gotten good at hiding the fact.

Because Pisces 1 individuals experience the world as unpleasantly mysterious and confusing, they have a strong incentive to figure out what's going on around them. The globe of the decan symbol represents a person's worldview—their internal model of the world, by which they make sense of their environment. Through ongoing analysis, people of this decan develop a clearer and more accurate picture of the world. Rather than getting overwhelmed by a flood of stimuli, they decide what's important and tune out the rest as "environmental noise." They then take the most-important data and use it to come up with some makeshift analytical structure. This analytical structure allows them to systematize and process information in an intelligent, practical way. It helps them clarify the situation to the point that they know what course of action they should take. Gary Goldschneider says of this area of the zodiac: "The goal of this path is for these individuals to become practical in their decision making. [They must] first create the structure for arranging information relevant to a question so that the answer or course of action they seek is made clear."[65] In my own decan image, the world globe, with its grid of longitude and longitude lines, represents this systematic ordering of information. Reality grids make it much easier to process information, since they help one quickly file each new piece of data in its proper place.

The old symbol for Pisces had two fish joined by a string. People of this decan understand that we are not that separate from other people—that we are interdependent. We share many of the same problems and are pretty much *all in the same boat*. To effectively tackle our problems, we therefore need to cooperate. We have to agree on how to proceed. This is not possible unless we are on the same page—unless we have the same understanding of the current situation. In traditional astrology, Pisces rules the feet. The feet are *where you are*. To make an intelligent decision about where you should go, you must first know where you are. You need to have an accurate analysis of your current situation. This is a function of the planet Mars, which is very important in this decan. Most astrologers do not identify Mars with Pisces, but Mars is actually important in all three Pisces decans. Mars is not reliably strong or focused in this sign, but out of sheer necessity, Piscean individuals are forced to develop their Martian skills. Mars gives them the ability to analyze their situation along practical lines. It helps them decide which elements in a situation are important, or operant, elements, and which elements can be effectively ignored. By simplifying the situation, Mars clarifies it to the point that they can make confident decisions about how to proceed. A strong Neptunian influence is also present in this decan, making these people sensitive to subtle emotions, aesthetics, and psychic perceptions. Mars ignores all of that. It has a much more practical focus. In the decan image, the issue facing the people on the ship is one of *survival*. Timely, practical decisions are required, and this involves thinking like a captain—thinking in a Martian way.

The decan symbol shows two people talking at cross-purposes. They have different ideas about their present situation and different ideas about where they should be heading. Because the young woman has less authority than the captain, she assumes that her views will be undervalued, yet she refuses to be silenced. She voices her opinions as persuasively as she can, varying her approach from mild-mannered explanations to impassioned tirades. She may even resort to sensationalism, if she thinks she can "make a splash."

People of this decan can often be found pointing out where other people have gotten "off course." They also point out where the "ship of state" has gotten off course. Pisces 1 individuals are very politically aware and are especially sensitive to abuses of power. A number of important feminists have planets here, including Betty Friedan, Gloria Steinem, Emmeline Pankhurst, and Germaine Greer. Pisces 1 individuals tend to be highly critical of the power elite's belief system—which they consider outdated, incoherent, prejudicial, and headed for disaster. They are championing an alternate interpretation and a new direction based on that interpretation.

Feminism is only one of the many "minority causes" that Pisces 1 individuals may embrace. To illustrate, the following crusaders have planets here: Madalyn Murray O'Hair, Phyllis Schlafly, Timothy Leary, William Kunstler, Hugh Hefner, Ralph Nader, and Pat Buchanan. This is a very opinionated, argumentative group. They have clearly articulated agendas, which they promote through various media, including books, radio, magazines, blogs, and speaking engagements. Their chief goal is to alert people to their cause and to convince them that the problems they are pointing out require immediate attention. As highly Jupiterian individuals, people of this decan take full responsibility for their worldview. Like the woman who grasps the globe in the decan symbol, they grasp their entire belief-system. They know what they believe and why, and what actions these truths require of them. Note, however, that some of the individuals listed above are clearheaded, while others are practically delusional.

The chief polarity of this decan is consciousness versus unconsciousness. Thus, in the decan image, the woman is awake to the reality of the situation while the captain is not. Pisces 1 individuals are aware of gross inaccuracies in other people's worldviews. However, they're not all that sure of their own worldviews either. They may be more conscious than others, but there are nonetheless times when life gets so strange and confusing that it doesn't seem real, but more like a dream or a phantasmagoria. This decan does, in fact, have a strong connection to dreams, as is evident in some of the artists with planets here. These include Alice Cooper ("Caught in a Dream," "Welcome to My Nightmare"), Audrey Hepburn (*Charade*), Ken Kesey (*One Flew Over the Cuckoo's Nest*), Keanu Reeves (*The Matrix, A Scanner Darkly*), Gene Tierney (*Whirlpool*), Jerzy Kosinski (*The Painted Bird*), Amy Tan (*The Hundred Secret Senses*), Giulietta Masina (*Juliet of the Spirits*), André Breton (leader of the surrealist movement), Mike Judge (*Idiocracy*), Woody Allen (*Sleeper*), and Winona Ryder (*Beetlejuice, Reality Bites*).

The dreamlike landscapes these people appear to inhabit are entertaining, but also sort of horrible. Pisces 1 individuals often feel like they're living in a madhouse, where the staff is as crazy as the patients, and incoherence and disorder are the rule rather than the exception. This can be funny, but it's also distressing. As warmhearted, sympathetic people, Pisces 1 individuals recognize how much pain all this confusion is creating in people's lives. Faced with all this human suffering, they help where they can—either by offering a sympathetic ear or by offering a practical solution. To keep their heads above water—to keep depression at bay—they try to develop a buoyant, humorous perspective. They focus on the fun and humor in people's behavior rather than the tragedies. Many hip, insightful comedians are found among the examples. These people specialize in humorous but warmhearted observations of human cluelessness and incompetence. Examples include Jeff Bridges (as the Big Lebowski), Woody Allen, Elvira, Kevin Smith, Jason Lee (*My Name Is Earl*), and Rainer Fassbinder. In real life, these people aren't particularly spaced-out or incompetent. They're just honest about the limits of their own understanding. They realize that their own picture of reality is probably distorted and incomplete. They can certainly remember times when they totally misjudged their situation.

While there are many activists with planets here, Pisces 1 individuals also have a strong impulse to *withdraw* from the chaos and suffering of the world. These people often set down roots in some peaceful rural retreat. There they can reestablish a peaceful emotional center and focus on music, meditation, or other spiritual pursuits. This may not be a particularly healthy response. Pisces 1 individuals are Martian enough to know when they are running away from life. There is no point in putting oneself in the way of trouble. However, some unpleasant things simply have to be faced. When these people fail to commit themselves to worthwhile goals, they tend to fall into a number of bad mental habits: procrastination, rationalization, and evasion—all side effects of a weak Mars. By refusing to take responsibility for what they are doing in life, they end up living life as if it weren't real—*as if it were a dream.* Instead of waking up to their situation, they sink into a confusing dreamworld. Some turn to drugs and alcohol, which, predictably, makes a big mess of their lives.

With a slight shift of perspective, it is possible to view the man and woman of the decan symbol as man and wife. People of this decan often consider marriage and intimate relationships the most important thing in their lives. By uniting with someone whose mind and spirit complement their own, they expand their world and their worldview. Generally, they put a lot of work into their relationships. They are always thinking about whether a relationship is going in the right direction, and what they might do to improve things. They take a genuine interest in their partner and communicate their feelings in some detail. Negatively, these relationships can run to clinginess and unrealistic expectations. Positively, they include a spiritual bond that provides stability and serenity amid the confusion and turmoil of modern life.

EXAMPLES

David Frost (Venus. Host of the political-opinion show *That Was the Week That Was.*)
Rush Limbaugh (Jupiter. Right-wing political commentator.)
Jon Stewart (Jupiter. Political commentator, comedian.)
Carol Burnett (North Node. Relaxed, forward-looking TV comic.)
Steve Allen (Uranus. Plain-speaking comic, emcee, songwriter.)
Bill Maher (Venus. Talk-show host—*Politically Incorrect.*)
Rosie O'Donnell (Mercury, Mars. Liberal talk-show host.)
Arianna Huffington (Jupiter. Onetime Republican who ran a liberal political website—the *Huffington Post.*)
Will Rogers (Jupiter. Humorist, political commentator.)
Joe Santagato (Sun. YouTube comedian—"Idiots of the Internet.")
Mike Judge (Jupiter. Cartoonist—*Beavis and Butthead*; film director—*Idiocracy, Office Space.*)

Murray Bookchin (Venus, Mars. Anarchist theorist promoting a decentralized society; social ecologist.)

Camille Paglia (Venus. Cultural gadfly taking aim at fascist tendencies within feminism and deconstructionism.)

Jean Paul Sartre (Saturn. Existentialist philosopher.)

Philip Roth (North Node. Novelist—*Portnoy's Complaint.*)

Helen Gurley Brown (Venus, Uranus. Editor of *Cosmopolitan.*)

Luis Alvarez (Chiron. Nobel physicist, with a wide range of controversial theories.)

Annie Besant (Saturn. Occultist, feminist, social reformer; campaigned for birth control.)

James Joyce (Mercury. Iconoclastic writer—*Finnegan's Wake.*)

Ken Kesey (Saturn. Wrote *One Flew Over the Cuckoo's Nest*; leader of the Merry Pranksters.)

Timothy Leary (Uranus. Promoted the use of LSD and opposed conventional culture—"Turn on, tune in, drop out.")

Geena Davis (Venus. Actress—*A League of Their Own, Thelma and Louise.*)

Alan Alda (Saturn. Sardonic, plain-speaking actor—*M*A*S*H.*)

Betty Ford (Venus. First lady, very honest about her alcoholism, founded a rehab center.)

Phyllis Schlafly (Mars. Republican, antifeminist propagandist.)

André Breton (Sun, North Node. Defiantly unconventional founder of surrealism.)

Sir Thomas More (Chiron. Minister of Henry VIII, executed for opposing the king's divorce.)

Riccardo Bauer (North Node. Socialist leader of underground opposition to Mussolini.)

Bob Dylan (Mars. Folk and rock musician—"The Times They Are A-Changin'.")

Dixie Lee Ray (North Node. Headed the AEC; propagandist for nuclear power.)

Kevin Smith (North Node. Thoughtful independent filmmaker—*Dogma, Chasing Amy, Mall Rats.*)

Germaine Greer (Jupiter. Feminist—*The Female Eunuch.*)

Eldridge Cleaver (Saturn. Black Panther activist, who later became a Moonie, a Mormon, a Republican, and a crackhead.)

Adam Carolla (Saturn. Host of TV's *Loveline* and *The Man Show*; libertarian Republican.)

James Baldwin (Mars. Black novelist and essayist—racial and sexual issues—*Notes of a Native Son.*)

Hans Küng (Mercury, Venus. Priest and theologian who rejected the doctrine of papal infallibility and was forbidden to teach Catholic theology.)

Pisces, 2nd Decan

IMAGE: *Having completed a circuitous sea journey, a group of seekers enter a domed temple in order to receive instruction from a spiritual teacher. On the altar, there are offerings of wine, fruit, and fragrant lotus blossoms.*

The individuals of this decan are explorers and seekers—both of the outer world and the inner world. They actively pursue adventure, wisdom, and love, confident that the universe will grant these things to anyone who actively seeks them. Among the examples, we find many actors and writers who have come to epitomize spunky adventure. These people can be found not only on dangerous sea voyages, but also on exciting road trips. Examples include Errol Flynn (*Robin Hood*), Bridget Fonda (*Rough Magic*), Laura Dern (*Wild at Heart*), Ben Stiller (*Flirting with Disaster*), Jackie Cooper (*Treasure Island*), Shelley Winters (*The Poseidon Adventure*), Erica Jong (*Fear of Flying*), Jules Verne, Helen Hunt (*Twister*), Tom Wolfe (*The Electric Kool-Aid Acid Test*), Lisa Kudrow (*Romy and Michele's High School Reunion*), and Jason Bateman (*We're the Millers*).

Pisces 2 individuals don't worry too much about the trajectory of their lives but trust the universe to get them where they need to go. Many would consider this approach impractical and overly romantic, but Pisces 2 individuals are not particularly concerned. They aren't afraid of making occasional mistakes in judgment, or in falling into delusion. As Jupiterians, they are attuned to the greater reality and are buoyed by that reality. Every now and then they may fall into error, but if they remain open, their course will be corrected, even as a boat on the waves will naturally right itself.

People of this decan do not shrink from life but are willing to explore completely unfamiliar physical or spiritual territories. They aim for great experiences but are not unwilling to experience a few harrowing adventures along the way. Armed with the optimism of Jupiter, they trust that even their bad experiences will have something valuable to teach them.

Pisces 2 individuals approach life with gusto. They are hungry for life, which they see laid out before them like a great feast. They aren't gluttons, however, but seek memorable, poetic experiences—experiences of real quality, which, like fine wines, uplift the soul. These people fully inhabit the present moment. They seek out the higher pleasures of life and then "drink them in." Among the various pleasures offered up by the world, this decan has an especially strong connection to classical music. The following composers all have planets here: Bach, Mozart, Schumann, Schubert, Mendelssohn, Chopin, Tchaikovsky. These lushly romantic composers all had strong spiritual commitments. They were channeling divine harmonies, then laying them out on some inner altar as offerings to God. On an emotional level, they all were adventurers, for they boldly followed their musical ideas wherever they led. In the process, they broke a lot of new ground, especially in the realm of harmony.

Many spiritual seekers have planets in this decan. These are people who travel long distances—both mentally and physically—to further their spiritual consciousness. Some seek instruction from spiritual teachers. They have no problem receiving these teachings, for they conceive of no barrier between their own mind and the minds of other people, or even the mind of God. They look upon consciousness as unified and oceanic, since like water, it has no intrinsic boundaries. Moreover, they believe that higher understanding is always available to those who seek it, and having found it, have the courage to drink it in. This wisdom can come from gurus and teachers, but it can also come from a direct intuitive connection to inner sources. The lotus blossom in the decan symbol refers to the crown chakra, which is often symbolized by "the thousand-petaled lotus." When the crown chakra is open, one's mind is open to spiritual wisdom from a higher plane of existence.

Pisces 2 individuals may experience a lot of "stormy seas" in their outer lives, but on the inmost level, they remain moored within the safe harbor of a calm and balanced state of mind. From this imperturbable seat of consciousness, they look out upon the disturbing events of life as if they were as unreal as a dream. One component of their consciousness has already awoken from the "Great Dream of Existence" and sits, like a Buddha, at the center of the lotus blossom. This component may just be a bud-like potential and not fully flowered. But it hardly matters where these people are in this process, as long as their overall direction is upward—as long as they are reaching toward the light of higher spiritual understanding, even as the lotus emerges from the water every morning and reaches toward the sun.

Pisces 2 individuals are naturally meditative, and much given to spiritual contemplation. They would like to develop a serene, uncluttered state of mind, which, like a still pool, reflects an undistorted image of the world. Some withdraw to the countryside to commune with nature. Others retire to a monastery, ashram, or religious retreat. Still others create an inner sanctum in their home or apartment—a room where they can listen to music, get high, or have metaphysical conversations. Many of the degree symbols of this decan show people coming together around shared beliefs and ideals. There is a church, an occult lodge, an art museum. These are all interior spaces devoted to group meditation.

All created things begin as rippling patterns in the waters of the collective mind. Musical ideas are emotional wave patterns that with time can crystallize into sheet music. Architectural blueprints, similarly, eventually take the form of actual buildings. People of this decan realize that what already exists is not that important, since any new pattern of thought can eventually replace it. Changes of consciousness are the ultimate source of worldly change. It is therefore more important to change people's consciousness than it is to change established institutions.

As with the first decan of Pisces, one finds a lot of activism here. People of this decan often join up with other like-minded activists in order to have a bigger effect. In these political, religious, or intellectual "cell groups," fellow travelers help each other clarify and develop their ideas. They also help each other resist the false beliefs of the dominant culture—beliefs that could erode their higher insights. Pisces 2 individuals are convinced that there is ultimately only one reality, since consciousness is naturally unified and oceanic. It is therefore inevitable that one day everyone will come together in that reality. This may explain why Pisces 2 individuals are so optimistic about their efforts. They believe that well-articulated ideals will attract followers, and that these followers will eventually bring these ideals into manifestation.

The "sea voyage" of the decan image can be seen as a journey of consciousness, but it may also symbolize the emotional journey by which one develops an intimate personal relationship. In their love lives, Pisces

2 individuals are looking for poetry and romance. Their ultimate destination is refined lovemaking that touches the divine. This refined eroticism is a product of Neptune, which has a very powerful presence in this decan. Pisces 2 individuals are capable of tender, poetic relationships. As emotionally sensitive people, they can sidestep their partner's sore spots and peculiarities and cultivate their better nature. Moreover, because Pisces 2 individuals are highly attuned to nature and already feel that they "belong," they are not particularly needy on an emotional level.

The Egyptian god Nefertum makes a good fit with this decan. Nefertum is a god of flowers, associated in particular with the blue lotus, which is a plant that contains a psychoactive drug that was used in ancient medicine. Nefertum is often depicted with a lotus flower emerging from the crown of his head. This is a fitting symbol for a decan associated with the crown chakra.

EXAMPLES

Frédéric Chopin (Sun, Pluto. Sublime classical composer.)
Franz Schubert (Jupiter. Classical composer.)
Johann Sebastian Bach (Mercury, Venus. Classical composer with an open crown chakra.)
Wolfgang Amadeus Mozart (Uranus. Classical composer.)
Felix Mendelssohn (Pluto. Classical composer.)
Robert Schumann (Pluto. Classical composer.)
Pyotr Ilyich Tchaikovsky (Uranus. Classical composer.)
Giuseppe Verdi (Operatic composer—*Aida*, *La Traviata*.)
Aretha Franklin (Mercury. Soul singer—confessional songs.)
David Gilmour (Sun. Spiritually attuned rock guitarist—Pink Floyd.)
Paul McCartney (Ascendant. Beatle.)
Hermann Hesse (Mars. Author sensitive to occult archetypes— *Steppenwolf*, *Siddhartha*.)
Dick Cavett (Saturn, stationary. Wide-ranging talk-show host.)
Ellen Burstyn (North Node. Actress—*Alice Doesn't Live Here Anymore*.)
Simon Pegg (North Node. Comic actor—*Paul*, *The World's End*.)
Norman Lear (Uranus. Produced *Maude*, *Mary Hartman*, *All in the Family*; founded a progressive advocacy group.)

Alix Shulman (North Node. Feminist writer—*Memoirs of an Ex-Prom Queen.*)

Emma Stone (North Node. Actress; gives off-screen narration of her story in *Easy A.*)

Howard Zinn (Uranus. Left-wing revision of American history.)

Charles Dickens (Venus. Author—*Great Expectations.*)

Jack Kerouac (Uranus. Beat writer—*On the Road.*)

Alan Bates (Mars. Actor—*King of Hearts, Women in Love.*)

Juliette Binoche (Sun, Mercury, Mars, Chiron. Actress—*The English Patient, Chocolat.*)

Rachel Maddow (Mercury. Political commentator who provides the inside story.)

Amy Adams (Jupiter. Actress—*Arrival*—with its time-independent narrative featuring flashbacks and flash-forwards.)

Nellie Bly (Neptune. Muckraking journalist; she faked insanity to get into a women's mental hospital, then did an exposé.)

Henry Miller (Jupiter. Writer of highly confessional books—*Tropic of Cancer, Crazy Cock.*)

Barnet Rosset (Uranus. Head of Grove Press; published *Lady Chatterley's Lover* and *Tropic of Cancer*; led court battles against censorship.)

Stanley Krippner (North Node. Studies human potential; leads personal mythology workshops and dream groups.)

Sam Phillips (Mars. Pioneering record producer; early recordings of Elvis, Howlin' Wolf, and Jerry Lee Lewis.)

Edgar Cayce (Mercury, Venus, Saturn, North Node. Mystic, healer; gave thousands of "life readings"; interpreted dreams.)

Philip Roth (Venus. Writer—*Portnoy's Complaint*, with its confessional personal narrative.)

Karl Marx and Friedrich Engels (Saturn, and Jupiter and the North Node, respectively. Class analysis of history; Communist theorists.)

Mary Tyler Moore (Ascendant, Saturn. Actress-—*The Mary Tyler Moore Show.*)

Tom Hanks (Mars. Actor—*Philadelphia, Big, Forrest Gump.*)

Guy Murchie (Saturn. Spiritual writer—*The Music of the Spheres, The Seven Mysteries of Life*; Baha'i.)

Gary Ross (Mars. Filmmaker, screenwriter—*Big, Pleasantville*; both of these movies involve time warps.)

Walker Evans (Jupiter. Photographed scenes of the Great Depression.)

Ellen/Elliot Page (Mercury, Stationary. Actor—*Whip It, Juno*; transsexual.)

Roger Daltrey (Sun. Rock star—the Who; lead actor in the rock opera *Tommy.*)

Dalai Lama (Saturn. Spiritual and political leader.)

Ralph Ellison (Sun. Author—*Invisible Man*; Communist.)

Vance Packard (North Node. Muckraking writer—*The Hidden Persuaders, A Nation of Strangers.*)

Marcello Mastroianni (Uranus. Lead actor in Fellini films—*8½*, *We Are All Fine*; lived much of his life within Fellini fantasies.)

Mircea Eliade (Sun, Saturn. Writer on yoga and alchemy; apologist for Mussolini, Salazar, and other Fascists.)

Jess Stearn (Chiron. Writes on reincarnation and other New Age subjects.)

Pisces, 3rd Decan

IMAGE: *On a nighttime mission, a knight steers a barge through a confusion of urban canals. When the moon comes out from behind a cloud, it becomes clear which canal he should follow.*

As a decan ruled by the moon, this is a place of mysteries and illusions, of secrets and revelations. People of this decan would like to have a clear picture of their situation but must often forge ahead in partial darkness. When the moon comes out from behind a cloud, elements of the landscape that had formerly been in darkness come into view. Similarly, when people of this decan turn a corner in their intellectual understanding, their situation comes into sharper focus, and they realize that their former interpretation was inaccurate and misleading. Pisces 3 individuals need to remain alert within their changing situations, for they could otherwise be blindsided by some disaster—some patch of "narrow rapids"—where they could easily lose control. These people hate to think that they don't know what they're doing, that they are adrift or floating down the path of least resistance. As self-aware individuals, they regularly ask themselves whether they are actually heading toward their goals—whether they are going in the right direction. If they decide they're not, they are quick to change course or to backtrack.

Pisces 3 individuals recognize that their understanding is under a cloud. They are therefore always searching for that essential clue that will give away the game—that will pull a veil away from the problem and reveal it in its true light. Sometimes these clues are self-explanatory. However, they can also be fairly arcane and may need to be deciphered or "uncloaked" through extended analysis. In the decan image, the clouds represent illusions and misperceptions, while the moonlight represents illumination and understanding. The basic idea is that one can arrive at the pure light of understanding only by piercing through layer upon layer of error and illusion.

People of this decan are often trying to illuminate some murky, poorly understood area of knowledge. The kinds of problems these people study are extremely varied. Elisabeth Kübler-Ross studied death and dying. Sigmund Freud studied the human subconscious. Einstein studied the physics of space and time. Seymour Hersh analyzed the My Lai massacre. Paul Foster Case studied the Tarot. Paul Ehrlich studied the population explosion. All these people were able to get to a deeper level of understanding than anyone before them. They peeled away their predecessors' illusions and delusions to arrive at a more accurate and coherent view of their subject.

Quite a number of scientists have planets here. These people follow out some murky line of research until their understanding has been illuminated by a major revelation. Einstein is among the examples, as is Alexander Graham Bell. Both Copernicus and Galileo have planets here. These pioneering astronomers were early proponents of the heliocentric theory. During their historical period, this was a dangerous position to take, for it undermined the authority of the Catholic Church, which had built an entire theology around the view that the earth was the center of the universe. Copernicus was a bit of a coward here. He allowed an introduction to be added to his book that basically said that heliocentrism was "just a theory." This failure to openly proclaim his position had major repercussions, since even fifty years after his book had been published, only a handful of people had accepted his theory. Galileo, writing some years later, was a lot braver. He openly promoted and fought for his beliefs, despite being threatened with torture by the Church. He made a cause célèbre of his discoveries, framing the conflict as a battle between demonstrable truth and dishonest dogmatism. In this he was quite successful, because fifty years after his death, the intelligentsia of Europe had accepted the heliocentric theory.

The theme of "cloaking and uncloaking" is important in this decan. Pisces 3 individuals must occasionally consider whether or not they should take a stand for their beliefs. The knight of the decan image is traveling through foreign territory—possibly enemy territory. For the time being, he has cloaked his beliefs and his loyalties from public view. Nonetheless, he looks forward to a time when he can openly proclaim these beliefs in a way that has potent cultural or political effects.

Quite a number of spies and secret agents have planets here. Spies are people who have strong loyalties but hide these loyalties in order to defeat their political enemies. Like spies, Pisces 3 individuals can live for any amount of time among people whose beliefs are foreign and even inimical to their own. Socially, people of this decan are fairly sophisticated and get along well with others. Privately, however, they consider themselves more conscious, more awake, and more moral than the people around them. Not surprisingly, they keep these beliefs under wraps.

When Pisces 3 individuals find themselves in situations where their moral and spiritual values are being challenged, they must decide whether to stop and fight. They must decide whether this is *their* battle or whether it will only retard their progress toward some more important goal. In order to make decisions like this, they need to stop and put the full beam of their attention on the problem. They need to shine a light on the situation, even as the Moon in the decan image shines down on the scene.

Through a sequence of revelations, Pisces 3 individuals gain a clearer and clearer picture of the world around them. But they are also gaining a clearer understanding of themselves. People of this decan are very self-reflective. They are highly aware of their own spiritual identity and very appreciative of that identity. It's as if they were looking at an upward reflection of their own divine self—their own highest potential. They feel that they already *are* that person, at least inwardly, but also realize that they may have trouble remaining true to this ideal self-image in the face of life's challenges.

This is a very demanding position. A knight is allowed very few compromises in life. Similarly, Pisces 3 individuals can't compromise a lot, because if they do, they will end up sullying their own self-image. The knight is a Martian figure, and Mars is in fact very strong here. Moral courage is a central issue in this decan. These people need to feel that they are meeting life both bravely and sincerely—that they are standing up for their ideals. Pisces 3 individuals are fighting not just for abstract ideals, such as truth and justice, but also for their right to be themselves—to live the life they were meant to live, and in the way they were meant to live it. On some level, they know that the gift they are bringing to humanity is in large part *themselves*. If they are to honor this spiritual gift, they must be absolutely true to themselves. They must maintain a high level of personal integrity, protecting their self-image by being careful about what kind of compromises they will allow themselves.

Once Pisces 3 individuals have seen through a number of life's illusions, they begin to share their wisdom more freely with others. Like keen-eyed archers, they deploy arrows of truth to shoot down exaggerations, illusions, and pipe dreams. A number of famous debunkers are found among the examples—people who have attacked mass delusions. These people are grappling with the phenomenon of mass hypnosis. The collective mind operates on a very low level of consciousness. It is as opaque as the dark waters of a canal. Because most people are very unconscious, they are extremely vulnerable to lies and propaganda, especially when these lies trade upon their fears. As compassionate individuals, Pisces 3 individuals are trying to awaken people from the grip of these falsehoods, for if these people can gain a more accurate understanding of reality, they will surely find it easier to navigate the troubled waters of life.

This is the last decan of the zodiacal cycle and is therefore involved in wrapping things up. Pisces 3 individuals are continually reflecting on the overall course of their life and reanalyzing it in light of new spiritual understandings. In the process, they begin to realize that they have been running into the same problematical situations time and time again—that on some level they have been going around in circles. These recurrent problems can be ignored for a long time, but not indefinitely. At this point in the cycle, the broader patterns of a person's life are becoming obvious. People of this decan are beginning to see where their beliefs about reality and their myths about themselves aren't working. They therefore stop to take a serious look at the problem. They concentrate the full beam of their attention on this recurrent situation and figure out how to escape its hold. They try to transform their intellectual and behavioral ruts into upward-moving evolutionary spirals.

The Egyptians often pictured the Nile god Hapi in this decan. Drawings of this hermaphroditic figure were often surrounded by a snake biting its own tail, which was a symbol of the river Nile. Since the Nile was the basis of life in what was otherwise a desert, this decan had a symbolic association with fertility and prosperity. The snake biting its own tail also symbolizes the circular nature of life, which moves through phases of spiritual comprehension and spiritual darkness, even as the moon passes through phases of light and darkness.

EXAMPLES

Katharine Hepburn (Saturn. Actress—*The African Queen.*)

Martin Goldsmith (Not me. North Node. Novelist; screenwriter for noir films—*Detour, The Narrow Margin.*)

Orson Welles (Jupiter, Chiron. Actor—*The Third Man.*)

Margaret Lockwood (Chiron. Actress—*The Lady Vanishes.*)

Herman Melville (Chiron, Pluto. Novelist—*Moby Dick.*)

Seymour Hersh (Saturn. Investigative journalist—My Lai.)

Grace Slick (Jupiter. Lead singer for the Jefferson Airplane.)

R. D. Laing (Ascendant, Jupiter. Psychiatrist who took the accounts of psychotic patients seriously; held rebirthing workshops.)

Hermann Hesse (Moon, Saturn. Wrote novels with spiritual and occult themes—*Steppenwolf, Demian*; friend of Carl Jung.)

Anthony Blunt (Saturn. Art historian and Poussin scholar; privy to the secret history of the Prieuré de Sion; Soviet spy.)

James Garner (Mercury, Venus. Actor—*Rockford Files, 36 Hours*—about an attempt to brainwash an American prisoner.)

Patrick McGoohan (Sun. Star and cocreator of *The Prisoner.*)

Angela Lansbury (Uranus. Actress—*The Manchurian Candidate.*)

Ed Harris (North Node. Actor—*The Truman Show, Glengarry Glen Ross.*)

John Carpenter (Moon. Director of horror films—*They Live, Halloween.*)

Upton Sinclair (Saturn. Muckraking writer—*The Jungle*—about food contamination.)

Rush Limbaugh (Moon, North Node. Right-wing talk radio host; purveyor of misinformation.)

Robert Stack (Chiron. Host of *Unsolved Mysteries.*)

Patricia Arquette (Venus. Actress—*Medium.*)

Laura Dern (Saturn, Chiron. Actress—*Wild at Heart, Blue Velvet.*)

Jessica Mitford (Chiron. Investigative journalist, civil rights activist—*The American Way of Death.*)

Sir Richard Burton (Sun, Pluto. Adventurer, writer; explored Egyptian brothels in disguise and also got into Mecca.)

Margot Adler (Mercury. Occultist—*Drawing Down the Moon.*)

Albert Einstein (Sun. Physicist in the "everything you know is wrong" school.)

Karl Marx and Friedrich Engels (Both have Pluto and Chiron here. Pioneers of the Communist economic interpretation of history.)

Umberto Eco (North Node. Semiotician, novelist—*The Name of the Rose, Foucault's Pendulum.*)

Nicolaus Copernicus (Mercury. Upset cosmology by arguing that the planets circled the sun, not the earth.)

Elisabeth Kübler-Ross (Uranus. Psychiatrist—*On Death and Dying.*)

E. M. Forster (Saturn. Novelist—*A Passage to India.*)

Mark Lane (Mercury, Venus, Uranus. Investigative journalist; wrote books on the JFK assassination—*Rush to Judgment.*)

Robert Jastrow (Uranus. NASA astronomer, helped found a disinformation think tank, to spread doubt about global warming.)

Eva Marie Saint and Cary Grant (Uranus and Jupiter, respectively. Actors in the spy thriller *North by Northwest.*)

Phạm Xuân Ẩn (Jupiter. Reporter for major US magazines; secret Vietcong agent.)

Viola Liuzzo (Uranus. Civil rights activist, killed by the KKK.)

Lusitania torpedoed (May 7, 1915. Jupiter. Sunk by German U-boat in WWI.)

Ingrid Bergman (Jupiter. Actress—*Suspicion, Casablanca.*)

Robert Bolt (Uranus. Wrote the screenplay for *Dr. Zhivago.*)

George H. W. Bush (Uranus. President, former head of the CIA.)

Lester Maddox (Jupiter. Violent, diehard segregationist, governor of Georgia.)

The Nature of Planetary Influence in Decans, Signs, and Houses

The nature of the planets is a fairly nebulous subject in modern astrology. It is rarely talked about. For the Babylonians, the planets were simply *gods*. Babylonian priests prayed to the planets to intercede in upcoming disasters. Thus, the planets, for the Babylonians, had consciousness, will, and power. The Greeks had a very different view. The Greek intellectuals who appropriated Babylonian astrology were scientific and atheistic in their basic outlook—so much so that they were persecuted by the government of Athens—not as astrologers, but as *atheists*. For Greek astrologers, the planets were not gods, but principles or archetypes, similar in nature to Platonic Ideas.

The Greek conception of the planets was very much in keeping with the Neoplatonic philosophical system, which was basic to Greek mathematics and astronomy. There were certainly other important philosophies in ancient Greece, but Plato's views, from the beginning, have been central to Greek astrology. The number-based disciplines of Greek mathematics, astronomy, and astrology were the most evolved sciences of the ancient world. In fact, astrology, with its "clockwork universe," provided a model, which is still basic to modern science—of the world as a machine constructed out of numbers and equations.

In its own time, Greek astrology was definitely a science. And the gods figured in this science hardly at all. The planet Mars, for instance, was only tangentially related to the Greek god Ares and was certainly not seen as a god. Greek astrologers considered traditional Greek religion and mythology embarrassingly primitive. The planets were principles, archetypes, and Platonic Ideas, rather than gods. Fate, on the other hand, was something they really believed in. Fate ruled over the planets and the worldly events within the dominion of each planet. Through the movement of the planets, Fate parceled out worldly events with the regularity of a well-oiled machine.[66]

Modern Western astrologers have uncritically accepted most of these Greek ideas. They still believe in Fate. If they did not, they would not be making astrological predictions. And the planets are seen as archetypes or principles rather than gods. Mars is not considered a god but is chiefly understood as the principle of aggression.

In more recent years, the Platonic Ideas of the Greeks have been replaced by Carl Jung's notion of archetypes, and the whole of astrology has been reframed within this psychologistic framework. However, this is less of a transformation than it first appears. Carl Jung was steeped in Neoplatonic philosophical concepts, since these ideas permeated the alchemical, astrological, and magical traditions he studied. In fact, his conception of psychological archetypes ultimately comes out of astrology and alchemy. Thus, the archetypes of Jungian psychology are simply a psychologically acceptable way of talking about the divine Ideas of ancient Neoplatonism.

Now, I have no argument with Jungian astrology; I consider it a step forward, since it makes astrology more of a counseling profession and distances it from predictions about love, money, and health. Nonetheless, it fails to address the metaphysical status of the planets and simply carries forward the philosophical biases of Greco-Roman astrology. This is not something astrologers have decided on; it is based on a passive acceptance of traditional teachings. We accept the Greek view because that is the tradition that has come down to us through medieval translations of Roman astrological works. It is our received tradition. Babylonian and Egyptian conceptions of the planets have no place in this tradition and have simply been consigned to the category of "the untrue." However, this adherence to the Greek view of the planets is ultimately based on little more than the Greeks' belief in their own cultural superiority, and their commitment to the basic tenets of Neoplatonic philosophy. The modern understanding of the planets is, in fact, an artifact of an unexamined ancient philosophy.

Let us look for a moment at modern Jungian astrology, whose most well-known practitioner is Liz Greene. First of all, Greene deals with the planets largely in terms of ancient Greek myths about the gods. There is a lot to be gained from this, but it is certainly *not* an approach known to ancient Greek astrologers. The Greeks had very little interest in Greek religion and mythology. In fact, by Ptolemy's time (the second century CE), astrology had become so rationalistic that the planets were characterized by whether they were cold, hot, dry, or moist—attributions that were used in Galenic medicine. Ptolemaic astrology was not really involved in mythology, or even symbolism. Thus the Jungian focus on planetary mythology has no ancient basis. It is new. Jungian astrologers still tend to see the planets as archetypal principles, rather than willful gods. However, they use the Greek myths as aids in interpreting the planets of the birth chart.

Jungian astrology may identify planets as archetypes, but the notion of a planetary archetype remains very vague. Are the planets divine Ideas, and if they are divine Ideas, just how divine are they, and in what way are they divine? For the Greeks, the planetary archetypes were at least *real*; they were aspects of nature, acting on worldly events from the celestial realm. With the adoption of a psychological perspective by modern astrologers, the planets lost their status as *divine* Ideas in the Neoplatonic mold. They were psychological concepts such as love, aggression, expansion, and limitation. More importantly, these planetary archetypes began to be seen as products of the human mind. This move has made astrology much more subjective and much less real than it was either for the Greeks or the Babylonians. The relativism of modern astrology, with its tolerance for alternative zodiacs, Uranian planets, and the like, shows just how far removed astrology has become from science—ancient or modern.

In the ancient world, astrology aspired to the objectivity of natural science. Nowadays, it is often just a psychological way of talking about things, where anyone's opinion is as good as anyone else's. While this descent into relativism has a long history, in more recent years, astrology has also divorced itself from serious occultism, where symbols were understood to have power. The planets have become increasingly conceptual, to the point that they are generally just reduced to words like "expansion," "aggression," and "love." The planets are viewed as mental concepts rather than as a part of external nature.

This negative turn is due in part to Christianity's rejection of nature-gods. The ancients, with their many gods and their ties to shamanism, very naturally perceived the Divinity within nature. This was certainly the case with the ancient Egyptians, with their many animal gods. With Christianity's rejection of all these nature-gods—animal gods, lake gods, mountain gods, sun gods, lightning gods—nature was robbed of its divinity. Everything non-human was viewed as a soulless thing. The Scientific Revolution, with its radically materialistic perspective, pushed this tendency even further. The relativism of modern astrology, with its subjective psychological perspective, is very much in line with this anti-spiritual perspective. To some degree this was inevitable, for it has become increasingly difficult for us to appreciate the divine intelligence within nature, or to see astrological influence as an aspect of the Divine Mind. This perspective, however, is false. Astrological planets may not be gods, but they are certainly spiritual and have an existence independent of the human mind.

How Powerful
Are the Planets?

Modern astrologers may not see the planets as conscious gods, but they still maintain the Babylonian view that the planets are the most powerful, independent agents in the astrological chart. Planetary power maintains its preeminence no matter what house or sign the planet lands in. Mars will always act as the principle of aggression wherever it's found. Its energies will merely be modified or colored by its house or sign position. My research into the planets, however, does not bear this out. Planets may retain much of their personality when one analyzes them in specific signs, but they do not retain much autonomy in decans, houses, or zodiacal degrees. In decans, their identity almost disappears. A specific decan expresses itself in the same way no matter what planet is located there. The physical planets energize the decan and the planetary rulers of that decan, but their own character more or less disappears.

As an example, if Saturn is found in the first decan of Aries, it expresses itself as Mars and Mercury, which are the two dominant planetary energies in the decan. The repressive influence of Saturn is nowhere to be found. As another example, if Saturn is found in the second decan of Capricorn, it expresses itself as Chiron, since that is the dominant planet of the decan. This is especially curious given that Saturn is the ruler of the sign as a whole. The Saturn in Capricorn energy is still there, but the *decan* expresses itself as a Chiron-ruled archetype, with very little Saturnian influence. Saturn may still express its character because it is in the zodiacal sign of Capricorn, but within the decan it merely activates the decan image and its underlying chronic energies. These sorts of overlays make astrology very complex, but that's simply the way it is. Over the last three hundred years, physical scientists have had to accommodate an increasingly complex understanding of the natural world. Eventually, astrologers too will have to relinquish their demand for a simplicity that just isn't there.

Traditional astrologers assume that the primary locus of the planetary archetype is the physical planet—that the archetype is like the spiritual body or astral body of the physical planet. But this may not be the case. I have found that the decans *contain* very strong planetary archetypes, and that the houses too are homes to planetary archetypes. Thus, the main locus of the Venus archetype may not be the astronomical body we call Venus. It may be located in the first decan of Taurus, the first decan of Libra, or the seventh house cusp of the natal chart.

Ancient astrologers assumed that the zodiacal energies came from the zodiacal constellations—that they were stellar in origin. Yet, the precession of the equinoxes shows that this simply isn't true, since the zodiacal signs no longer match up with their ancient constellations. Because almost all modern astrologers accept the reality of the precession, they have *already* put aside ancient ideas about the source of astrological influence. They can no longer argue that the energies of the zodiacal constellations are the active agents of astrology. But have astrologers come up with a *new* explanation for the location and origin of zodiacal energies? Not really.

Since the tropical zodiac, accepted by most astrologers, is based on the equinox and solstice points, we need to be looking at the relationship of the earth to the sun, and particularly to the electromagnetic field of the earth, as it is affected by solar movements. In other words, the zodiac, as a band of energies, does not reside "out there" in the realm of the stars but is part of the earth's electromagnetic field. Planetary archetypes, similarly, may also have their primary locus in the earth's electromagnetic field, rather than in the physical planets.

In the Western astrological tradition, the planets are the most powerful, active elements. They do not affect the chart from within, but from above. My research on the decans, however, shows that the planetary archetypes also reside within the decans independently of the position of the physical planets.

The idea that planetary influence can be independent of the physical planets occurred to me over thirty years ago when I was studying the moon phases. At that time, I realized that the moon phases, which are essentially aspects between the sun and moon, are ruled not by the sun or the moon, but by a planetary energy specific to the zodiacal decan associated with that moon phase. This planetary ruler, though very powerful, has no relation to the physical planets of the birth chart. It is a planetary archetype residing within the moon phase itself. For instance, a waning sextile between the sun and moon has Saturn as its ruler, since this marks the beginning of the first Capricorn moon phase, which is ruled by Saturn. The only two *physical* bodies involved here are the sun and the moon, yet the influence of Saturn is extremely powerful when the sun and moon are in this aspect—this, despite the fact that the physical planet Saturn is not involved. The Saturnian influence emerges from an archetypal planetary presence within the moon phase itself. As another example, the waxing square between the sun and moon begins the Gemini moon phase and therefore has a Mercurial influence that is quite independent of the *planet* Mercury. In short, planetary archetypes can operate from *within* the zodiacal signs, and not just through the influence of the physical planets. The implication here is that the zodiac is the *primary* astrological reality, and that the planets generally operate in subservient positions to the zodiacal signs and decans in which they find themselves.

Generally, we think of the planets as being outside time; we see their archetypal nature as a constant throughout history. Yet, the physical planets, because they *are* physical, are never outside time. Planetary transits are by nature time-bound and transitory in their influence. The birth chart, on the other hand, operates as a fairly stable energy field—an energy field that is in large part defined by the activated decans and their underlying planetary "rulers." As stationary energy fields, practically outside time, the decans have enough density to retain a complex consciousness. They are therefore a key element in the basic *character* of the individual, and their basic psychology. They show what kinds of dramas they will habitually play out, what kinds of people and situations they will encounter in life, and what issues they will be trying to address. Planetary transits, by contrast, are ephemeral external influences. The basic reality of any situation is not what happens *to* you; external events are just that—external. The basic reality of a situation is defined by who you are—and what you are likely to make of your situation.

I am convinced that planetary archetypes dwell *within* astrological signs, houses, and decans. Still, it is not clear what these planetary archetypes actually *are*. They seem to have a lot more energy, power, and consciousness than mere *ideas* and should certainly not be reduced to simplistic concepts such as aggression, love, expansion, or limitation. They have a lot more complexity, consciousness, and will than that. Still, they don't seem like gods, since they don't operate independently of specific zodiacal or decanal scripts but serve the purposes of the house, sign, or decan in which they are found. Jupiter may function very differently from one sign to another or from one Jupiterian decan to another. Jupiter is not merely "colored differently" because of these placements but is spiritually adapted to the purposes of the decan or house it resides in. It is subservient to the larger purposes of the signs, houses, and decans. The Greeks may not have seen the planets as gods, but they still ascribed to them too much power and individual identity. It is not natural for planets to operate in isolation from each other. It is natural for them to operate as part of an integrated system. Some planets may be more adaptable than others, but all of them will naturally adapt themselves to their function within the whole.

There are still a lot of unanswered questions here. However, I offer this incomplete analysis in the hope that it will stimulate further discussion.

ENDNOTES

1. It is interesting to note that Gary Goldschneider, in his own empirical work on the decans, found in *The Secret Language of Destiny*, also threw out the rulers of the Indian decans. He is the only other person I know of who has done serious empirical research on the decans. There is an intuitively derived book on the decans by Austin Coppock, which I will discuss later.

2. It is important to note that the spirit was considered to reside within the body for a while after death. The funerary rites, in fact, were devoted not only to the preservation of the body, but to the preparation of the *ba*, or soul, for its imminent journey through the netherworld, or Duat. The funerary rites were a form of spiritual *alchemy*—a technique for manipulating spiritual energies.

3. In their earlier history, Egyptians believed that only the pharaoh could unite with the sun god. Later on, anyone who could afford embalming and expensive funerary rites could participate in these mysteries. See Simson Najovits, *Egypt, Trunk of the Tree* (New York: Algora, 2003), vol. 1, 201.

4. Otto Neugebauer claimed that the decans were originally used as a clock to measure the hours of the night. From there, they degenerated into a less scientific religious usage. Though this view is generally accepted within academia, a careful examination of the extant decan lists found in Egyptian temples does not support it. These lists often vary from 36 in number, and neither are they divided geometrically. Moreover, this mathematically imprecise use of the decans in Egyptian burials continued long after the introduction of Greco-Babylonian astrology with its rigorously mathematical view of the heavens. I am not saying that the decans never had a time-telling function, but this was a secondary usage of the decans that was quite independent of the decans' magical, funerary function. The Egyptians may not have been as mathematically advanced as the Greeks, but they were certainly capable of dividing a circle into thirty-six parts.

5. Jan Assmann, "Death and Initiation in the Funerary Religion of Ancient Egypt," in *Religion and Philosophy in Ancient Egypt*, ed. William K. Simpson, Yale Egyptological Studies 3 (New Haven, CT: Yale Egyptological Seminar, 1989), 140. See also Siegfried Schott, "Nut Spricht als Mutter und Sarg," *Revue d'Égyptologie* 17 (1965): 81–87.

6. The text is *Papyri Graecae Magicae* IV. See Garth Fowden, *The Egyptian Hermes* (Princeton, NJ: Princeton University Press, 1986), 83–84.

7. To prepare for death, a person had to have a lot of esoteric knowledge. He had to know the secret names of the parts of the ferry that would be transporting him in the Duat. Perhaps this is to transfer the individual parts of the ferry into the luminous "Akh sphere," even as the individual parts of the body were

transferred to the Akh sphere through the procedures of embalming and burial. The achievement of the akh state is not that different from the achievement of self-awareness in the dream state. The Tibetans developed sophisticated techniques to achieve lucidity in dreams, which were considered equally valid for navigating the after-death, or "bardo," state. See Tenzin Wangyal Rinpoche, *The Tibetan Yogas of Dream and Sleep* (Ithaca, NY: Snow Lion, 1998).

8. Jeremy Naydler, *Shamanic Wisdom in the Pyramid Texts* (Rochester, VT: Inner Traditions, 2005), 216.

9. Firmicus Maternus, a Roman astrologer of the 4th century CE, mentions the Egyptian decans, but does not provide either images, names, gods, or descriptions for the separate decans. See chapter 12 of his *Matheseos libri octo*.

10. See Martin Bernal, *Black Athena* (New Brunswick, NJ: Rutgers University Press, 1987). The book has a lot of problems, but the Greeks' attitude toward Egypt is well documented.

11. Fowden, *The Egyptian Hermes*, 22–25. Ptah, Isis, and other Egyptian gods were also associated with magic.

12. Fowden, *The Egyptian Hermes*, 25.

13. László Kákosy, "Decans in Late-Egyptian Religion," *Oikumene* 3 (1982): 164–79.

14. Dorian Greenbaum, *The Daimon in Hellenistic Astrology* (Leiden and Boston: Brill, 2016), 234. See Otto Neugebauer and H. B. Van Hoesen, *Greek Horoscopes* (Philadelphia: American Philosophical Society, 1987).

15. Frances Yates, *Giordano Bruno and the Hermetic Tradition* (Chicago: University of Chicago Press, 1964), 3.

16. Briant Bohleke, "Survey of the Indigenous Egyptian Contribution to Ancient Astrology in Light of Papyrus CtYBR inv. 1132(B)," *Studien zur Altägyptischen Kultur* 23 (1996): 11–46. Dorian Greenbaum argues that the ascendant was added to Greek astrology through the influence of the Egyptian decans, which were, after all, based on the eastern rising of decanal constellations. However, since the Ascendant has always been calculated mathematically, a Greek origin seems more likely. See Dorian Greenbaum and Micah Ross, "The Role of Egypt in the Development of the Horoscope," in *Egypt in Transition: Social and Religious Development of Egypt in the First Millennium BCE; Proceedings of an International Conference, Prague, Sept. 1–4, 2009* (Prague: Czech Institute of Egyptology, 2010), 146–82.

17. Antiochus of Athens, of the first century BCE, names "Timaeus" as an earlier interpreter of Hermes Trismegistus. It seems clear to me that the more philosophical literature in the *Corpus Hermeticum* is in large part an extrapolation of the line of thinking found in Plato's *Timaeus*. See Fowden, *The Egyptian Hermes*, 3n11. The exaltation of man in the *Hermetica* is entirely foreign to the Egyptian religious tradition and is clearly derived from the speculative metaphysics of Alexandrian Gnosticism, built up from an underpinning of Alexandrian Neoplatonism. See Najovits, *Egypt, Trunk of the Tree*, 2:307–10.

18. Stobaeus, Excerpt VI, from *Hermetica*, translated and edited by Walter Scott (Boulder, CO: Hermes House, 1982), 415.

19. Augustine, *City of God*, translated by Henry Bettenson (London: Penguin, 1984), book V, chap. 7, 188.

20. See Jan Assmann, *The Price of Monotheism* (Stanford, CA: Stanford University Press, 2009), on the intrinsic intolerance and violence of all forms of monotheism.

21. A. Labhardt, "Curiositas," *Medievalia et Humanistica* 17 (1960): 206-224. See also Hans Blumenberg, *The Legitimacy of the Modern Age*, translated by Robert M. Wallace (Cambridge, MA: MIT Press, 1983).

22. See Yates, *Giordano Bruno and the Hermetic Tradition*, 9–11. The *Picatrix* was the main European source for the astrological decans. However, the Florentine Neoplatonists took their views on the decans from the philosophically oriented *Corpus Hermeticum*, and not from the decanal magic of the *Picatrix*. The ascendancy of Christianity in the Roman Empire was in part a reaction against the widely accepted fatalism of Greco-Roman astrology. Christ, it was thought, could break the chains of planetary domination. Early Christians still believed in the Roman gods but considered them demons who enslaved the soul through astrological agencies.

23. Yates's ideas made a splash but have also been vigorously attacked. Western academia is Christian; all the Ivy League schools, outside of Cornell, are Protestant in origin, as are Oxford and Cambridge in England. The idea that paganism, and especially *occultism*, should be a positive force in human history is something that the academic establishment does not want to admit. Meanwhile, they seriously underplay the disastrous effect of institutionalized Christianity on the scientific and intellectual life of the Middle Ages and the Renaissance.

24. See Erik Iverson, *The Myth of Egypt and Its Hieroglyphs in European Tradition* (Princeton, NJ: Princeton University Press, 1993). Also Brian Curran, *The Egyptian Renaissance* (Chicago: University of Chicago Press, 2007).

25. The *Corpus Hermeticum* contains highly philosophical works that often take the form of metaphysical dialogues between Thoth and one of his disciples. However, the underlying philosophy strongly recalls the metaphysical dialogues in Plato's *Timaeus*. Almost everyone in the Renaissance thought the *Hermetica* were ancient Egyptian treatises written long before Plato. Renaissance scholars therefore believed that Egyptian philosophy was the original source of all the Neoplatonic and Pythagorean ideas found in Plato's dialogues. Renaissance myths about Egypt have been persistent within the Western occult tradition, particularly within Freemasonry. For an intelligent discussion of pseudo-Egyptian lore within Western occultism, see Najovits, *Egypt, Trunk of the Tree*, 2:307–13.

26. The Egyptian decans depicted in the *Sala dei Mesi* had little relation to their Egyptian originals. For instance, the third decan of Taurus has a man with tusks. This is a corruption of the evil god Set, whom the Egyptians sometimes placed in late Taurus in the form of a boar—thus the tusks. See Marco Bertozzi, *La Tirannia degli Astri: Gli Affreschi Astrologici di Palazzo Schifanoia*, (Bologna:

Capelli, 1985). This is an excellent treatment of the Palazzo Schifanoia and the medieval precursors of its decan figures.

27. The Index of Prohibited Books, instituted at the Council of Trent, banned the works of almost all the major Italian philosophers of the period, including Patrizi's *Nova de universis philosophia*, Telesio's *De rerum natura*, and the *Opera omnia* of Campanella and Bruno. In its new intolerance, the Catholic Church executed Pucci and Bruno, imprisoned Campanella, and subjected Cremonini and Della Porta to inquests. In short, in its pursuit of theological orthodoxy the "reformed" Catholic Church was willing to stamp out creative thought altogether. See Luigi Firpo, "Filosofia Italiana e Controriforma," *Rivista de Filosofia* 41 (1950): 153.

28. Yates, *Giordano Bruno and the Hermetic Tradition*, 155.

29. Ibid., 211.

30. Scott Hagwood, who has won the US memory Olympics four times, uses luxury homes described in *Architectural Digest* to organize and store his memories. See Joshua Foer, *Moonwalking with Einstein* (New York: Penguin, 2011), 97.

31. The seventeenth-century witch hunt was consciously initiated by the Catholic Church as a weapon against Protestantism. Rosicrucianism was the initial target, since for a time, many Lutheran theologians favored this form of alchemical Christianity. One of the more important tracts against the Rosicrucians was a book titled *Horrible Pacts between Satan and the Pretended Invisible Ones*. See Frances Yates, *The Rosicrucian Enlightenment* (Boulder, CO: Shambhala, 1978), 103-117.

32. Najovits, *Egypt, Trunk of the Tree*, 2:312–13.

33. Gary Goldschneider and Joost Elffers, *The Secret Language of Destiny* (New York City: Viking Studio, 1999).

34. Sophie-Anne von Bomhard, *The Naos of the Decades* (Oxford: Oxford Centre for Maritime Archaeology, 2008).

35. Franz Boll, *Sphaera* (Leipzig: B. G. Teubner, 1903); and Wilhelm Gundel, *Dekane und Dekansternbilder* (Glückstadt-Hamburg, Germany: J. J. Augustin, 1936).

36. Martin Goldsmith, *Moon Phases* (West Chester, PA: Whitford, 1988), 218.

37. Curiously, the first decan of Gemini, which also stresses the creative emergence of personality, is ruled by Mercury. Both Aries 1 and Gemini 1 are associated with Mercury and deal with identity issues. One must ask whether Mercury itself is associated with identity issues. Given its proximity to the sun, this would certainly make sense.

38. In Hermetic literature, the decan was said to provide protection against harmful animals as well as demons. Its fierce decan god was seen as the "guardian at the door."

39. Austin Coppock, *36 Faces* (Richmond Vista, CA: Three Hands, 2014), 59–60.

40. See Johannes Kepler, *The Harmony of the World*, epilogue.

---

41. Veronica Ions, *Egyptian Mythology* (New York: P. Bedrick, 1968), 47.

42. As the mutable decan of a mutable air sign, Gemini 3 has a rarified energy, closer to "ether" than to air.

43. The constellation located here has always been a boat. The Egyptians had Isis in a boat. The Greeks saw it as the Argo. It was also a boat in the Indian and Arabian traditions. My own symbol for the decan has deep roots. See Richard H. Allen, *Star Names* (New York: Dover, 1963), 64–66.

44. The stars Castor and Pollux both are in this decan. The Latin roots signify purity and chastity on the one hand, and corruption and pollution on the other.

45. See Adolphe Gutbub, "La tortue animal cosmique bénéfique a l'époque ptolémaïque et romaine," *Hommages à la Mémoire de Serge Sauneron* 1 (1979): 391–435. In the Palazzo Schifanoia, Cancer 3 is represented by a man with clawed, webbed feet, and a small winged dragon sitting on his knee. This is taken from Albumasar, whose image includes a man with feet like a tortoise. These images hark back to the two turtles of ancient Egypt.

46. In the Palazzo Schifanoia, this decan is represented as the maiden Persephone, with a sheaf of wheat in one hand and a pomegranate in the other.

47. In some of the ancient Egyptian decan lists, this decan was called "the seat-mat of the judge."

48. As a point of interest, my symbol for Gemini 3 features an aviator, and my symbol for Aquarius 3 features a butterfly emerging from the chrysalis. Flying is therefore a common characteristic of this airy trine.

49. This type of romantic comedy is closely associated with Venus. Other planetary influences in this decan include Jupiter, Neptune, and the sun.

50. The ancients associated Arcturus with dangerous storms. See Allen, *Star Names*, 98–103.

51. Babylonian priests at the time of Sargon called α Draconis or Thuban "The Judge of Heaven." This star is now at the first degree of Scorpio (by right ascension) and was the pole star in 2750 BCE. See Allen, *Star Names*, 206.

52. This decan is associated with the Hanged Man of the Tarot, which is in turn associated with Christ consciousness.

53. Thoth was often associated with Khonsu, another lunar god. Khonsu had a special association with healing and medicine, for he wielded power over the demons that cause sickness and decay.

54. Coppock, *36 Faces*, 198.

55. The exaggerated, cartoonlike social personas of this decan come from Chiron, but the aggressive independence and bold, devil-may-care attitude show a strong secondary influence from Mars.

56. In a somersault, we see the human figure both in the upright and upside-down positions. This is the upright pentagram of noble human attainments and the inverted pentagram of the devil and dark magic.

57. See Serge Sauneron, *Les Songes et Leur Interprétation* (Paris: Éditions du Seuil, 1959).

58. This decan has a strong connection to the astral plane—thus its association with magical beings.

59. The theme of the hidden path is common in fantasy literature. We see it, for instance, in Platform 9¾ in the Harry Potter stories. In *The Magicians* there is an entire college of magic hidden away within Manhattan.

60. Thoth is pictured as a long-beaked ibis. He is a great teacher, possibly of alien origin, who has a map in and out of the various dimensions of the cosmos—rather like the magical map in *The Time Bandits*. An alien traveler, after all, must know how to get around. Time warps, time travel, and precognition figure strongly in this decan. The shaded path of the decan image may, in fact, symbolize a kind of lunar time tunnel. Perhaps the explanation lies in the last degree of Capricorn, which is home to a large black hole.

61. Erik Hornung, *Idea into Image: Essays on Ancient Egyptian Thought* (New York: Timken, 1992), 134.

62. Saturn's glyph is a stylized scythe.

63. Assmann, "Death and Initiation in the Funerary Religion of Ancient Egypt," 136–37. The deceased must become an *akh* (ȝḫ), by entering into the spirit state. Phonetically, this word is related to light and radiance; thus, the deceased must become a being of light. The feminine form ȝḫt (*akhet*) refers to the radiant place where the sun rises, but also to the land of the blessed that is inhabited by immortal souls who have entered the "akh-sphere."

64. Ions, *Egyptian Mythology*, 85.

65. Goldschneider and Elffers, *The Secret Language of Destiny*, 765.

66. "Astrological determinism is a product of the inexorably logical Greek thought, which could not have come about if it had not been Greeks who constructed the astrological system. Thus arose the problem of the relation of the gods to fate, which was lacking in the oriental religions because in them fate was simply the will of the gods. Religion is man's protest against the meaninglessness of events, which is contained in mechanical causality....

The pressure of blind, merciless, unavoidable destiny drove men into the arms of religion, which offered them a refuge from its insensate rule. They took their revenge by making the planetary gods into evil powers. For the Babylonians, the stars were tyrants and arbitrary, but they were not exclusively bad, for they could send not only evil but also good, namely, good luck. The mystical forms of religion in late antiquity made them into evil powers, which clad the soul, when sent down from heaven to earth to be incarnated into a human body, with its vices. This condemnation of the planetary power arose as a protest against the doctrine of fate as mechanical causality which fettered man in bonds of iron and hung over him like an intolerable burden, since it excluded every kind of freedom, stripped him of his free will, and shut off his hopes of the grace of the gods." Martin Nilsson, *Greek Piety*, 114-115.

Babylonian and Gnostic ideas about the planets are still present in modern astrology, in the view that Saturn and Mars are "malefic" planets—that the very structure of the universe includes powerful, demonic elements.

BIBLIOGRAPHY

Allen, Don Cameron. *The Star-Crossed Renaissance: The Quarrel about Astrology and Its Influence in England*. Durham, NC: Duke University Press, 1941. Treats the astrology of Ficino and Pico della Mirandola. Allen also wrote *Doubt's Boundless Sea*, on Renaissance skepticism.

Allen, James. "The Cosmology of the Pyramid Texts." In *Religion and Philosophy in Ancient Egypt*, 1–28. New Haven, CT: Yale Egyptological Seminar, 1989. Important for an understanding of the travels of the soul and the transformation into an akh.

Assmann, Jan. "Death and Initiation in the Funerary Religion of Ancient Egypt." In *Religion and Philosophy in Ancient Egypt*. Edited by William K. Simpson, 135–59. Yale Egyptological Studies 3. New Haven, CT: Yale Egyptological Seminar, 1989. Important.

———. *The Price of Monotheism*. Stanford, CA: Stanford University Press, 2009. Here Assmann takes on the violence and intolerance inherent in monotheistic religion.

———. *The Search for God in Ancient Egypt*. Ithaca, NY: Cornell University Press, 2001.

Attrell, David, and David Porreca. *Picatrix: A Medieval Treatise of Astral Magic*. University Park: Pennsylvania State University Press, 2019. The *Picatrix* is the chief source for the decan images in medieval and Renaissance Europe. It was derived from Arabic sources. Contains a far-ranging historical essay.

Baigent, Michael. *From the Omens of Babylon: Astrology and Ancient Mesopotamia*. London and New York: Arkana, 1994. A popular but excellent work based on academic sources, written by the author of *Holy Blood, Holy Grail*.

Bertozzi, Marco. *La Tirannia degli Astri: Gli Affreschi Astrologici di Palazzo Schifanoia*. Bologna, Italy: Capelli, 1985. Excellent treatment of the Palazzo Schifanoia and the medieval precursors of its decan figures.

Bohleke, Briant. "In Terms of Fate: A Survey of the Indigenous Egyptian Contribution to Ancient Astrology in Light of Papyrus CtYBR inv. 1132(B)." *Studien zur Altägyptischen Kultur* 23 (1996): 11–46.

Böker, Robert. "Über Namen und Identifizierung der Ägyptischen Dekane." *Centaurus* 27 (1984): 189–217. Attempts to correlate Egyptian decans with Greco-Roman constellations.

Boll, Franz. *Sphaera*. Leipzig: B. G. Teubner, 1903.
On the constellations of the ancient world.

Boll, Franz, Wilhelm Gundel, and Carl Bezold. *Sternglaube und Sterndeutung: Die Geschichte und das Wesen der Astrologie*. Leipzig: Teubner, 1917.
Older but excellent history of ancient astrology.

Bouché-Leclercq, Auguste. *L'Astrologie grecque*. Paris: Leroux, 1899.
Lester Ness says that all later historians of astrology have mined the information in this book.

Brennan, Chris. *Hellenistic Astrology*. Denver, CO: Amor Fati, 2017.
An ambitious, scholarly book that adds important material to earlier histories of Hellenistic astrology.

Coppock, Austin. *36 Faces*. Richmond Vista, CA: Three Hands, 2014.

Cumont, Franz. *Astrology and Religion among the Greeks and Romans*. New York: Putnam's Sons, 1912.
Excellent.

———. *L'Égypte des Astrologues*. Brussels: La Fondation Égyptologique Reine Élisabeth, 1937.
The misleading title suggests a treatment of ancient Egyptian astrology. Actually, the book treats Egyptian culture as seen through the works of Roman-era Alexandrian astrologers.

Curran, Brian. *The Egyptian Renaissance*. Chicago: University of Chicago Press, 2007.
Egyptian themes in Renaissance art, from the former editor of *Zontar*.

Davis, Whitney. "The Ascension-Myth in the Pyramid Texts." *Journal of Near Eastern Studies* 36 (1977): 161–79.

Desantis, Giovanni. "Pico, Pontano e la polemica astrologica." *Appunti sul libro XII del De rebus coelestibus di G. Pontano. Pubblicazioni della facoltà di lettere e filosofia della Università degli studi di Bari* 29 (1986): 155–91.

Dieleman, Jacco. "Stars and the Egyptian Priesthood in the Graeco-Roman Period." In *Prayer, Magic, and the Stars in the Ancient and Late Antique World*, 137–53. University Park: Pennsylvania State University Press, 2003.

Faulkner, R. O. "The King and the Star-Religion in the Pyramid Texts." *Journal of Near Eastern Studies* 25, no. 3 (July 1966): 13–161.

Federn, Walter. "The 'Transformations' in the Coffin Texts." *Journal of Near Eastern Studies* 19 (1960): 241–57.

Festugière, André-Jean. *La Révélation d'Hèrmes Trismégiste*. Paris: Lecoffre, 1944–54.
Untrustworthy.

Fortune, Dion. *Moon Magic*. Boston: Weiser, 1956.
Contains a ritual for creating an astral temple that becomes an actual place that can be entered into. Carries forward the Renaissance tradition of fantasy temples, associated with early Freemasonry.

Fowden, Garth. *The Egyptian Hermes*. Princeton, NJ: Princeton University Press, 1986.

The best treatment that I have found on the origins of Hermeticism in Ptolemaic Egypt. A major advance in a poorly studied field.

Frankfort, Henri. *Ancient Egyptian Religion: An Interpretation*. New York: Harper, 1948.
Insightful book on Egyptian religion and the "teaching" literature of ancient Egypt. An excellent introduction to Egyptian thought and culture.

———. *Kingship and the Gods: A Study of Ancient Near Eastern Religion as the Integration of Society and Nature*. Chicago: University of Chicago Press, 1978.

Fraser, P. M. *Ptolemaic Alexandria*. 3 vols. Oxford: Clarendon, 1972.

Goldschneider, Gary, and Joost Elffers. *The Secret Language of Destiny*. New York: Viking Studio, 1999.

Green, Tamara. *The City of the Moon God: Religious Traditions of Harran*. Leiden: Brill, 1992.
Discusses the ancient city of Harran, which was the last surviving outpost of Babylonian paganism.

Greenbaum, Dorian. *The Daimon in Hellenistic Astrology*. Leiden and Boston: Brill, 2016.

———, and Micah Ross. "The Role of Egypt in the Development of the Horoscope." In *Egypt in Transition: Social and Religious Development of Egypt in the First Millennium BCE; Proceedings of an International Conference, Prague, Sept. 1–4, 2009*. Prague: Czech Institute of Egyptology, 2010.

Gundel, Hans. *Weltbild und Astrologie in den griechischen Zauberpapyri*. Munich: Beck, 1968.
Lester Ness considers this an excellent analysis.

Gundel, Wilhelm. *Astrologoumena: Die astrologische Literatur in der Antike und ihre Geschichte*. Wiesbaden, Germany: Steiner, 1966.
This is a list of all the known astrological works from classical antiquity.

———. "Astronomie, Astralreligion, Astralmythologie und Astrologie: Darstellung und Literaturbericht." *Antiquité classique* 4, no. 1 (1935): 289–90.
A bibliography of works on astrology and astral religion.

———. *Dekane und Dekansternbilder*. Glückstadt-Hamburg, Germany: J. J. Augustin, 1936.
This is an early treatment of the Egyptian decans. It is often inaccurate.

———. *Sterne und Sternbilder im Glauben des Altertums und der Neuzeit*. Bonn, Germany: Schroeder, 1922.

Hart, Vaughn, ed. *Paper Palaces: The Rise of Architectural Literature*. New Haven: Yale University Press, 1998.
Essential for an understanding of the "invisible temple" literature of early Freemasonry.

Hornung, Erik. *The Ancient Egyptian Books of the Afterlife*. Ithaca, NY: Cornell University Press, 1999.

———. *Conceptions of the Gods in Ancient Egypt: The One and the Many*. Translated by John Baines. Ithaca, NY: Cornell University Press, 1971.

————. *Idea into Image: Essays on Ancient Egyptian Thought.* New York: Timken, 1992.
Has a chapter titled "The Temple as Cosmos."

Hutchison, Keith. "What Happened to Occult Qualities in the Scientific Revolution?" *Isis* 73 (1982): 233–53.
A very important article explaining the decline of occultism and astrology in the seventeenth century. Hutchison doesn't give enough emphasis to political factors. Robin Barnes's *Prophecy and Gnosis* provides a good corrective.

Ions, Veronica. *Egyptian Mythology.* New York: P. Bedrick, 1968.

Jones, Alexander. "The Place of Astronomy in Roman Egypt." In *The Sciences and Greco-Roman Society.* Edited by Timothy D. Barnes. Edmonton, AB: Academic Printing and Publishing, 1994.

Kákosy, László. "Decans in Late-Egyptian Religion." *Oikumene* 3 (1982): 163–91.

Labhardt, A. "Curiositas." *Medievalia et Humanistica* 17 (1960): 206–24.
Curiosity, as a Christian sin epitomized by astrology.

Letronne, A. J. "Analyse critique des représentations zodiacales de Dendéra et d'Esné." *Mémoires de l'Institut Royale de France. Académie des Inscriptions et Belles-Lettres* 16, no. 2 (1846): 102–210.
Post-Napoleonic attempt to decipher the Denderah circular zodiac. Historically interesting, but highly inaccurate.

Leventhal, Herbert. *In the Shadow of the Enlightenment: Occultism and Renaissance Science in Eighteenth-Century America.* New York: New York University Press, 1976.
This contains a long chapter on astrology in the American colonies and also deals with the eighteenth-century decline of astrology.

Lichtheim, Miriam. *Ancient Egyptian Literature.* 3 vols. Berkeley: University of California Press, 1975, 1976, 1980.

Long, A. A. "Freedom and Determinism in the Stoic Theory of Human Action." In *Problems in Stoicism.* Edited by A. A. Long, 173–99. London: Athlone, 1971.

Morenz, Siegfried. "Anubis mit dem Schlüssel." In *Religion und Geschichte des alte* Ägypten, 510–20. Köln: Bohlau, 1975.

Najovits, Simson. *Egypt, Trunk of the Tree.* New York: Algora, 2003.
Najovits is a journalist and as such asks the bigger questions that Egyptologists often neglect. Highly intelligent overview of Egyptology, which includes a bibliographic essay on the most important modern Egyptologists. He also gives a history of the persistent myths about Egypt that pervade esoteric and New Age writings.

Nasr, Seyyed Hossein. *An Introduction to Islamic Cosmological Doctrine.* Cambridge, MA: Harvard University Press, 1964.
Treats the Islamic elaboration of Hellenistic cosmology, in which astrology played an important part.

Naydler, Jeremy. *Shamanic Wisdom in the Pyramid Texts.* Rochester, VT: Inner Traditions, 2005.

Groundbreaking work on the Egyptian religion and the real purpose of the pyramids. Solidly researched and fascinating.

Ness, Lester. *Written in the Stars: Ancient Zodiac Mosaics.* Warren Center, PA: Shangri-La, 1999.

See his extensive online bibliography on ancient astrology at http://www.smoe.org/arcana/bibs.html.

Neugebauer, Otto. *Astronomical Cuneiform Texts.* London: Lund Humphries, 1955.

————. *The Exact Sciences in Antiquity.* Princeton, NJ: Princeton University Press, 1952.

Groundbreaking when it came out, but narrow-minded in its vision of ancient science.

————. "Tamil Astronomy: A Study in the History of Astronomy in India." *Osiris* 10 (1952): 252–76.

————, and Richard Parker. *Egyptian Astronomical Texts.* London: L. Humphries for Brown University Press, 1960–69.

The third volume gives detailed information on the decans taken from many extant archeological sites. Neugebauer had a prejudicial and highly inaccurate understanding of Egyptian astrology. As a source of raw data, however, the book is fundamental to any serious work on Egyptian astrology.

Nilsson, Martin. *Greek Piety.* Translated from the Swedish by Herbert Rose. New York: Norton and Co., 1969.

A clear outline of the complex spiritual environment of the Hellenistic Age. The book is important in accurately positioning astrology and occultism within this mix.

North, John. "Medieval Concepts of Celestial Influence: A Survey." In *Astrology, Science, and Society: Historical Essays.* Edited by Patrick Curry, 5–17. Woodbridge, UK: Boydell, 1987.

————. *Stars, Mind, and Fate: Essays in Ancient and Medieval Cosmology.* London: Hambledon, 1989.

Parker, Richard. "Ancient Egyptian Astronomy." In *The Place of Astronomy in the Ancient World,* 51–65. London: Oxford University Press, 1974.

Pingree, David. "Between the Ghaya and Picatrix." *Journal of the Warburg and Coutauld Institutes* 44 (1981): 27–56.

————. "Some of the Sources of the Ghayat Al-Hakim." *Journal of the Warburg and Coutauld Institutes* 43 (1980): 1–15.

Pollard, Justin, and Howard Reid. *The Rise and Fall of Alexandria: Birthplace of the Modern Mind.* New York: Viking, 2006.

Ruelle, C. E. "Hermès Trismégiste, le livre sacré sur les décans." *Revue de Philologie* 32 (1908): 250–77.

Sauneron, Serge. *The Priests of Ancient Egypt.* Translated by David Lorton. Ithaca, NY: Cornell University Press, 2000.

Schott, Siegfried. "Nut Spricht als Mutter und Sarg." *Revue d'Égyptologie* 17 (1965): 81–87.

Scott, John Beldon. *Images of Nepotism: The Painted Ceilings of Palazzo Barberini.* Princeton, NJ: Princeton University Press, 1991.
Though essentially an art book, one also finds an account of the astrological intrigues behind Urban VIII's condemnation of Galileo's *Dialogue on the Two Chief World Systems.*

Shackelford, Jole. "Rosicrucianism, Lutheran Orthodoxy, and the Rejection of Paracelsianism in Early 17th-Century Denmark." *Bulletin of the History of Medicine* 70, no. 2 (Summer 1996): 181–204.

Tester, Jim. *A History of Western Astrology.* Woodbridge, UK: Boydell, 1987.
Reliable and interesting, though it leaves a lot of gaps in the story.

Thorndike, Lynn. *A History of Magic and Experimental Science.* 8 vols. New York: Columbia University Press, 1923–58.
Reliable academic treatment of astrology and occultism during the Middle Ages and Renaissance, with detailed synopses of major texts. Thorndike's work has aged remarkably well.

van der Waerden, Bartel. *Science Awakening: The Birth of Astronomy.* Leiden: Noorhoff, 1974.
Stresses or overstresses the astral religion of the ancient world. Very interesting.

Vickers, Brian, ed. *Occult and Scientific Mentalities in the Renaissance.* Cambridge: Cambridge University Press, 1984.
See especially Mordechai Feingold's article on the teaching of occult sciences at English universities.

von Bomhard, Anne-Sophie. *The Egyptian Calendar: A Work for Eternity.* London: Periplus, 1999.
Has frequent references to the decans.

———. *The Naos of the Decades.* Oxford: Oxford Centre for Maritime Archaeology, 2008.
A groundbreaking book. Gives a highly coherent explanation of the place of decanal constellations in the religion of ancient Egypt.

Wente, Edward. "Mysticism in Pharaonic Egypt?" *Journal of Near Eastern Studies* 41 (1982): 161–79.

White, Lynn, Jr. "Medical Astrologers and Late Medieval Technology." In *Medieval Religion and Technology,* 297–316. Berkeley: University of California Press, 1978.
White shows that the fine technology of the Middle Ages, including the clock, was designed in large part by and for astrologers.

Wippel, John. "The Condemnations of 1270 and 1277 at Paris." *Journal of Medieval and Renaissance Studies* 7, no. 2 (1977): 169–201.
Treats the religious repression of deterministic Arabic astrology in medieval European universities.

Wright, Paul. *The Literary Zodiac.* Edinburgh: Anodyne, 1987.
Wright explains each zodiacal sign by examining the dominant themes in the literary works of people who have the Sun in that sign. Unusually insightful.

Yates, Frances. *The Art of Memory.* Chicago: University of Chicago Press, 1966. Reprinted in 2001.
This treats the memory tradition, including the occult memory palaces of the Renaissance.

————. *Giordano Bruno and the Hermetic Tradition.* Chicago: University of Chicago Press, 1964.
Groundbreaking book on the importance of astrology and occultism in the intellectual life of the Renaissance. The single most important book on the history of occultism and Hermeticism.

————. *The Rosicrucian Enlightenment.* London and Boston: Routledge & Kegan Paul, 1972.
The book treats Hermetic culture in the seventeenth century and its importance in the development of modern science. This book is reviled within history-of-science circles, first because it shows the connections between Rosicrucianism, Freemasonry, and the Royal Society, and second, because it shows the importance of alchemy, astrology, and occultism in seventeenth-century evangelical Protestantism.

Martin Goldsmith has been a serious astrological researcher for over 50 years. He has a PhD in the history of science, where he concentrated on the intersection of occultism and science during the Scientific Revolution. Using a methodology that combines intuition and empirical analysis, he has been able to arrive at a deeper understanding of astrological basics. His previous books treat moon phases, degree symbols, and the planet Jupiter. He is currently working on a book on the luminaries and the planets.